"THURSDAY'S CHILD"

THE STORY OF THE FIRST FLIGHT ROUND THE WORLD BY A WOMAN PILOT

BY

RICHARDA MORROW-TAIT

WITH ADDITIONAL MATERIAL BY
MICHAEL TOWNSEND & NORMAN H. ELLISON

CIRRUS ASSOCIATES

PUBLISHED BY:
Cirrus Associates (S.W.),
Kington Magna,
Gillingham,
Dorset,
SP8 5EW UK.

All rights reserved. No part of this publication may be reproduced, stored in a retrieval system, or transmitted in any form or by any means, electronic, mechanical, photocopying or otherwise without the prior permission of the publisher.

© Michael Townsend 2001

ISBN 1 902807 11 1

PRINTED IN ENGLAND BY:
Bookcraft Ltd.,
First Avenue,
Westfield Trading Estate,
Radstock,
BATH,
BA3 4BS.

PHOTO SCANNING BY:
International Graphics Services Ltd.,
24-31 Fourth Avenue,
Westfield Trading Estate,
Radstock,
BATH,
BA3 4XE.

DISTRIBUTORS:
Crecy Publishing Ltd.,
1A Ringway Trading Estate,
Shadowmoss Road,
MANCHESTER,
M22 5LH.

COVER PAINTING: Maurice Brett.
PORTRAIT OF DIKKI: Henry Carr R.A. (1946).
PHOTOS: all from the authors' private collections unless otherwise stated. Provenance unknown in many cases, but due acknowledgement given wherever possible.
MAP ON PAGES 94-95: by permission of *Flight International*.

DEDICATION

(by Michael Townsend)

For Anna and Giles, without whom our lives would not have been complete.

Sadly, Norman H. Ellison died in August 2001 a few days before this book went to print.

CONTENTS

FOREWORD: *(by Norman H. Ellison)*   10

INTRODUCTION: BACKGROUND TO ROUND-THE-WORLD FLIGHTS   11
(by Norman H. Ellison)

CHAPTER 1: BIRTH OF THE IDEA   13
January 1946. "I will and I'll fly round the world." April 1948. An experienced navigator appears and presents the difficulties. Choice of route and timing.

CHAPTER 2: CHOOSING AN AIRCRAFT   17
Auster to Chrislea Super Ace to Proctor IV.

CHAPTER 3: CAMBRIDGE–MARSEILLES   23
Goodbyes and a start at last. Taxying accident at Marignane.

CHAPTER 4: REPAIRS AT MARIGNANE   26
Good repair work cannot be hurried. "Personne ne travaille le Samedi ou le Dimanche!"

CHAPTER 5: MARSEILLES–MALTA–CYPRUS   31
Change of route to conserve foreign currency. Consumption and equipment checks. Help from the RAF Spitfire squadron.

CHAPTER 6: CYPRUS–HABBANIYA–BAHREIN   35
Avoiding the Arab-Israeli war. Three bacon & egg meals in one day. First night landing.

CHAPTER 7: BAHREIN–SHARJA–KARACHI   40
A note on Pakistani lawn-mowing.

CHAPTER 8: KARACHI–DELHI   44
Nehru and his daughter at the airport. Struggles for an early take-off to defeat the monsoon.

CHAPTER 9: DELHI–CALCUTTA   48
Flying below the monsoon.

CHAPTER 10: CALCUTTA (ONE)   51
Engine overhaul. The fuel tankage problem. Foray to a dump for a Spitfire drop tank.

CHAPTER 11: CALCUTTA (TWO)   54
Air test and a ground loop.

CHAPTER 12: CALCUTTA (THREE).   58
Enforced idleness. Calcutta Swimming Club

| CHAPTER 13: | CALCUTTA (FOUR)
Social observations. Dire weather warnings for the North Pacific. | 62 |
| CHAPTER 14: | INTERLUDE IN A PALACE
Leopard hunts, hornets and a Durbar. | 65 |
| CHAPTER 15: | CALCUTTA (FIVE)
Nefarious deeds at Dum Dum. | 73 |
| CHAPTER 16: | CALCUTTA–RANGOON–VIENTIAME –HONG KONG–OKINAWA
Change of planned route. Desirability of achieving maximum distance from India in minimum time. USAF welcome in Okinawa. | 79 |
| CHAPTER 17: | OKINAWA–ITAZUKE–TOKYO–CHITOSE
Hiroshima, Mt. Fuji and an ambassadorial lunch. Frustration re escort. | 85 |
| CHAPTER 18: | CHITOSE – WAITING FOR THE WEATHER
Silent forests, Japanese tea time and salmon traps. Squabbles over a cherry. | 90 |
| CHAPTER 19: | THE NORTH PACIFIC
Instrument flying, astro-navigation and "finding the island." 13¼ hours of rain, gales, icing, snow showers and, finally, sunshine. 15 minutes' fuel left on landing. | 96 |
| CHAPTER 20: | THE ALEUTIAN ISLANDS
Shemya to Adak. "Dry and dusty down the Chain." | 103 |
| CHAPTER 21: | ADAK–COLD BAY–ANCHORAGE
Volcanoes, photography, pilot icing. Fog and three GCAs at Anchorage. | 107 |
| CHAPTER 22: | ANCHORAGE
Technical help from the 10th Rescue Squadron. Out with the temporary fuel tanks. In with seats and safety belts and M/F radio range receiver. Condensation in the ignition harness. | 110 |
| CHAPTER 23: | ANCHORAGE–TANACROSS
Engine failure in the mountains. Forced landing in 30 degrees below. My birthday treat – survival! | 117 |

CHAPTER 24: FAIRBANKS, ALASKA   121
             *Recovery and repair of "Thursday's Child"
             arranged. Mike recalled to Cambridge.*
CHAPTER 25: CHRISTMAS ALONE IN EDMONTON   126
             Goodbye to Mike. Living on a shoestring.
CHAPTER 26: END OF THE PROCTOR   132
             *Hitchhiking the Alaska Highway in January
             to find out who was responsible.*
CHAPTER 27: NADIR OF THE FLIGHT   137
             Stuck in Dawson Creek, Yukon.
CHAPTER 28: ESCAPE FROM DAWSON CREEK   141
             *The coldest hotel in my life. Ice on the shower
             room floor and soot from the central heating vents.
             Snowdrifts and outside sanitation.*
CHAPTER 29: BACK TO ANCHORAGE   144
             *Night in a snowdrift. Arguments at the border
             post.*
CHAPTER 30: ANCHORAGE AGAIN   148
             *The Fur Festival. I acquire a Husky pup. Kindness
             of an Alaskan bush pilot: Don Dorothy helps.*
CHAPTER 31: SOUTH TO SEATTLE   151
             *Theft of my wallet whilst singing at a night club.
             Job as acting stewardess on an unscheduled
             flight to Seattle saves the day.*
CHAPTER 32: ENTER A NAVIGATOR   157
             John Mackennan Ellis volunteers.
CHAPTER 33: BUYING AND FLYING A BT-13   159
             *Doc Campbell to the rescue. Generous help from
             two citizens of Vancouver makes the purchase
             possible. Named "Next Thursday's Child."*
CHAPTER 34: SEATTLE–VANCOUVER–EDMONTON   169
             On our way at last in the BT-13.
CHAPTER 35: EDMONTON–TANACROSS–EDMONTON   175
             *An uneventful trip back to start again at the
             Proctor crash site.*

CHAPTER 36: EDMONTON   179
             *Increasing the fuel tankage for the Atlantic
             crossing. Kindness of North West Industries.
             Dossing down in Hargreaves & Dick's
             Emergency Equipment store. The crew
             undertake supervised overhaul work of
             the aircraft whilst a ventral tank is designed
             and fitted. Poor Shemya dies.*

CHAPTER 37: EDMONTON–MINNEAPOLIS   182
             *Problems of an 'X'-Category aircraft. The Press
             to the rescue – "Moses from* The Sun.*"*

CHAPTER 38: MINNEAPOLIS–CHICAGO   187
             *Joining the circuit of Chicago International with
             radio on the blink. Rude remarks from the Tower
             about "a dirty silver BT-13 on the south-west
             corner." "Next Thursday's Child" impounded.*

CHAPTER 39: BREAKING THE SEALS   194
             *Chicago to Toronto on reduced power. Speaking
             engagements and a police escort in Buffalo. Jake
             quits to rejoin his family in Toronto.*

CHAPTER 40: BUFFALO INTERNATIONAL   200
             *Waiting for a CAA export licence. The blow falls –
             "Pay a $300 fine by tomorrow or you lose your
             aircraft." Generosity of Buffalo friends.*

CHAPTER 41: BUFFALO–MONTREAL   209
             *Mike returns from England to navigate. Still
             awaiting an export licence. We carry out overhaul
             work under professional supervision. A dirty job –
             sealing leaky integral wing tanks.*

CHAPTER 42: MONTREAL–BURLINGTON–MONTREAL   213
             *Preparing "Next Thursday's Child" for the
             Atlantic crossing. Difficulties with the Canadian
             Department of Transport: "If it's the last thing I do,
             I'll see you don't fly this aircraft to England."*

CHAPTER 43: ESCAPE FROM MONTREAL   218
             *Appeal to the Minister. Officialdom trumped
             but still hostile. Attempt at the high Arctic
             route to Greenland thwarted by fog en route.
             Diversion to Goose Bay, Labrador.*

CHAPTER 44: GOOSE BAY 224
Amongst friends in the RCAF and USAF but
the DOT turns up and insists on an escort – but,
which way? Dawn escape to Greenland.

CHAPTER 45: BLUIE WEST 1 235
Amongst friends again. An enforced rest and a
mountaineering expedition.

CHAPTER 46: GREENLAND–ICELAND–UK 236
An uneventful completion of the Atlantic
crossing. Press and Gaumont British News
at Croydon. The 366th day of the flight.

EPILOGUE: (by Norman Ellison) 238

POSTSCRIPT: RICHARDA MORROW-TAIT 240
(by Michael Townsend)

APPENDIX 1: FINAL PRESS COMMENTS 241
(by Norman H. Ellison)

APPENDIX 2: TECHNICAL DETAILS OF EACH AIRCRAFT 242
(by Norman H. Ellison)

APPENDIX 3: AIRCRAFT PERFORMANCE DATA COMPARED 245
(by Michael Townsend)

APPENDIX 4: A BRIEF HISTORY OF ROUND-THE-WORLD 246
FLIGHT ATTEMPTS
(by Norman H. Ellison)

FOREWORD

(by Norman H. Ellison)

This is a true story of perseverance, mainly against bureaucracy initiated by individuals who were just trying to do their ordinary everyday official jobs. However, when one is trying to do something to prove a point, officialdom uses two tactics. It either turns a blind eye to what is being proposed, and hides behind its natural inertia to do nothing, or it uses every rule in the book to protect the employment of its officials. These fear to use their own initiative in case they then suffer retributions.

In the romantic period of aviation between the two great World Wars, women pilots, or *aviatrices* to quote a Press description of the time, took a leading role in long-distance flying. Encouraged by the popular press for publicity in order to boost circulation, many pilots became instant heroes. They were celebrities to the general public, most of whom had never travelled further than a rail trip to the seaside on an annual holiday.

However, compared to student pilots in the aviation world at the end of the millennium, people learning to fly in the twenties had to complete only relatively a few hours of instruction before they were considered fully trained. Other than basic airmanship, there was not much to learn: no electronics, radios, rules of the airways, airspace classifications etc., and navigation was often a matter of just following a road map.

Many of the now-famous women who took up long-distance flying had very few hours in their log books when they started out on their flights. Here there is a similarity between the pre-WWII lady pilots and the pilot in this story.

Very few of the round-the-world flights were made by pilots flying solo. Most of the point-to-point flights *were* solo, particularly England–Australia, America–Europe and other intercontinental flights. However, there were exceptions, such as the 1934 MacRobertson Race to Australia and the 1936 Schlesinger Race to South Africa. Some aircraft in these two races even carried passengers. There were a few solo flights around the world, but these were mostly after WWII. Most of the world flights had a crew in addition to the pilot, sometimes just a navigator, but other flights had more, such as radio operators and mechanics. The pilot usually received all the publicity, but the crew worked just as hard and endured the same trials and tribulations.

This story is about a woman pilot and a navigator; in fact two navigators took part at different times, for reasons which will become clear in the book. No records were set for speed or duration, and in fact this was one of the longest (in time) round-the-world flights ever recorded.

INTRODUCTION
BACKGROUND TO ROUND-THE-WORLD FLIGHTS

(by Norman H. Ellison)

To the average romantic person living in the twenties, looking for excitement after the dull and dreary WWI and its aftermath of chaos and reorganisation, the thought of a voyage of escape to travel around the world must have been very appealing. The visionary writer Jules Verne probably originated early dreams of a great romantic voyage when he wrote the novel *Around the World in Eighty Days*. Hardly mentioned in the book, but a long early feature in the film version, Mr Phileas Fogg used a balloon to cross the Alps. When air travel became an attractive practical reality, at a reasonable cost, it was not long before people, generally considered as dreamers, connected together air travel and round-the-world voyages.

Shortly after WWI, long-distance flights began in America and Russia, and between the great continents. As aviation technology increased, so did greater distances become a possibility. It was another gas-filled aircraft that completed one of the earliest journeys around the world when the German airship *Graf Zeppelin* circumnavigated the world in 1929. However, the first actual flight all the way round was by two amphibious aircraft of the United States Navy in 1924.

As smaller aircraft became more reliable in the latter half of the twenties, they became available to private owners. Then the great adventures of the flying romantics commenced.

One of the first of these was The Hon. Mrs Victor Bruce, a journalist whose passion was fast automobiles. One day, when passing by one of the major department stores in the centre of London, she saw a small aircraft for sale in the window. It occurred to her that in it she could fly around the world – so she purchased it. Then she learned to fly it, and set off on the 25th September 1930, flying around the world in five months. However, she did take the precaution of crossing the Pacific and the Atlantic oceans on a passenger ship, as had the Vicomte and Vicomtesse de Sibour the previous year. This was a well-planned arrangement for the time, and was probably a lesson learned from the early Trans-Pacific Race, the Dole Derby of 1927, when three of the starters in the race from Oakland to Hawaii were lost at sea.

The first private owner to fly all the way round the world without using any sea transport was the American Wiley Post who, with Harold Gatty navigating, completed the trip in June 1931. He repeated the flight in 1933, solo this time, but was killed in Alaska along with comedian Will Rogers on a flight in 1935. Circumnavigation then became a race as larger, faster aircraft became involved. There was Amelia Earhart's attempt in 1937 and Howard Hughes' successful flight in 1938.

Then came WWII, and everything changed. The world politics, the aircraft, the people, aviation technology, and all the support facilities such as radios, navigation equipment and airports, all had advanced over the world. Sponsorship now had to show the versatility and dependability of the product. The global flight of two Piper Super Cruisers in 1947, piloted by George Truman and Clifford Evans, was sponsored by the aircraft manufacturer. However, there were still a few aviation romantics after WWII, and one of these was Mrs Prudence Richarda Evelyn Routh Morrow-Tait.

Richarda Routh was born in Ickleton, Cambridgeshire, on the 22nd November 1923. She received a private education at the Perse School for Girls in Cambridge from September 1932 up to July 1940. After leaving school she dropped the name Prudence and was called by her second name, Richarda, sometimes shortened to "Dikki." On the 21st July 1945, in Cambridge, she married Norman Robert Morrow-Tait, a Cambridge mechanical engineer. They had a daughter, Anna Victoria Airy, who was born on 9th October 1946.

When the wartime ban on civil aviation was lifted on the 1st January 1946, the Cambridge Aero Club was the first civilian training club to resume peacetime operations. Leslie Worsdell, who was the Club's Chief Flying Instructor at that time, wrote to me recently recalling that on the day the Club reopened for Private Pilot's Licence training, eight persons joined. Amongst them was the then Mayor of Cambridge, Prince Birabongse – a racing-car driver who later flew gliders at the London Gliding Club at Dunstable – and a very glamorous redhead named Mrs Richarda Morrow-Tait.

Norman H. Ellison
Seattle, USA
July 2001

CHAPTER 1
BIRTH OF THE IDEA

It's funny how things begin. My daughter fell into a bed of nettles that afternoon, and being only a baby she cried a lot, so my husband and I, instead of going into the town to meet Michael Townsend, suggested he came to the flat to chat over a friendly pint of beer. He said in passing that he'd have to get a job for the summer during the long vacation until the university term started again in October. He sat on the old leather-clad sofa cradling Anna's silver christening mug between his hands. My husband paused by the door in his habitual prowling of the room and, turning, said: "Why don't you navigate Dikki round the world?"

My husband's remark, Michael's mock astonishment – "Not me!" – and subsequent declaration that it was impossible gave me the chance to put into words the dreams which took shape from the shadows. This idea wasn't entirely new, not for me anyway. Way back in November 1945, after having been to a concert in town, Morrow and I were lying in bed talking about flying when he told me that the Schools and Clubs were starting up again in England on January 1st.

He said: "Why don't you learn to fly?"

I fought shy: "I couldn't."

"You could, you know," he told me.

So I thought a while, and then said: "All right, I *will*, and I'll fly round the world."

Then when I first learned to fly – it was indeed the first time I stepped into an aeroplane – I just got bitten by it. To me it was the most wonderful thing in the world and the battered, beat-up little Tiger Moth, the only one the School possessed at that time, became more sacred to me than the Holy Grail. I started on January 7th 1946, for the Flying Clubs were not permitted to open until 1st January.

Lord, how cold it was! At that time of year one could stand barely half an hour's flying before one's brain congealed and refused to absorb any more instructions. However, I went solo in about 12 hours and did two rather untidy circuits and landings, and went home crowing with joy. We were wonderful, God and I. Yes, I "wouldn't even call the King my uncle." I grabbed pencil and paper and burst into poetry:

"*The smooth green turf slips past and I fly skyward,*
No soul on that small earth is quite like me,
For I am God, for these few hours immortal,
I own myself; I'm life, I'm death, I'm free!
The pretty plots they nurture down below me
Are everything or dust beneath my hand.
Shall I go back to humble daily failure
Or shall my deeds be cried throughout the land?

And will the vows I made in drunken valour
All be translated into brilliant fame?
And can I set the highest heavens ringing
And little children murmuring my name?
The skies are mine, they stretch until forever
And night and day was made by God for man.
No trembling at the edge of great endeavour
When I climb skyward – for I know I can."

I came down to earth, though, pretty soon, because too much jumping out of cockpits nearly made me have a miscarriage and I had to rest for about a month. I always did try to do too many things at the same time.

In April I learnt to fly an Auster, but the hot sun on the perspex roof created conditions somewhat similar to a greenhouse and caused me to feel very faint one day, so I had to pack it up at least until Anna was born. My hands were full after that and there wasn't so much time for flying, but I still got the odd hour or two here and there.

I had it all planned in my mind but it was only a daydream, the sort of story one tells oneself to forget the everyday whilst waiting for sleep. But I could produce for Michael a map of the world with all the route marked out and with hops short enough for an Auster to fly, with a small extra fuel tank.

Strangely enough Michael was quite impressed but, being Michael, he verbally poo-poohed the idea. "Quite impossible," he said, after we had spent a good three hours lying on our tummies on the floor working out mileages and stopping places; yet when he went home that night, he got his own maps out and found that maybe it *could* be done. He knew much of the route for he had been a navigator in the RAF Transport Command and on the UK–India route for BOAC And a damn good navigator too! At the time he was with BOAC there were only two men on that route with their First Class Navigator's licence – and he was one.

We talked it over next day. There were, it seemed, an incredible number of difficulties and Michael certainly did his best to make sure I knew them. We would need to land at RAF Stations in the Middle East, United States Military Aerodromes in the Pacific theatre, French Air Force Stations in Indo-China and countless foreign civil airports throughout the world. Worst of all, it would be necessary to land in Russian territory on our way across the North Pacific. Why should we, a couple of civilians on a madcap chase around the world, be allowed to land where others were refused? My reason took over momentarily and my heart sank.

Then there was the problem of weather and the ocean crossings. Up to 1939 no regular landplane flights took place over either the Atlantic or Pacific. Under the stress of war, however, routes had been developed for ferrying bombers from the American factories, both to Australia and Europe. These were used by twin- or multi-engined military aircraft equipped with full de-icing apparatus, radar, and other heavy safety equipment.

Private flying, however, had been in abeyance all this time and what data on it there was had been gathered from the few scattered flights of pioneers like Charles Lindbergh and Kingsford-Smith. But Lindbergh's desperate solo across the Atlantic and Kingsford-Smith's crossing of the Central Pacific were two of the minority of ocean flights that did not end tragically. These men had many hundreds and even thousands of flying hours' experience. How could *I*, with my 80 hours, expect to cross safely both the Atlantic and the grimmer and almost unknown North Pacific?

Both oceans would have to be crossed by their far northern rims in order to cut down the length of the non-stop flights necessary. Furthermore, both would have to be crossed in the summer. The route from Labrador to Scotland, via Greenland and Iceland, would present very dangerous icing conditions by mid-October. The Atlantic hops were short, however, compared with the Pacific flight. This, more than once the stumbling block of round-the-world flights already, was the vital part of our whole flight. Although both the Kurile and Aleutian Islands were largely shrouded in fog in the summer, a winter crossing was unthinkable with its headwinds, icing and savage weather. If we did not reach Japan by mid-September, our flight was an almost certain failure. It was the end of April already and we were only just beginning to make our plans.

Yet another hazard, Michael pointed out, was that, in order to reach Japan by September, we should have to fly through the height of the South-West Monsoon in India and Burma. He had personally known of at least two heavy transport aircraft that had been torn apart in mid-air in June 1944 through flying into monsoon clouds in India!

This all sounded positively gruesome and yet, behind it all, did I detect a note of enthusiasm creeping, quite unbidden, into his voice?

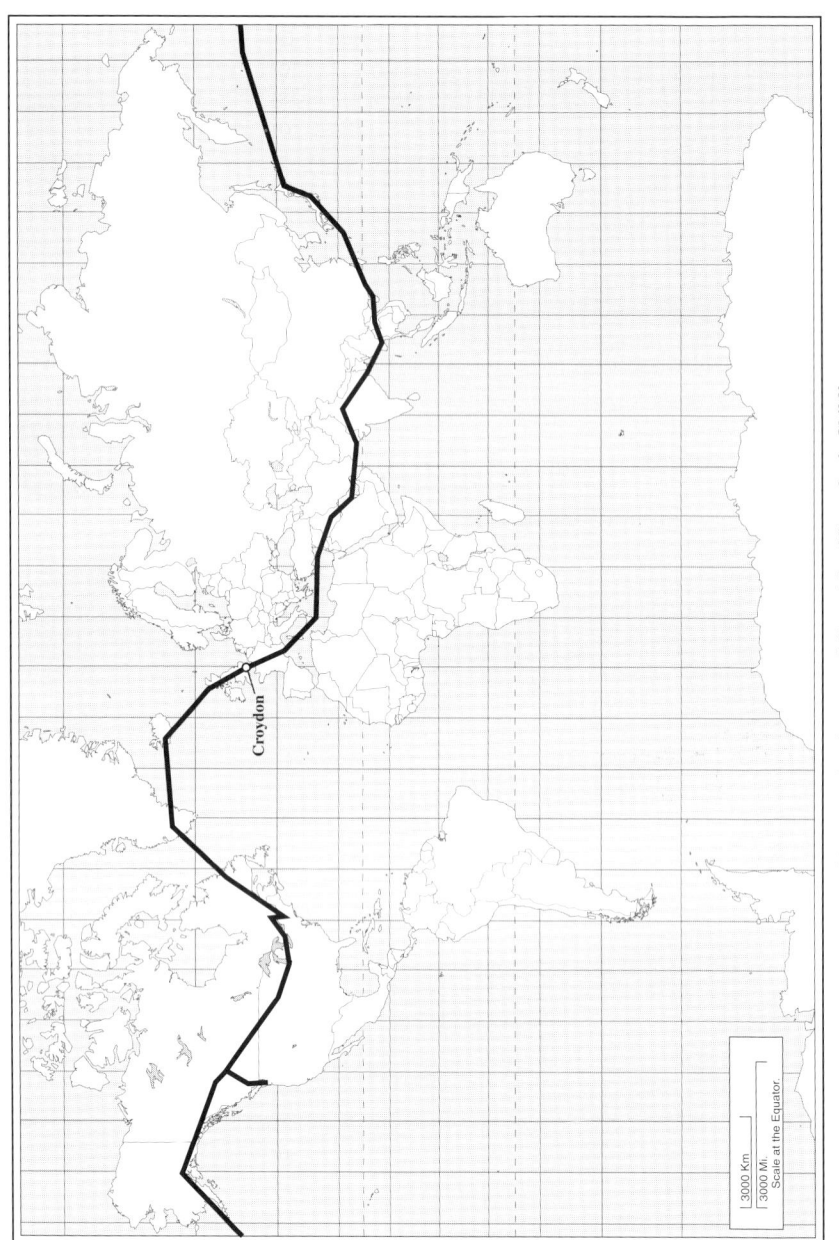

CHAPTER 2

CHOOSING AN AIRCRAFT

I was really quite a bit surprised that Mike should take me as seriously as he did. I needed no more encouragement; I rang the American Embassy for permission to land on American military airfields and made an appointment to meet the Russian Air Attaché for permission to land on Kamchatka and on the Kurile Islands in the North Pacific.

As I entered the sacred portals of the Soviet Embassy the guards looked suspiciously at the little personal radio that I was carrying (they were still very new in England at the time) and I am sure that they thought that it was some kind of electronic 'bug.' I was eventually ushered into an enormous room with the inevitable portraits of Lenin and Stalin and waited there. After a while a man came in, shut the door and said *"Offskiddlepopski"* or something like that. I hadn't a clue what this meant and gazed blankly at him, wondering if it was Russian for "Good Morning," but apparently he was just announcing his name. Unfortunately he wouldn't take me seriously about the flight round that world and kept saying: "A pretty young girl shouldn't do things like that." He also would insist on referring to my navigator very chummily as my "navvy," which I found rather disconcerting at the time.

However, when eventually we got down to discussing landing fields, although he was very friendly and quite charming, he gave me the inevitable Russian *"Niet."* He explained that not even their own civil aircraft were allowed to land on Kamchatka and that the former Japanese airfields in the Kurile Islands would only be operated in time of war.

Michael and I visited the American Embassy, and told them where we wanted to land; they were very helpful, asking what facilities we would need at each. I personally remembered very little about that visit as the subtropical temperature of the room – the normal requirement of the American indoors – induced such agonies of sleep that I can only remembering fighting against this overwhelming desire.

The refusal of the Russians to permit our landing doubled the length of the non-stop flight across the Pacific and we knew that the range of the Auster could never be stretched to cover the 1,450-mile flight from Japan to the Aleutian Islands.

Looking through some back numbers of *Flight*, I showed Michael details of another aircraft on the same lines, only a little heavier. It was a completely new British plane of rather revolutionary post-war design called a Super Ace and its performance compared favourably with any plane of its price or type in the world. A world flight in this plane would give the British light aircraft industry some much-needed advertisement in overseas markets. Negotiations with the firm, the Chrislea Aircraft Company of Exeter, ended in a visit down there and I ordered an aeroplane. It was just like ordering a suit or a hat or anything else. How grown-up I felt! On the second visit to Exeter I received flying lessons on the aircraft, which was confusing in that it had unconventional flying controls. The control column, which had a wheel and came out of the instrument panel, was fixed to a ball-joint and, instead of pulling it towards you to climb, you had to push it *down*. Michael, the test pilot (Rex Steadman) and I flew it to Gravesend, where we had arranged with Essex Aero to build the extra tanks which would give us the long range necessary to cross the North Pacific.

It was at this point that we met our second major setback. The day after the aircraft had been delivered, I read in the papers that the manufacturers had closed for an indefinite period. No spares would then be available during the flight and Essex Aero were unable to get the necessary stressing data for the modifications. They thereupon refused to have anything more to do with the job.

It was at this crucial time that information was received from Japan that Nemuro airfield, on the extreme north-east tip of Hokkaido, had been demolished and our take-off point for the Pacific flight was pushed back two hundred miles to Chitose. In addition, Attu, the westernmost island of the Aleutian chain, was now only an emergency field and our destination was advanced fifty miles eastward, to little four-miles-by-two Shemya Island!

The start of the flight had been planned for July 15th and now, July 6th, when diplomatic clearances, foreign currency and inoculations had all been completed, I found myself with an aircraft incapable of doing the job! There followed two gloomy days when I thought that the whole idea was off and it suddenly struck me how terribly important it had become. What was worse was that I had already committed myself. The papers had given the intended flight publicity and the fact that I had pressed on this far against the advice of many people made it even more difficult to turn back. One round-the-world flight had already fallen through this year, too.

Where did we go from here? Michael and I talked it over . . . sure, and my husband, our Nanny and the woman in the next-door flat all had a word. Eventually Mike and I decided to hand the new plane in as hostage, more or less, for a Percival Proctor Mk. IV, on condition that I paid for modifications of the Proctor, which included the substitution of two 38-gallon tanks for the rear passenger seats and a complete overhaul. The Proctor was an ex-RAF wartime derivative of the Percival Gull which had made several record flights in the immediate pre-war period.

I christened the Proctor *"Thursday's Child"* after the old nursery rhyme. Remember it?

"Monday's child is fair of face,
Tuesday's child is full of grace.
Wednesday's child is full of woe,
Thursday's child has far to go.

Friday's child is loving and giving,
Saturday's child works hard for its living.
But the child that is born on the Sabbath Day
Is bonny and blythe and good and gay."

I, of course was born on a Thursday.

Michael and I went to Luton airfield, the home of Percival Aircraft, where he discussed modifications and probable performance with the chief designer, whilst I was checked out by the Chief Flying Instructor. I liked the feel and the handling of the aircraft and particularly the way she used to go "wonk" and drop just after you put the flaps down when coming in to land. It's a great thrill having an aeroplane, a whole aeroplane all of your own, even if the bill wasn't really paid. Other people own cars and horses, some own yachts, but I had an aeroplane! I must confess I purred!

The snowball had gathered speed by now. Michael and I rushed up to London and back again and ran round in tight circles, whilst my husband stood by, slightly bewildered but nonetheless rooting for me all the way, bless him.

They kept playing the song on the radio, *Civilisation*. It was whistled on station platforms and hummed in the hangars, and haunted me for weeks. I still get thrills when I play that record – thrills of excited anticipation! That wonderful "something is going to happen" feeling.

I was making lists by this time; lists of what things I wanted to take, lists of what I was going to do next day, losing lists, writing new ones, finding the originals and ticking the wrong items . . . oh what a delightful flap and panic! "D-Day" had been put off three times until it was now August 18th, but it crept nearer, inevitable and unbearable but never quite soon enough until the last moment, when it was much *too* soon.

Two days before I took off, I had to fly the other plane from Gravesend to Tollerton, where it would lie as hostage. Unfortunately I hadn't yet been solo on it but lightheartedly decided it didn't matter. The grass on Gravesend field was terribly long so we took off, Michael and I, on the perimeter track. This was curved, of course, and downhill, but slightly into the wind.

We took off and climbed like a scalded cat, missing a little hut (the sort people have at the end of their gardens) by what seemed like inches, and pressed on to Cambridge, where we were going to stop the night.

After a while Michael said: "Let me take over, I should like to try what she's like." He tried for a while and handed her back to me. "You can keep it!" he cried disgustedly.

She was difficult to fly because the weight of the hands on the wheel made her climb. When we got to Cambridge, joining the pattern at 1,000 feet, Michael remarked: "I wouldn't be in your shoes for all the tea in China," quite regardless of the fact that he wasn't in my *shoes*, he was in my *ship*.

[Dikki was writing this account shortly after spending much time in the US & Canada and so naturally tended to use the word 'ship' rather than 'plane' or 'aircraft'; I've left things that way throughout the book. – M.T.]

I came in, inevitably choosing the roughest place on the airfield to land on, and dug the nosewheel in. I had tried to pull the stick towards me to raise the nose as one does in a conventional plane, forgetting, of course, I should have pressed *down*. The propeller cracked and splintered and pieces flew everywhere, and in the "deathly 'ush" which followed the crash, Michael said: "Oh dear!" I thought this rather an understatement but declined to comment.

When the "blood wagons" (the ambulance and fire truck) had sauntered back again disappointedly, and I had avoided the reproachful eyes of the men who pulled the ship into the hangar, I went to Flying Control, where sat the Chief Instructor.

"How much do I owe for landing fees?" I asked.

I felt most horribly ashamed; I would rather have crashed anywhere else in the world than in my own field. He swung round in his chair and exposed me to one of his flashing, boyish grins.

"Nothing, Mrs M-T," he said. (How I hate being called Mrs M-T!) "You see, you didn't make a landing."

I smiled weakly and squirmed out under the door.

Richarda ("Dikki") Morrow-Tait and navigator Michael Townsend; the Chrislea Super Ace G-AKUV, originally intended for the flight, is in the background.

Dikki says goodbye to husband Norman and daughter Anna at Cambridge Airport before she and Michael leave for Croydon to start their epic flight in Percival Proctor IV G-AJMU. August 18th 1948.

CHAPTER 3
CAMBRIDGE–MARSEILLES

I cried the night before I took off – like a baby, to myself in bed. My husband hugged me and said: "You don't *have* to go, you know." But I did. I knew only too well that if I hadn't gone, if somehow it was stopped, I'd have hated it twice as much and regretted it all my life.

I had asked Morrow many, many times: "Could I go? Do you mind my going?"

And he said: "No, you go. If *you* want to go, *I* want you to go."

He is a rather wonderful person. I was afraid. Anything might happen; anything *would* happen. There might be death, there certainly would be adventure and, maybe much more dreadful than death, I could crash and be maimed. And suppose I never saw Morrow or my Anna again?

However, at dawn in the bright sunlight, my fears had gone and I was breathless with excitement. I met Michael at Cambridge airfield, while the dew was still wet on the grass and there was that unforgettable smell of an English early morning in summer. We pulled the ship out of the hangar, packed the bags in the back and ran to and fro doing little things. A handful of people saw us off, my daughter and my husband and just a few friends from the local pubs. We all shook hands, like the end of a tennis match. I kissed Anna and Morrow goodbye, turned and clambered blindly into the cockpit.

We bumped across the turf and soon were airborne over England. We flew over Hatfield trying to contact de Havillands to test the special lightweight radio receiver and transmitter made by Murphy Radio for us on two channels, 116.1 mHz and 126.18 mHz. However, we couldn't make contact as they were not listening out at the right time, so we flew on to Croydon with the radio untested.

Did I say we ran hither and thither at Cambridge? It was ten times worse at Croydon. There were Press and photographers; there were things to organise and last-minute equipment to pack in. The Croydon company, Field Aircraft, who had sold us the ship, were very helpful and we had a quick meal in one of their offices. Eating and talking and rushing away in the middle made a rather disquieting meal.

I was beckoned away to an empty office by one of the men of the firm, who said that they had been sorry but they could not fix us up a relief tube wide enough at the top for me to use and he produced the most obscene article I've ever seen in my life. It was like a small size in hot water bottles, with a large top and a small bottle and what he assured me was a non-return valve between. I was utterly appalled at this hideous contraption, vowing immediately to die rather than ever use it. But I saw why he gave it to me when I inspected the ship, for even Michael remarked that the equipment at present installed was an insult to a grown man.

With the ship piled high with odd things like flowers and sandwiches, we took off and flew south. I was almost sick with excitement, little thrills were chasing up and down my spine and my back teeth chattered quietly. But we were on our way. Very soon we could see the south coast of England roll under the wings, with the yellow sand dotted with hundreds of utterly unconcerned and completely happy people. They didn't know I was flying above, saying goodbye to England for six weeks, maybe even two months. Oh brother! I never made a greater underestimate in all my life.

How young I was! Maybe not so much in years, for I was 24, but I'd never really left home before, had never been abroad – bar a couple of family holidays in France to try to learn the language – and far, far worse, I had less than 100 flying hours to my name. And here was I setting blindly off, with a certain amount of trust in myself and the rest in God and Michael.

Soon France was underneath us, the northern part very like England again, and we were taking turns in flying so that we could eat sandwiches – and quite unconcerned, as the weather report at Croydon had been reasonably good. We flew over Versailles and I immediately thought, of course, of the Petit Trianon and the beautiful, foolish queen and how the fashion was to imitate the "simple life," dressing as shepherdesses and telling fairy stories, whilst the most brutal revolution in history was just breaking out.

We were almost over the Massif Centrale when clouds suddenly came down on us. We did a quick 90 degree turn to port, descending rapidly, aiming for the Saône Valley. Not a nice feeling, descending through cloud – there might be nothing underneath, or again there might be a nasty jagged mountain. Besides which the rain on the windshield made visibility so poor we had to throttle back and hang our heads out of the windows to see anything at all. Chugging down the Saône, flying quite low, we could see plainly how, when after the Rhône joined in, the two rivers ran side by side, one brown and the other blue. Oh – memories of my old school days and being told about it in French lessons!

Very little of those lessons remained but a few facts will stand out to my dying day. That the Champs Elysée is the widest road in the world and that Jeanne d'Arc was born at Dorémy. Both facts I was able to produce with great aplomb in the course of conversation later on, much to Michael's intense admiration and surprise.

Later on, when we were not quite sure where we were, I saw an airfield with 'AVIGNON' written on it. "*Sur le Pont d'Avignon,*" I hummed, peering over the wing. "Oh, Michael, there's the *bridge*!" and there it was, broken, just as it should be.

The even rows of olive trees and the vineyards had given way to sandy valleys and, as the warm sun was lengthening the shadows, Michael said: "There's Marignane, over on the far side of the lake." (Marignane airport was our destination, near Marseilles.) I flew over the lake, cautiously circled the field twice, looking for ground signals and that elusive thing, the windsock. It is unbelievable how cunningly some airfields can contrive to hide their wind-T or windsock. Sometimes they are amazingly well camouflaged and much trouble is apparently taken to make them tone in exactly with the surrounding grass.

I landed and followed the taxi strip round, heading for the control buildings. Before we got there, however, Mike suddenly yelled out: "Look out, there's a heap of earth ahead." I braked, cut the throttle and swung off the strip on to the grass.

Sure enough there *was* something ahead. A whacking great unmarked trench had been dug, right across the taxi strip and to both sides of it. We fell into it. The wheels sunk in, the nose tilted forward, we hovered and then slowly settled down on to the tailwheel again. We sat there, Mike and I, saying alternately in agonised tones: "No, no, no!" We couldn't believe that such a thing should happen. The first landing and then this. Briefing at Croydon had failed to mention the obstruction, and we had received no red warning light from Marignane control tower. No, it couldn't be true. It just couldn't.

Crash trucks came up and then turned away again sadly as we slowly climbed out. Then people started rushing up and we realised for the first time that this was France and that the inhabitants insist on speaking French. They kept it up all the time we were there. Never shall I forget seeing Michael standing there, chin in hand, struggling in schoolboy French, the cynosure of uncomprehending eyes. The Esso representative, on the lookout for us, eventually sorted things out and had the ship pulled out with the help of ten men and a crane and towed into the hangar.

CHAPTER 4
REPAIRS AT MARIGNANE

I was tired that night. I found that the sound of the engine was a great strain on my ears, which kept up this singing all night. We were late when we were driven into Marseilles by the fuel representative, so we just had a quick meal in a noisy little café, so very French, before we went to our rooms, previously booked, in an appallingly expensive hotel.

We were in France for nine days. The second night we spent in a cheaper hotel in Marseilles and later we moved into a little hotel in a village called St. Victoret. This had been recommended to us by some of the mechanics in the hangar and we were driven there, each on the back of a motor bike, over a dusty, bumpy road. I found it incredibly difficult to cling on and I am sure my driver must have been mildly surprised at my ardent embrace on so short an acquaintance, but it was the only way of staying on.

The hotel was very small and bare. The downstairs room was dining room, bar, and everything else all rolled into one. It had a concrete floor and two doorways covered by bead curtains. The food, needless to say, was excellent and we had the local wine at every meal, though the midday meal, we found, was too heavy and too conducive to quarrelling in the afternoon.

We used to walk up to the airfield in the morning to watch the repairs being carried out, for we had damaged four ribs in the leading edge of the starboard wing as well as bending the propeller and the wheel spats. The men in the hangar were very chummy and our appearance in the morning was the signal for them all to stop work whilst we shook hands; after that they would lean against the mainplane and work could not be resumed until every man had had his say. The work they did, however, was excellent and, in view of later experiences, miraculously speedy. Their foreman, Monsieur Druon, seemed quite confident of being able to repair it but gave his time as 6½ days and, to our suggestion that they might work overtime over the weekend, the reply was: *"Personne ne travaille le Samedi ou le Dimanche!"* We should just about manage the trip in a year with a week's stay at each place!

I tried to discuss the matter of the accident with the airport manager, with, of course, the aid of an interpreter, my French not being able to hold out in an argument. At the Croydon briefing there had been no warning of work in progress at Marignane airport and, worse still from my point of view, no international ground signal (the red square with an orange diagonal) had been displayed at Marignane. Besides which, it was downright careless of him to leave a large unmarked trench lying around like that. However, I got nowhere!

We were glad of that nine days' rest, though, for we were tired with the stress of the preparation for the flight and there was an awful lot of nothing to do there, as we had to be careful of our small fund of currency. We went into Marseilles a couple of times, once with a Frenchman from Nancy, who said he wanted to show us the town but, since his idea of showing us Marseilles was to go from bar to bar, we saw remarkably little. We eventually got brassed off with that and, having bought two vacuum flasks (thirsty work, flying), one small funnel (modification to the relief tube) and one big floppy straw hat for me, we returned to our little hotel.

The sanitation there was incredibly primitive; the lavatory didn't work and we never did discover if there was a shower. We swam in the nearby lake a lot and had showers in the Esso representative's office, where one had just been installed. Oh how Mike kidded me about that man! I had incautiously stated at one time that I considered him good-looking. He was tall, fair, wavy-haired and slim and his clothes the last thing, but what used to hold my eye was the gold tooth at the end of his smile, a thing so rarely seen in England nowadays. Mike kidded me so much about his "lithe shape" that when one day I did see him in swimming trunks I was hopelessly embarrassed.

Our French was very poor but we had huge fun trying to use it. There was a time when my brassière did not come back from the laundry and I had to explain to mine host that it was missing. This involved a protracted and intensively vivid display of gestures on his part before it was finally settled as to what part of my anatomy the garment covered.

We found the walk from the airfield to the hotel hot and tiring and, when one day we had a lift by the foreman in his car, we really were grateful. Mike, however, became a little involved in his profuse "thank you" and told the man he was *"tres joli"* instead of *"tres gentil."* The foreman looked a little surprised but took it in good part.

We should have gone off on the eighth day and in fact packed ourselves up, complete with bottle of brandy (a very present help in times of trouble) and the French idea of a sandwich. (This was a long loaf, split in two lengthwise, with a row of pieces of ham as a filling.) Unfortunately we had plug trouble, causing a big drop in RPM when we tried to take off. However, we got that just about all right by running it up at full revs in lean mixture. But I did not appreciate it when, as we went for our test flight, Mike leaned over and tested the magnetos on our climb over the lake.

We slept the eighth night in a different hotel in St. Victoret because we went back with a British European Airways man who had been helping us. The sanitation there was something I had never met before. There was a little room at the end of a passage which, bare of ordinary facilities, had only a hole in the floor and two bricks on which one balanced precariously. The knack, I discovered too, was that one should get out of the little room before leaning back to pull the chain, otherwise one became awash to one's ankles.

That night for me was memorable for the most appalling nightmare. I remember waking three or four times sweating with fear and I was most horribly tired the next morning; maybe that's why I forgot to pack my one and only dress.

UPPER: M. Druon (extreme left) and the S.N.C.A.S.E. repair team at Marignane Airport (Michael Townsend at extreme R.).
LOWER: Arranging for fuel with the Esso representative at Luqa, Malta.

UPPER: The repair team at Dum Dum (Calcutta) Airport. From L. to R.: Himalayan Aviation mechanic (unknown), Jerry Jermyn (DH engineer), Dikki, "Lofty" Wall (Himalayan Aviation engineer) and Michael (see Ch. 11).
LOWER: His Highness the Maharajah of Cooch Behar (see Ch. 14).

CHAPTER 5

MARSEILLES–MALTA–CYPRUS

We took off at 8.55 in the morning and climbed up over the clouds, setting a course for Malta. There were six tenths cumulus clouds for half the way and after that CAVU (Ceiling And Visibility Unlimited). We had decided to go there rather than our original planned route via Castle Benito and El Adam, in North Africa, as we were now short of currency for what was called on our travellers' cheques "Other Countries." Our money was divided into three groups, Sterling area, dollars and "other countries"; in Malta, of course they use Sterling.

It wasn't a very long flight, 6 hours and 15 minutes, but because of the nightmare, I suppose, I was very jittery. Every time the propeller changed its note, as it often seemed to do over water, my heart was in my mouth. In fact, as far as I remember, it was there most of the time in that flight. Michael had no maps of the area over which we were flying as it was not part of the original route; but we managed quite nicely with the knowledge that we had to fly directly over the highest (6,017 ft) mountain in Sardinia, skirt the toe of Sicily and finally land on the third island on the right. Sardinia duly turned up and its wild, mountainous terrain made all the old stories of brigands and vendettas seem very real. Ninety minutes later we were passing between Sicily and Pantellaria; then came the little island of Gozo, almost joined on to Malta.

We touched down at Malta soon after three o'clock. Actually we did more than touch down for I bounced her and, much to my intense mortification, they reported me in the papers as doing so. The land looked very brown from the air and puzzled me because it seemed to be entirely composed of walls, like lots of houses with no roofs. I found out later that these walls were built to keep earth on the island when the wind blew. We were again welcomed by the fuel representative, even though he didn't know we were coming, and he drove us around over the island so that we could see what it looked like.

Apparently my absence caused some worry up at the camp at Luqa airfield because my bare arms and bare legs and very short shorts would have caused no minor stir had I been seen on the streets that day; there was some sort of religious festival going on and, as the women had to be clad from the wrist to the ankles, they were afraid I might be cast into jail. Apparently, too, two-piece swimsuits are not allowed on the island so some women sew a piece of tape between the brassière and the pants, thus making it a one-piece costume.

The Shell representative took us back to his beautiful home and we sat on the terrace drinking whisky and watching the sun go down over the bay where St. Paul's ship was wrecked. He gave us a huge bag of grapes and took us back to Luqa airfield, where we had supper before retiring to our quarters in the Transient Officers' Mess.

I tried to have a shower before going to bed but, as water in Malta is very scarce in August, so little came out of the sprinkler that I had great trouble in getting all of me wet at the same time without bits of me drying off. After I had finished there was just about a pint of dirty water left in the bottom of the bath, that's all. It was cool and pleasant but I found difficulty in composing myself until I mesmerised myself with my magic formula for sleep. It's nearly infallible and consists of lying comfortable and motionless in bed, consciously relaxing from feet to neck and then saying softly and sibilantly to oneself: *"There is sweet music here that softer falls . . . "* etc.

The next morning we took-off at 0642 hours, all keen and ready for Cyprus, another bit of "Sterling area." This we knew would take about 9 hours but we wanted to do a test flight for the fuel consumption. How blue the Mediterranean was, just as they say. We flew at 6,000 feet, just a little silver ship 40 feet wide and 28 feet long of pulsating energy, suspended between deep blue water and deep blue sky. There wasn't a cloud and we talked and laughed and spat grape pips at each other, perfectly confident and perfectly content. *"We were young, we were merry, we were very, very wise."*

This time we ate ordinary sandwiches: the French one, which had been left in the aircraft overnight, had become case-hardened and though Mike tried his best with my sheath knife he could make no impression, so he gave it up and extracted the fatty pieces of ham, which he consumed with obvious relish but to my intense disgust.

We flew for 9 hours and 13 minutes; Michael taking over from me for about 10 minutes every hour so that I could rest my eyes, for there was no horizon, just blue everywhere and it was best to fly on instruments. Mike did a few sun-shots with his sextant, just to see how easily it could be done, and would point out to me: "Over there is Turkey," and so on. I sang little French songs to myself and quoted endless poetry. We were as young and happy as if the world had only been made for us that day. When the contents of each fuel tank ran dry, the engine would cough and quit, and, as we dropped the odd hundred feet or so, before that tank was turned 'off' and a new one 'on,' we would turn to each other and laugh and say: "Quiet, isn't it?"

I must admit that was the easiest flight for that length of time we had ever done. The best flights are those when nothing happens, but my, my, aren't they tedious? I even caught myself on that trip wishing something would happen and then I'd turn round to myself and say hurriedly: "Don't be silly." Of course the mountain rim of Cyprus turned up eventually, though at one time I felt it never would. After a short flight over the dusty inland plain, we touched down at Nicosia at 4.55 in the afternoon, having made three shots at the runway. It happened to be lying dead into the low evening sun and my first attempt blinded me, so I opened the throttle and went round again. The second time I thought I would be smart, come in very low on the base leg and sneak it on to the strip quickly. But I wasn't quite low enough and had to go round yet again. Mike then called up on the RT and explained, and so we were given another runway to land on.

"*Thursday's Child*" was a very noisy ship and, despite our using cotton wool in our ears, we still shouted at everybody when we landed and everything had to be said to us twice, for the constant hum stayed in our ears. We had only one microphone and headset, which I encouraged Michael to wear as much as possible. But it made no difference, his ears still stuck out. "*With monstrous head and sickening cry and ears like errant wings, the devil's walking parody on all four-footed things.*" I used to tease him often but he had his own revenge in his description of me in a tight black suit walking towards him on a station platform, with a smug smile covering my face and double chin – "Just like a self-satisfied seal," he told me a year later, whilst sitting waiting for a visa in a hushed, efficient office.

I taxied the ship over to a man waving the bats, meditating meanwhile on how little they realized the danger in which they stood, particularly with our type of ship, when they insisted on lining us up with the other ships just so. For there was only a handbrake like on a sports car with differential brake control through the rudder pedals, and the amount of pressure applied by the hand controlled the speed and manoeuvrability of the ship. This meant that any close manoeuvre meant a sudden burst of engine being applied, as well as a lot of brake on one side. It's very much a question of hit and miss; normally I miss but I'm afraid one day I won't, particularly when so little can be seen from the cockpit.

As I stepped out, pulling the cotton wool from my ears, a little man with a strong Greek accent rushed up and said confidentially into my ear: "Who handled you the last time you were here?"

Somehow this didn't make sense to me, besides which it didn't sound quite nice. I made him say it again and then a third time. The little man, red in the face by this time, stood on his toes, with his hands clenched at his sides and screamed at me. And still it didn't make any more sense and sounded exactly like: "Who handled you the last time you were here?"

An RAF officer standing nearby had to explain that the man was a representative of one of the fuel companies and he was referring to the servicing or "handling" of my aeroplane. Evidently he must have thought I was a regular visitor.

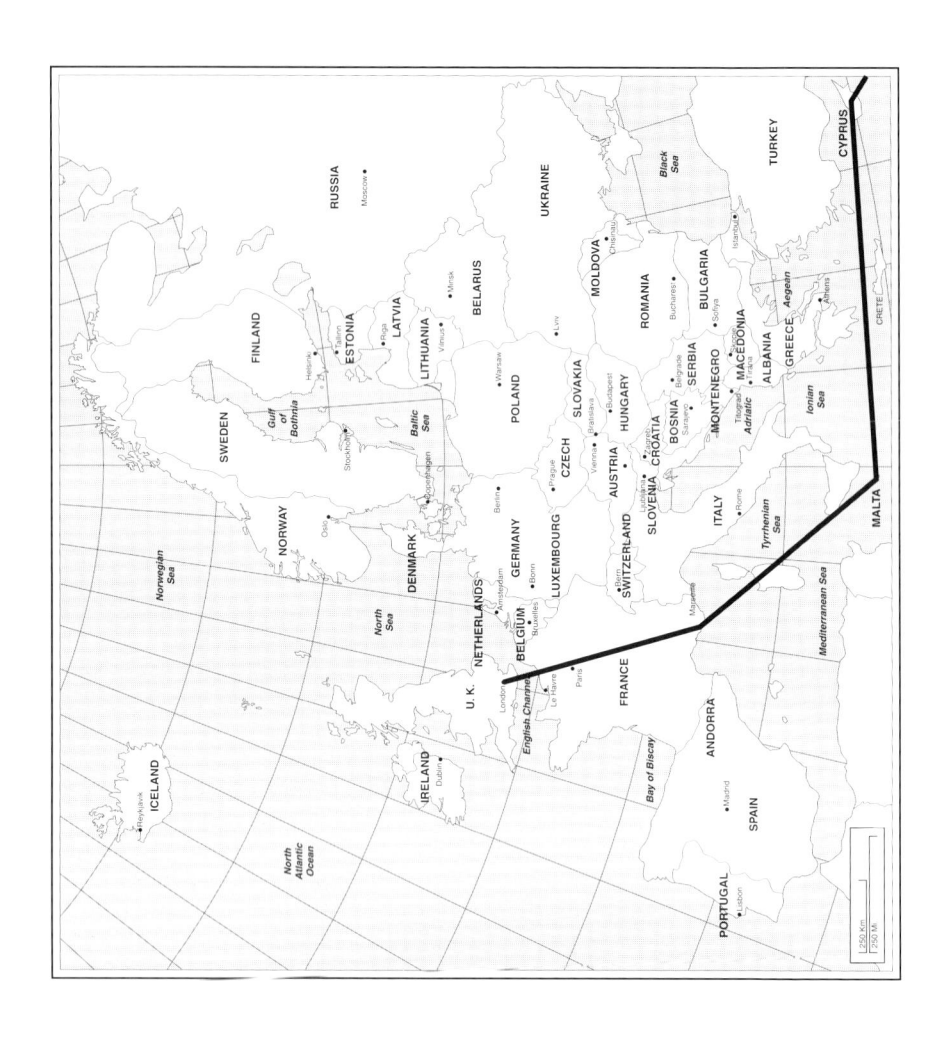

CHAPTER 6
CYPRUS–HABBANIYA–BAHREIN

We rested a day at Nicosia, Cyprus. It was very pleasant. The hotel was cheap, the sun was warm and we were pleased with ourselves. The aircraft hadn't done too well, for though she had only used 10·7 gallons per hour, her speed had been 10 mph less than we had been led to believe. However, we expected her performance to improve in the cooler conditions abiding when we would fly our Pacific flight. That was the one, of course, we were very worried about. In fact Michael and I had got what we referred to as "yellow feet" about that bit. "Yellow feet," of course is being 'yellow' and 'having cold feet' at the same time.

We had a little party one evening at the RAF station at Nicosia and everything would have been fine but for us again having plug trouble when we tried to take off. A young fighter pilot and his cheery little fitter came over to help us investigate a very large rev drop on one magneto and there followed an exhausting morning working in the sun, taking the plugs out, cleaning them and putting them back again and playing with the contact breaker gaps in the magnetos. This is a harassing pastime anyway, but with a temperature of nearly 110° F even in the shade of our wings it became even more so. It was here that we first learned not to leave metal tools and plugs in the sun if we wished to escape with a full complement of unscorched skin. Eventually we ran her to our satisfaction, there being a drop of less than 75 rpm each mag.

We took off at midday and tried to fly our next leg. The heat of the day made flying terribly bumpy due to up-draughts and our progress seemed so imperceptible that for fear of not reaching Habbaniya before sunset we gave it up and after half an hour came back again. The return journey was one of those nightmares which I feel sure happen to all pilots at some time or other. Not only had we been making slow progress on the eastward flight, but the engine had been worrying us. I kept hearing changes of note in its tune and I know Michael did too, as we kept glancing at one another nervously and I had asked him more than once whether we ought not to turn round and go back. The arrival of the east coast of Cyprus decided us and back we went. All the way to Nicosia the engine kept faltering and both of us were in an absolute fever of anxiety after 30 minutes of glancing surreptitiously first at one another and then at likely-looking forced-landing places beneath us. After what seemed ages, we reached the aerodrome and I somehow landed her with her heavy fuel load.

Once on the ground I ran the engine up and it sounded perfect! Just to make sure I invited our RAF pilot friend to do a test flight with me and give his unbiased views on it. Of course he checked it OK. Funny things, nerves, all very well in moderation but for Mike and I to have the same hallucinations at the same time was something to guard against in future.

We were not without our diplomatic problems at Nicosia, too. Our planned route lay to Baghdad and then down the Persian Gulf to the Arabian Sea. We had reckoned, though, without political conditions.

Damascus control refused us clearance to fly over Syria, where they were liable to fire on strange aircraft. Palestine, to the south, was busy with the Arab versus Jew war and both sides shot at anything in sight, whilst Egypt, which was on the normal air route to the East, was involved in the same *melée*. The problem was fraught with all manner of interesting possibilities. These were duly discussed in the RAF Mess and, out of the tangle of somewhat alcoholic suggestions, our only plan became clear.

We set off next morning, August 31st, at dawn, when the land was cool and the air quiet, and climbed high above the broken cloud that mantled the mountains of Cyprus and the Levant coast. Michael had chosen a somewhat erratic route, far from any settlements, and we scarcely saw any sign of habitation, only just desert, looking precisely as desert is supposed to look – low rock plateaux separated by wide desert basins and cut into by steep-sided *wadis* and not a sign of life or vegetation. So this was the Middle East, the place there was so much international fuss and feuding about. The politicians should come and take a good look at it some time.

It was terribly hot and I sat there in the cockpit, with the sweat streaming down my arms and legs, quoting things like *Ozymandias of Egypt* and anything else deserty that I could quote. There's nothing much else to do in an aeroplane when you are flying a straight course. Believe you me, it had to be straight, too, for if I wavered off course, Mike's hulking great feet would come thudding down on the rudder bar, a thing which made me 'madder'n'hell,' but taught me to fly a straight course. Middle name "George," that's me. But it doesn't need a lot of effort, though, and as often as not, I used to fly entirely on instruments, for we would be flying eastward into the sun, and I would sit my big floppy hat on the bridge of my nose, like Daddy in a deck chair, so that all I could see would be the instrument panel and my own hands and feet. I would watch the gauges, of course, but there again it is something that you see as a whole combined shape rather than as individual dials. But I would soon notice if something wasn't right. There I would sit, quoting endless poetry (there's too much noise for singing) for, having a retentive memory for verse and not for anything really useful, there was an enormous amount hoarded away.

After desert and more desert, we finally picked up the Euphrates, which we followed until we reached the RAF airfield of Habbaniya, 40 miles west of Baghdad. It looked utterly deserted and I wondered vaguely whether it was Sunday or Early Closing, but it sprang to life when we taxied up to the hangars. It's lucky that I am always a firm believer in the theory that runway in front of one is much more useful than runway behind, and if anything I'm inclined to land a little short. For the concrete was hot and after cutting the engine our little plywood and fabric ship floated on and on due to the up-draughts. It sure was hot there!

We refuelled the ship outside the hangar in the blazing sun and as each can was opened the evaporation made the whole sky seem to shimmer and it almost sizzled going in. It was a very fiddly ship to refuel and we spent as long as an hour and a half supervising the natives doing the job. For of course they had to go back and get things (they could knock spots off an English plumber); and we had six fuel tanks, two outer wing tanks containing 20 gallons, two centre-section tanks with 10 gallons each and two cabin tanks in the back, containing 38 gallons apiece. Then quite often we would mix it because there would be only 100 octane or 73 octane and we ran on 80 or 87. It was a very complicated business, for, with a little bit of 100 octane here and a little bit of 73 octane there, it was like someone fussing with their tea and wanting milk poured in first.

We had lunch at Habbaniya at a most superior RAF Mess, complete with a swimming pool and everything, and then climbed into our ship, heading for Bahrein Island, in the Persian Gulf. Did I say "climb" into the ship? We didn't, we hopped around like jumping beans for she had been sitting in the sun and the leather upholstery is not the best thing to sit on wearing only cotton shorts. Twice during the refuelling I'd put my hand on the metal and quite hurt myself.

I was very impressed at this time by the fact that though I had drunk at least two quarts of water, it just disappeared. If course it was sweated out but I didn't notice it.

Conditions were unbelievably bumpy when climbing up from Habbaniya and I was quite exhausted when we gained 6,000 ft (our most economical level) for it took such a lot of will power. The oil temperature would go way up and the little extra oil tank, which nestled between the two fuel tanks behind us in the cabin, would sweat beads of paint on the pipe which led to the engine. When the sun warms up the earth it reflects the heat, as you can see by the ground shimmering on any summer day, and the greater the heat and the rougher the ground, the bumpier it is.

That flight was the only one wherein my dinner troubled me, for at Habbaniya we had made a hearty meal of the inevitable RAF eggs and bacon and I confess I wasn't feeling any too good on that trip. The two sluggishly meandering rivers below us, the Tigris and Euphrates, with their dull green borders of date palms, were merely a source of irritation because they seemed to stretch for ever in front of us. The thought that under our wings were the ruined cities of the world's oldest civilisations left me almost unmoved. Nebuchadnezzar and his city of Babylon, Sargon of Akked and Ur of the Chaldees were pushed into the background by the turbulence and up-currents reflected from the mounds of their ruined temples. However, when Mike took over at the end of an hour, I ate a Benzedrine tablet and two aspirins and had a nap for five minutes, woke up, saw there was still five minutes left, had another nap and woke up as good as new. That was the only time, too, that I've ever slept in an aircraft. Mike should be very flattered that I trusted him that well!

As the afternoon wore on and we flew over the Persian Gulf, conditions became much smoother, but what was rather worrying was that the sun was sinking and we still had many miles to cover. Apparently we had been given the wrong local time at Habbaniya for sunset, and we certainly were not enamoured of the idea of having to land on some strange field after dark. Mike was distinctly perturbed until I pointed out to him that he was still wearing his dark glasses. But even so the blue of the afternoon turned to deeper & deeper shades of violet, and along the Arabian coastline on the starboard side little lights sprinkled the shore. I put the ship down into a shallow dive to make as good a speed as possible and presently Mike called up Bahrein on the R/T. The tower told us to call them on our downwind leg of the circuit and, very soon after, we saw a row of lights. I came down to 1,000 ft and lined myself up parallel with the runway, Mike dutifully putting in his call.

It wasn't until then that he suddenly realized that the row of lights did not mark out a runway but a jetty, for there across the other side of the island was the real runway with its double row of lights. I got into position again, muttering instructions to myself, telling myself what to do, for I was just scared rigid. I'd never done a night landing before and the last thing I felt I wanted to do at that time, tired and hungry, was to learn how. However, I was up there and I had to come down some way. Mike had told me that I had to touch down by the third runway light and much to my intense surprise, I did. There followed then the most ghastly row of clanking and crashing metal, which utterly unnerved me, causing me to look all ways at the same time.

"Mike, what's the matter?" I yelled. "Has something dropped off?"

We hadn't put any lights on for landing because sometimes the lights reflect on to a bank of dust maybe 10 ft above the actual runway and one looks silly doing a three-point landing 10 feet off the deck. I'd even forgotten to put the navigation lights on. When the ship came to a standstill, Mike said: "No, you mutt, it's only a metal-strip runway." It was the first I'd ever landed on and it sure did sound horrible. Whilst we were chatting, I suddenly noticed we had one wingtip over a runway light, which in this case was a flare, so I opened the throttle hastily and hoped Mike hadn't noticed. My shirt clung sweat-soaked to my back.

When we taxied to the hangar, everyone came out and took us in to the Mess. It was an RAF station and they were so kind to us. They even seemed glad to see us, which is always an encouraging start. They gave us drinks. I had a brandy – and I needed it – and Mike had cold beer, which unfortunately gave him collywobbles later on in the evening. A cold beer should not be drunk on an empty stomach when you're hot and Mike had to be sent to bed.

One of the problems there was the noise of the air-conditioning. Everyone slept in air-conditioned quarters but they managed to drag an extra bed from somewhere into someone else's room for Michael, whilst I slept in the bed of an officer out on night duty. I was bitterly tired that night – we both were, really. We had a flight of 4¾ hours in the morning and 5 in the afternoon, to say nothing of a couple of hours at lunch time, when we superintended refuelling and organized passports and papers and what-have-you, always an exhausting and an exacting labour, as everyone talks at the same time and I can never remember the name of the place I am going next. Come to think of it, you know, they must have thought me incredibly clueless at times.

CHAPTER 7

BAHREIN–SHARJA–KARACHI

In my imagination Bahrein, climatically speaking, is a particularly horrid spot. Hell will be exactly like that. "It's not the heat, it's the humidity" and "Don't ask me, ask my pal, I'm sweating," are the by-words of that place. Every moment makes one sweat and it never dries, it just runs down in rivers. People walk around with towels round their necks. Most of them look soaked to the skin.

They were so good to me that night. After a supper of the eternal eggs and bacon (would you believe it, for the third time that day) and when Michael had gone to bed, I chattered for a while over another brandy and they sent a wire off to my husband for me, loaned me a dressing gown and led me into the shower where they stood outside, as there were no locks on the door, while I performed my ablutions rather hampered by the complete darkness, there being no light in the place. They then escorted me back and I was given strict instructions to keep my tummy covered with a towel as I would be sleeping under a fan. If you don't, you get cramps, as I found out later.

I took a phenobarbitone tablet, as I always used to when I got overtired, for being one of those people who dream a lot, I used to go on frantically doing all night the things I'd been doing all the day. Dreams to me are very vivid and I dream every time I close my eyes. Sometimes I would dream that somebody had made a remark to me about something, or I would dream that I'd done a certain thing to the ship that I'd meant to do and I would often have trouble separating fact from fiction next day. However, that night I slept comparatively soundly until woken by the bearer with a morning cup of tea. He was horrified to find a woman in his master's bed and insisted on telling everyone, who one and all got quite the wrong idea and, though applauding heartily, thought it a bit of a nerve on the part of the officer concerned.

We decided to make only a short flight the next day, and anyway we'd left it too late to make Karachi, so we took off for the little fort of Sharja, at the south end of the Persian Gulf, which is also a RAF station. That was quite an uneventful trip; it was calm and only took 2 hours and 40 minutes. Before we took off, I heard one man make a remark to another, calling him "Charlie Oboe," and I thought to myself "That's a funny name, isn't it?," and it wasn't until the thought struck me again whilst I was flying that it dawned on me he was talking to his CO. *[Charlie stood for "C" and Oboe for "O" in the international phonetic alphabet then in use. – M.T.]*

Sharja stands in the desert and the runways are made of sand, marked by a narrow tarred strip in the centre. These puzzled me for a while, I couldn't think quite what they were. Being only about 3 feet wide, I thought they couldn't possibly be runways. I came in on a slow, low, wide pattern that Mike would refer to as "low-level cross-country" but even so I couldn't judge my distance from the ground at all. Normally you tell by the blades of grass and the surface of the runway. You really can't see the grains of sand and 100 ft looks very much the same as 10. I was just about to ease the stick back to put the ship in a stalling position, when I discovered that I'd already touched down and done a wheel landing.

We stood in the sun for an hour while the ship was refuelled. Oh what a tedious process that was and I was getting thirstier and thirstier till my mind conjured up fantastic images of beer bottles on the wall of the Fort. I was very fascinated, though, by a little gazelle, which stood in the shade made by the aeroplane, watching the refuelling process with big, wise eyes. It was a beautiful and delicate little thing, standing about two feet high, and lived apparently entirely on a diet of cigarettes and toffee, which it consumed in the paper. It struck me as an expensive way to feed a gazelle but maybe it was faddy that way. I must say, though, that I quite fell in love with it and very much embarrassed Michael by beseeching the CO to send me one home. We had dinner that night in a beautifully air-conditioned Mess but our quarters were unbearably hot and stuffy.

Before supper that night, I lay down and tried to sleep, lying on the bed with absolutely nothing on, wishing I could even take my skin off. Of course the moment I'd just dropped into sleep some beastly little Arab boy came crashing in saying: "Tea, sir?." I said "No" firmly and loudly, trying hard to pretend that the brief towel over my tummy covered me from head to heel. The boy backed out, only to return in a few minutes with a large and steaming brew.

"I don't want any tea, take it away," I yelled irritably and he said: "Yes, sir," and put it down by my bedside table. I growled gently and Mike told me afterwards he had received exactly the same treatment.

Having discovered where the bathroom was, I thought I'd try and get a little washing in, as I never did care for showers. I found, however, that this again was easier said than done. The taps produced a warm fluid of a strong orange colour and there was no plug. I found, however, with a little manoeuvring, one heel could be kept in the hole most of the time. At least it was wet and moderately cool. I got very brassed off with the water which we drank, which was so chlorinated and so salty that it created a very vicious circle between desire and effect.

The next morning was comparatively cool and, after briefing and the payment of our debts, we climbed out over the Mountains of Oman and headed for Karachi, on the west coast of India. Actually our rate of climb after take-off was always embarrassingly slow and I was almost ashamed of the little ship. She also flew perpetually in a nose-up position which irritated me, for I could do nothing about it. We usually climbed up to at least 6,000 ft though there again it depended on the clouds and everything. The first thing in the morning there would be no cloud and then one or two little cumulus clouds would dot the world beneath us, here and there, as though they were pretending they weren't there at all. By degrees they would become thicker and more numerous until sometimes the whole ground was obscured. Then they would rise slowly with the heat of the day, some of them reaching as much as 30,000 ft by mid-afternoon and spreading out at the top. These had to be avoided at all costs for, being full of up-draughts and down-draughts, they were kind-of dicey for a Dakota, let alone a little plywood matchbox like us.

As we invariably flew east into the dawn, I always wore my floppy hat which I bought in France. It might look a bit funny and really there was hardly room to wield it in our little ship and sometimes Mike complained it tickled his ears, but it looked a darn sight funnier on Mike when he used to take over the controls, particularly as he always religiously tied the bow under his chin. It used to be agony sometimes to keep awake on those still, shining days, when there was nothing to do but just sit. All the navigation needed for the first half of that leg was to follow the Persian and Baluchistan coastlines, keeping just over the Arabian Sea so that there would be no up-draughts. I used to eye the little clock in the panel, trying to hurry the hand round to the hour when Mike would take over for that brief ten minutes. I would never ask him to take over; I'd rather die than do that but oh how glad I used to be when he did, for my eyelids would flicker and droop and then jerk upwards again in the continued effort to stay awake.

After a while, when the clouds were thick beneath us, and we thought we were not far from the coast line of India, we decided to come down. I throttled back and down we came, through the thick white clouds, which felt as though they were pushing at you through the windows, giving you a feeling of intense shut-in-ness and of vague hostility outside. We took so long to come through the clouds that we started being anxious as to whether we were over the coast or the sea and, if we were over the coast, what we would hit in our descent. We came out of the clouds about 500 ft over water, in poor visibility and being very much tossed around. We had to spot a mountain on the coastline but we couldn't see any coastline or mountain – or anything. We chugged on however and I kept gulping water from the thermos flask, my throat feeling unnecessarily dry.

Looking back on it now, I seem to have wasted an awful lot of time feeling scared but of course this is *now*, and that was *then*. I used to cast sidelong glances at Mike scowling over his maps and pulling the most horrifying faces, and it wasn't for quite a while that I discovered that this was Mike's way of concentrating. I used to worry, thinking that all sorts of dreadful things had happened – that we had lost our way, or that the tail section had dropped off without my noticing. Surely we couldn't miss India altogether. It was the same sort of useless panic I used to get into when my mother would suddenly start one of her spells of asthmatic coughing and I would look all ways at once, wondering if fire had broken out somewhere and she was unable to tell us. But of course the hills and the coastline soon came into view beneath a threatening monsoon sky. Mike spotted his position: what a wonderful man, how did he ever do it? To me, navigation, even yet, seems to be mostly magic, due to my confirmed inability to grasp any form of calculation whatsoever, however elementary.

The map marked Karachi but did not inform us that there were three airfields, which confused us a little bit and we landed on the wrong one. We landed at Drigh Road, taxied up to the control tower which was closed, all the doors being locked, and then we taxied down to the other end, where we thought we saw signs of life. Sure enough there, sitting in the sunshine, were a few RAF "erks," of whom we asked the way. Kinda silly, isn't it, when you cross the sea and everything and have to come down and ask your way to the right airfield? We had a few gulps of water from a pitcher and took off again to the next airfield about a mile away. This was the big airfield with the airship hangar built for the R.101 and we pretended we had just come in.

It was just as well we did, too, for the Pakistan officials are very rigorous on the health regulations. I was highly incensed when an Indian official opened the door, shoved a disinfectant bomb on my lap and slammed the door shut again. I took it as a direct insult until Michael explained it to me. There were hordes of suspicious officials to be pacified and all of them seemed to be darkly suspecting the worst, whatever that might have been. But we came through triumphant, having suffered agonies in England of injections of all kinds; in fact, my arm had been sore for weeks and by the time we had got round to having the plague injection, I'd had to have it done in the right arm.

CHAPTER 8
KARACHI–DELHI

Karachi was cool and we stayed at bright, clean BOAC quarters, long low rooms connected by a veranda, with fans and bright chintz curtains. We stayed there two nights whilst the BOAC engineers gave *"Thursday's Child"* a 50-hour inspection. There wasn't an awful lot to do actually but I was a little perturbed to notice that one undercarriage leg was lower than the other; and there wasn't anything I could do about it either, because they were not filled with fluid but had some sort of spring arrangement. They changed the oil, checked the engine, cleaned the plugs and looked inside all the inspection panels to see what had dropped off. Then we stood around, watching her being refuelled; this refuelling was the record, taking precisely an hour and a half, together with a quantity of swearing by Mike and scurrying to fetch things by the natives. One clot of an Indian even stood on the wingtip which, being made only of plywood and fabric, moved Mike to quite profound eloquence. Nothing happened, however, probably as the culprit had bare feet, so we all went back to lunch.

The square of grass upon which the hotel windows faced was being at this time cut by the Indians. It took about six of them squatting near each other to cut the grass, which was done with small scissors, each Indian covering about 3 sq ft in a day. The idea intrigued me and I tried to get Mikey to do a sum for me to find out how many days it would take the six of them to cut the square.

I wish I had had time to see something of the town of Karachi. However, on the last evening of our brief stay, which we had meant to be a quiet one and to have gone to bed early, I was asked if I would do a broadcast for Pakistan radio. I said yes, I would, and a car was sent for me. Mike didn't like me going alone so he came too. We were driven into the town in the dark and along a meandering way to the studios. These were quite small, for Pakistan radio was a very new institution. However unfortunately the power had failed and, though we stayed there nearly an hour, nattering about what I was to say etc., Mike eventually announced that we really had to get back and get some sleeping hours in, so back we were driven and I still saw nothing bar the silhouette of a camel on the road, the first I'd ever seen out of a zoo.

Now that we had entered the monsoon area, a special flying programme was necessary. The great danger to small aircraft like ours was the severe turbulence which, in its milder forms, would toss us about like a leaf in an autumn gale and, at its worst, could easily tear off a wing. All this was very undesirable, but it could be avoided by an early-morning take-off. The severe vertical air currents which were our *bête-noir* were clearly visible as they only occurred in cumulo-nimbus clouds. These would not begin to develop as a rule until well after sunrise and did not reach a dangerous size until after midday, when the ground had been really well heated. If we took off at 3 am and landed before 11 o'clock, we should be quite safe. In these dawn flights we would keep at 6,000 ft as long as possible and thereafter climb as necessary to keep above the cloud. The only time this plan came unstuck was on the long flight from Delhi to Calcutta.

We were perfectly determined when leaving Karachi to get off really early, and got up all keen and ready (at least that was what we swore we were) in the pitch-black night. Whatever made Keats refer to it as *"the honeyed middle of the night"*? Personally, I can find nothing 'honeyed' in it whatsoever. I would crawl out of bed sleepy and sore-eyed, with a strong suspicion that my head is really only filled with wool, as it feels. We would drag our bags to the ship with weak unwilling arms, but once out in the night air I'd slowly wake up. There's something about a night take-off that I find excruciatingly thrilling. There's a bustle of expectancy and I hope I never get too blasé not to feel childishly important and excited when making out a flight plan, however casual I might appear on the surface.

We got through everything in Karachi quite quickly: Customs, Health, Security, Weather and the Control Tower. There was even little delay about the reclaiming of our armaments (a ·303 rifle and a Walther 7·65 automatic) and sundry spares that we had put in bond. We always get up two hours too early, knowing full well how long the departure formalities can take, involving as they do, all these things to be seen to; but though we dawdled in Karachi, it never seemed to get much lighter. The dawn must have been a lot later than they said, for eventually, as everything was packed in and the little tail compartment was all neatly stowed, we thought we had better do a night take-off. Gulping in a few last breaths of exciting night air with all its wonderful smells, we climbed into the cockpit, I taxied her out and we took off.

My constantly flying with my head in the 'office' certainly taught me how to fly on instruments. I'd never done any Link training but somehow blind-flying has never been very difficult for me. The runway lights slid beneath us and we climbed off into a deep velvety sky with patches of stars and here & there a dark smudge of cloud. Only a few scattered lights showed where Karachi lay and anyway it was soon far behind us.

We watched the Indian dawn rise. The land became greyer and at 6,000 ft we could see the first rays of sunshine long before it broke into the drowsy little huts beneath us. Soon the coils of the Indus glittered beneath us in the half-light and we headed out over the 400 miles of Sind desert to Jodphur, where we changed course for Delhi.

So this is India, I thought, as the plains stretched out flat and patterned beneath us, and here begins the mysterious East, where everything is utterly different and *"the wildest dreams of Kew are the facts of Khatmandhu and the crimes of Clapham chaste at Martaban."*

This land my father knew, I thought idly to myself, wondering if he had ever campaigned in the country underneath us right now. I, too, had read

When the Rains Came and also many of Somerset Maugham's books and, feeling all mystical and Eastern about the whole thing, tried to transmit these thoughts to Michael. Mike grunted and said "Ten degrees left." Speaking in that ship involved a lot of "What?" and "Did you say so and so?."

The lands were very much flooded beneath us and many, many miles were covered by water, for the rivers had spread with the rain. I discussed the growing of rice with myself and "casting one's bread upon the waters." I watched the ground as much as I could but soon clouds started forming beneath us and we could see less, but before it became quite ten tenths we slid down beneath them. Here it was stormy and rough but we found Delhi airfield and dutifully tried to make contact with the tower but, because their English was so bad, we could not understand what they said and just came on in. Influenced still by the up-draughts on the runway at Habbaniya my circuits were becoming wider and lower, and although Mike normally didn't mind, he got a trifle anxious on that approach because I seemed to be hedge-hopping for at least a mile before I touched down.

We taxied up to the tarmac, parked our ship and climbed out. We seemed to have chosen our arrival at just the right time, for Pandit Nehru was being seen off by his family and I had a glimpse of him (I wondered why the face looked vaguely familiar until I asked) and of a tall, slim woman in the most beautiful blue *sari* I've ever seen in my life. I can see her standing waiting there now on the steps of the Admin. Building.

The aerodrome manager took charge of us and, after our paperwork had been sorted out, we were taken to lunch. We were offered curry, of course, but I decided I did not know enough about the procedure and I should leave it until I learnt more, contenting myself meanwhile with a small chop.

We decided that we would rather sleep in the disused barracks nearby than drive into the town because we wanted to make an early start the next day, and any rate it would be cheaper. The aerodrome manager was a trifle surprised, I think, but realizing we were English and of course a trifle mad, complied with our request and led us over there. The quarters we were shown were not exactly the best we had on this trip: a bare room each with a table, a bed and two blankets, one to lie on and one to fold and put under your head, but fortunately an overhead fan. The only distinction between Mike's room and my own was that I was apparently the lucky possessor of a frog; this I shut in a cupboard for the night, from where it croaked mournfully.

Mike volunteered to supervise the refuelling – after we had given a little demonstration of taxying and jumping out of the ship for the newsreels – and I went back to my room and had a nap. Mike woke me at five, hot, sweaty and bad-tempered. After refuelling he had apparently run the engine up and found a big mag drop, and he had cleaned and replaced all the plugs more than once. His excruciatingly bad temper came from my having unwittingly parked my chewing gum on the left-hand throttle lever (the one used for taxying so that your right hand can clutch the brake) and he had blindly put his hand down on it and found to his intense disgust that his hand had adhered to the knob and thereafter to anything else with which he had come into contact. I felt most frightfully mean about this, particularly about his having worked in the sun all the afternoon. There was nothing I could do however and after supper he went straight to bed. I very foolishly stayed up awhile drinking brandy with the airport manager, which resulted in my not getting to bed until about eleven.

CHAPTER 9
DELHI–CALCUTTA

We had arranged with the bearer to wake us at four, as we wanted to be airborne by six. He woke us at 4.30 am for some reason of his own, me feeling decidedly the worse for wear due to a pronounced hangover. I took a couple of Benzedrine tablets and swore to Mike that I never felt better, but the half-cooked onion omelette which was served up in the dimly-lighted Mess very nearly proved my undoing. Together we went to Met., manned by two drowsy Indians. One sat and snored, utterly oblivious, in a room so thick with insects I had to keep my arm waving like a windshield wiper to see anything at all, whilst the other compiled a met. forecast for Calcutta.

Mike went on down to the ship with the bags, leaving me to make up the flight plan, take it up to Control and clear Customs, Health and Security. Head swimming, I went up to the Control tower where a fat, sleepy Indian told me that the flight plan couldn't be cleared until it had been signed by Customs, Health and Security. I tried Customs first; I banged on the door until my fist was sore and eventually a towsled head popped out but he couldn't speak English, so I gave it up. There was no one in Health at all. At Security I eventually understood by means of signs that there was an officer asleep upstairs, who would be down some time after six.

Brother, was I ever mad? I strode back to Control, burning with righteous anger and a hangover, and pitched into that Indian at the top of my voice. He wouldn't clear me to go and I wouldn't wait on his drowsy compatriots. We had just about reached a deadlock, two other Indians having joined him, and were all shouting in unison when an officer came in, struggling into his tunic. I was burnt up with righteous anger and, thumping my fist on the table, so that all the inkwells danced, I announced loudly and firmly that I was leaving, clearance or not, and if they didn't like it . . . etc. etc. I banged out of the room, rather spoiling my exit by falling down the last three stairs, and pattered out into the grey dawn, where I found Mike impatiently taxying up and down; I hopped in and we left for Calcutta.

The performance of *"Thursday's Child"* was poor that day. Somehow she didn't seem to be trying. It was peculiar about that ship but she really was strictly feminine. She had her 'on' days and her 'off' days and no amount of honeyed words or cussing would make any difference. It might have been the order in which we packed things in the back of the ship in a tiny little compartment aft of the cabin tank. But somehow I don't think it was. To me she was always a capricious creature, with a malicious tendency to dart off the runway on both take-offs and landings.

Incidentally, aft of the baggage compartment a small panel could be unscrewed and the works of the radio installed. We had two frequencies but the change could only be made on the ground, one crystal being taken out and another put in. Somehow or other Mike would squeeze into this tiny compartment through a space about 18 inches square, perform the necessary installation and emerge like the genie from the leaden vase, an operation which never failed to move me into prolonged hilarity, particularly the day he got stuck halfway in and halfway out.

We followed the River Ganges to Cawnpore and Allahabad, and tried to keep above the clouds and well out of the way of the cu-nims. They got higher and higher and I pulled her up and up and up, until our climbing speed, 80 knots, was all we could get in straight and level flight. This was at about 9,500 ft. Eventually we gave up the struggle and came down into the monsoon. Due to the low, black, sweeping clouds, we had to fly at 800 ft and follow the railway line to the south of Gaya, instead of proceeding on track. We had a moment's worry when the railway dived into a tunnel but we managed to pick it up again. Of course if I was really shooting a line, I would say that we flew through the tunnel – like the fatuous story of the guy who decided to fly through the hangar when he saw the doors were open but, just as he got in, they completed shutting the further door and by the time he had turned round again, they'd shut the other door. As far as I know he is still flying round and round.

"*Thursday's Child*" at this time was making quite definitely peculiar noises. A cockpit check resulted in my shoving the mixture control into rich mixture, but even so it didn't seem to help. The ship was popping like a two-stroke motor-bike and every mile of the 200 miles we battled through the pouring rain into Calcutta, I was watching the ground below and making emergency landings mentally. Just in case . . . These might not have been too easy actually, as the fields were nearly all very small and many of them were sown with 'wet' rice. One thing that particularly impressed me was the perfect levelness of the Ganges flood plain. It was monotonous, too, with its thick sprinkling of almost identical villages and tiny rectangular fields.

Having found Calcutta, we had to find the airfield and, as we hadn't a large-scale map, this in itself took quite a while. Eventually Mike spotted Dum Dum and we came in. We got through the formalities fairly quickly. Whilst we were in the process of doing this, a woman spoke to me, a smart middle-aged Frenchwoman. She was the wife of the French Consul, M. Kolb-Bernard, but she said: "You might have heard of me under my stage name." I looked politely intelligent. She must have said she was an "artiste" because before she told me her name, I got hopelessly confused whether she was an artist or an artiste, the 'e' being too mute for my insensitive ears. Her name, she said, was Alice Délicia. I was instinctively impressed and said "Coooh! Are you really?," which comment quite amused her; fortunately, I met her again later and thought her charming.

We had arranged with the de Havilland Aircraft Company that they should give us free maintenance, so we looked up their representative there, a Mr Jermyn. He was a charming young lad and became a great pal.

He said he would check our engine and so we started to look round for quarters to stay the night. We met the airport manager, a swarthy Sikh in a green turban, who held my eyes hypnotised by the cunning way in which his beard was brought back under his chin, parted in two and tucked into his turban behind his ears, the whole blooming issue being covered by a hairnet. He said we could stay in the "VIP room" if we liked, which belonged to the catering firm who ran the café and bar. He collected the key and marched us off, unlocked the door and threw it open; he then proudly showed us the room, quite nicely furnished but, to my great embarrassment, with two beds in the one room, demurely separated by a table. We thanked him politely and sat down to think about it. Since, however, the room also contained a room with a bath in it, a room with a lav in it, and a big room with a washbasin in it, we solved everything to our own satisfaction.

CHAPTER 10
CALCUTTA (ONE)

Mike was very tired that night, and after supper I sent him to bed while I went and discussed matters with Mr Jermyn, known as Jerry. He had worked at that engine all the evening, and the more he worked on it, the more troubles he found. We sat on the concrete steps outside the VIP room and talked in hushed whispers lest Mike should hear, swigging alternate shots from our bottle of French Cognac. He said it would be very unwise to take off the next day and, though I realized Mike wanted to press on, I decided we had better stay. As for myself, what I thought was kinda confused. Sure, I wanted to finish the flight in a hurry and get home but Mike had been abroad and seen places and I hadn't, and this big wide world with its strange lands and customs was too wonderful to be hurried over. I laugh now when I think how earnestly we debated about an extra day; we came in on the 6th September and we didn't leave Calcutta for another seven solid weeks.

Next morning Michael was in better spirits and had quite an animated discussion on India's social and economic problems with Reuter's Calcutta representative. After the departure of the Press reporter we worked with Jerry on the ship, trying hard to find out what was the trouble with her, whilst I made little jaunts to the airport restaurant to collect long, tall glasses of lemonade.

Mike and I also got into a huddle over the fuel consumption of the ship: she was using a little over 10½ gallons – say 11 for safety – per hour, which wasn't too bad, but our speed was only 125 mph. This was really serious as the extra fuel capacity had been calculated on the basis of a consumption of 10 gallons per hour at an economical cruising speed of 135 mph. These figures had been passed by the highest authorities and Air Registration Board approval had been given for a fuel overload of 380 lb. We had been refused petrol coupons (which were then necessary) for a long test flight in England and had relied on the acceptance of our performance specifications by those who knew more about Proctors than we did. Alas for our innocence! Here we were, 7,000 miles out on our trip and with insufficient fuel capacity to get us across the North Pacific, even in calm weather. Moreover, we were already over a week behind schedule and every delay would decrease the chances of a favourable wind across the ocean. We would need an extra 20 gallons of fuel to give us the very barest of safety margins.

Three questions immediately arose:
1. Could our little plane lift still another 150 lb of fuel off the ground?
2. Even if it could, where would we carry it? It certainly could not go in the luggage compartment as the weight so far aft would upset the aircraft's centre of gravity. It could not go in the cabin because there was hardly room

to move as it was. The only alternative was to fit an extra tank outside and that would cut down the speed.

3. Where were we going to get this extra tank and who could we persuade to fit it without approval from England? The task suddenly began to seem a bit hopeless, particularly in view of the time factor.

We talked it over and decided that, as we looked like being there a couple of days, we would see if we could find a 30-gallon belly tank from an old Spitfire. There must have been Spits somewhere in South-East Asia during the war but it was a question of finding out where. The trouble was that South-East Asia covered rather a largish area to search, and anyway SEAC Spitfires might not have had any belly tanks, and even if they did they might not have left any behind. We asked Jerry about it and he said he didn't know where any were himself, but he knew a couple of guys who, he thought, could help us and he would have a word with them.

That afternoon we retired to our rooms to rest, and we were just chatting, taking off our shoes, when there was a heavy pounding on the door and two men entered. One was tall and lean and lantern-jawed, with a strong resemblance to a highly intelligent ape. The other was short and plump and rather bored-looking. They had already been told about our need of a tank and, on talking the question over, they said that they knew a dump at Barrackpore, where old aircraft and components were to be had for the taking. We piled into their station wagon and went off to investigate.

It was a short journey, but it was my first trip outside the airfield and I just couldn't see things fast enough: palm trees, moist, tangled undergrowth and a road lined with decrepit huts and overrun by innumerable Indians, bullocks, dogs and children. A little swift talking got us past in the gatekeeper and we soon swung in past a disused hangar, where the *gharri* stopped. We climbed out and there, scattered about like prehistoric monsters, were fuselages and mainplanes, boxes, tanks, wheels and propellers: all sorts of aircraft junk, slowly and inevitably being swallowed up in the jungle vines. We were warned "'ware snakes" as we started lifting and turning over the piles of slim, sled-shape tanks. We found one admirably suited to our purpose but unfortunately made of steel instead of dural. It would have done fine but the extra weight would have pulled our speed down and quite counteracted its purpose. One scarcely-damaged Harvard struck Mike's interest and, though many of the fittings had been extracted from inside the cockpit, when Mike turned the prop over she moved easily with just the right amount of compression.

Mike trained as a pilot once in the RAF on Harvards in Arizona and loved it. He reached the "wings" standard and was terribly pleased. He was so happy he slow-rolled one over an airfield at 300 ft where, unfortunately, a lot of officers were gathered together in conference. He was reported and was told that he could not receive his wings but would go back to Canada as an AC2. Poor Mike! He just couldn't believe it was true, but instead of just quitting trying, as I'm sure I would have done, he started again from the bottom and got his commission instead as a navigator. I've never said much about this to Mike but that is a thing I really take my hat off to. I wholeheartedly admire the sort of moral courage that can make you start again at the beginning. I know I couldn't.

In some of the boxes, splitting open with the damp and the heat, we could see brand-new propellers and, in others, unused Merlin engines. We amused ourselves for a while and then climbed back into the car. That tank wouldn't do and that was for sure. Where then were we going to put the extra fuel?

"Put it in Jerricans and pour it into the cabin tanks when we need it," was somebody's suggestion.

Not a bad idea, but where were we going to put the Jerricans? We thought of building another tank high up in the baggage compartment to drain into the cabin tank but she was nose-high already, so that was no good. Eventually I came up with the suggestion: "Why not take the seats out and put one big tank about six inches deep right across, which we could sit on?"

Everyone condemned my suggestion, saying that you couldn't turn on the other fuel cocks because they were between the two seats and how would you get the fuel into the cabin tanks?

I said: "Well, two tanks then, one for each of us to sit on and a hand pump to raise the fuel into the cabin tank."

It was the brightest suggestion I've ever made in my life. I was hopping with enthusiasm but nobody took the least bit of interest until Mike produced the idea later on as his own, when everyone heartily agreed. Every time Mike needs putting in his place, I tell him that. It used to annoy me so much because he would never let me play with the engine and always treated me as though I couldn't have two thoughts in my head at the same time when it came to the groundwork. Never mind, I vowed, I'll show him one day.

Mike and I, because we had done so many of the same things, were always competing with each other. He can play squash a bit better than I, but I'm the stronger swimmer. He can beat me on a target with a pistol but I can beat him with a rifle, and that sort of thing. But there's one thing I've done and can do that he can't, and that is, have a baby. I've got him whacked there! *[I really have no inclination that way. – M.T.]*

CHAPTER 11
CALCUTTA (TWO)

On the two engineers' suggestion, I taxied the ship into the hangar owned by Himalayan Aviation, for whom they worked, so that Jerry could work in the shade and we could see about the tanks.

It struck me the whole time we were there how odd it was to see modern streamlined aircraft against a background of the eternal meandering bullock and the lush green jungle. There were bananas within sight and coconut palms actually overhanging the taxi-apron. The coconuts always seemed such an anti-climax grouped in their tiny cluster right at the top of fifty feet of completely bare tree trunk. One could expect something at least as large as a pumpkin to make up for so little foliage on the way up. Perhaps, though, it was just as well they were not pumpkins: the effect of a small coconut crashing down onto the concrete from such a height was devastating enough.

The tall lanky engineer, Gordon Wall, known, of course, as 'Lofty,' suggested we should come and live in his flat since his wife and offspring had just gone back to England and he said he was lonely. We accepted gratefully and he took us back that night in time to change and go out to the Skating Club. It wasn't a particularly classy night club but the Indian women must definitely have taken Mike's fancy for, after a lot of summoning up of courage and a few drinks, he took one out on to the dance floor. He was definitely intrigued, I know, and said he thought the Indian *sari* a very beautiful garment. I heard him ask Lofty *sotto voce:* "How do they come undone?" Lofty laughed and said you pulled the end, which went over the shoulder smartly and the girl spun round like a top, unwinding as she went.

We spent a nice leisurely morning in Lofty's flat and then he drove us the ten miles to the field in the afternoon. When we arrived, Jerry was working on the engine and we hung around handing him wrenches and trying to look intelligent. He worked on that ship twelve solid days. First of all there would be a mag drop on one side, then one on the other side. He put a new magneto in and there had to be a change in the ignition harness; the induction manifold leaked at one joint; the automatic mixture control was just about seized solid and the scraper rings on the pistons were found to be very badly fitted, added to which it was running with the wrong type of plugs. Jerry couldn't believe that it had had a complete overhaul just before we left England, in fact he swore it had not, and the times that boy built the engine up, ran it up and took it to pieces again was a real example of perseverance. I was very impressed.

Mike was getting more and more depressed during this time. Our original deadline for reaching Japan, September 15th, had passed and now we would have the weather to worry about as well as the engine and the inadequate fuel capacity. To complicate matters even further, our Military Permits for entering Japan would soon be out of date and we had just discovered that we should need a visa for French Indo-China. This we had thought unnecessary, as holders of a British passport did not need a visa for France itself. A visit to the French Consulate in Calcutta elucidated the fact that we also need a permit to fly over Indo-China, this restriction being enforced due to the activity of *"les insurgents"* – the Annamites, I guess – who, it seemed, were inhospitable to downed fliers.

It was hot in Calcutta and very humid – a weather combination which Michael seemed to find more exhausting than I did. However, rather than lie and meditate upon our numerous troubles, he pestered Jerry so much that he was occasionally allowed to help with the engine. Drenched with sweat and barking their knuckles on the incredible number of projections which go to make up an aero engine, they would curse quietly into the works until the particular little nut or washer they were wrestling with had fallen into its allotted place. Frequently, of course, it would fall into some other quite inaccessible place where it would defy recapture. After removing another section of the cowling or fishing around with a screwdriver, it would be retrieved and the whole agonising process would begin again.

These overhaul operations had their lighter side, however. There was the occasion of the testing of the new joints on the carburettor air intake manifold. This was made in several sections which were sealed with rubber joints and normally held together by each being bolted in position to the engine. It was quite impossible to test our new joints on the engine so the manifold was removed and all outlets were sealed, except one, which was duly connected to an air compressor; the whole issue was then plunged into a trough of water, whilst Jerry and Michael attempted to hold it rigid and watch for tell-tale bubbles. Lofty's Indian mechanics were nothing if not enthusiastic, and the order to release only a few pounds pressure from the compressor must have seemed awfully half-hearted when they had all of 150 lb at their disposal. Jerry's new joints were no doubt masterpieces of assembly and would have held under the most arduous flying conditions but . . . ! The effect, watched from a safe range, was like the explosion of a depth-charge in miniature – a crack like a revolver shot, accompanied by a tremendous uprush of water that temporarily obscured Mike, Jerry and all the Indians who had been clustering round the trough to offer encouragement. Needless to say, exactly the same performance was repeated at least twice before sufficient restraint was exercised on the compressor.

The manifold incident was a source of amusement even to the participants, once they had got over the first shock; in fact I secretly wondered whether they repeated it deliberately in order to get a cool shower.

The other bright memory that stands out from our dreary days at Dum Dum is not shared quite so wholeheartedly by Michael. We had been there about ten days and, the engine being temporarily re-assembled, Jerry suggested a run-up. As the seats had been removed there was not room for Michael in the cabin; so wanting to watch the instruments for himself (he still didn't trust me, really!), he stood on the port wing and scowled through the perspex. That didn't last for long! Either Mike didn't realise that I would run the engine full-out or else he overestimated his powers of adhesion under the full blast of the slipstream. Anyway, intent on the boost gauge and rev-counter, I was slowly opening the throttle when his fingers gradually began to slide on the cabin roof. Heedless and in fact unknowing (he always denies this), I remorselessly edged up to full boost until, with a last despairing cry, his fingers let go and he was blown backwards off the wing, momentarily retarded by losing half the front of his new shirt on the door handle.

I always disliked that shirt anyway!

These exhausting days were followed by evenings during which Lofty introduced us to a couple of night clubs and the Calcutta Swimming Club, where we were made honorary members. We spent much time there later on and it was a very pleasant place in which to relax. There was one swimming pool under cover, the water about 80°F, and one huge swimming pool in the sun, where the temperature would be about 86°F. All round it were tables, covered by a little wooden roof, and you could arrive there in the morning at about eight, have your breakfast and stay there all day, having lunch, and then dinner there at night. Drinks were served whenever you wanted and if you had any money, you could have a super time beside the sparkling *pani*. All day there was chatter, chatter, chatter, as reputations were torn to shreds and new affairs planned by women with too much time and too few interests, dawdling their days in the sun and the water.

Towards evening, a few people would be getting a little high and twice I was pushed in, complete with glass and cigarette holder and I would rise like Venus from the waves, glass still in hand, cigarette holder in mouth, gibbering with indignation. Once or twice, of course, I, too, was made a little mellow. It's very delightful to gambol in the water in this state, but rather conducive to intense breathlessness and dives from a height that made you shiver the next morning. We made many friends there; they are probably still sitting there. But despite the pleasure and the surroundings, the anxiety and restlessness to be on the way and the worry about our ship spoilt an awful lot of it for me.

On the 18th September the engine was ground-tested and pronounced to be in good condition. I also decided on a test flight as we had altered the angle of incidence of the tailplane. This had been found necessary due to the unnaturally nose-up attitude of our aircraft in flight, even with a light load. When a duly licensed engineer came to check it he found the incidence to be far too small. This meant that the tail had been giving insufficient lift and was therefore too low in level flight. Had I been more experienced on Proctors, I might have noticed this before I left England. In any case one does not look for such trouble only a few weeks after overhaul.

It was very foolish, I suppose, but because I knew many people thought Michael flew the ship I decided I would take Jerry on the test flight instead of Mike. Mike objected but I insisted and we took off. The engine sounded good and the flight attitude had greatly improved. After the test flight, as we touched down on the one runway, with quite a strong crosswind, the ship swung into wind and before I could stop her did a violent, vicious ground loop.

Jerry looked bleakly at me. "Does this always happen?" he asked.

"Oh! yes, quite often," I said, as nonchalantly as possible.

And in a way that was true. When the tail was down, rudder control was blanked off by the rather high cabin and even if I was using hard right or left rudder and brake, she tended to swing into wind. This time the swing was probably accentuated by having the cabin tanks over half-full; 300 lb of fuel swishing about aft of our centre of gravity was a factor to be considered. The swing got out of control and we left the runway, turning to the left and skidding to the right at the same time.

I taxied her back to the hangar, horribly ashamed of myself for letting such a thing happen (of course it would happen when Mike wasn't there, too). Could I ever live it down? Possibly not, but I was very relieved that I hadn't wiped off a wingtip on one of the Bartow lights, as can so easily happen.

None of the aerodrome staff seemed to have noticed and we put the ship back in Himalayan's hangar. At lunch in the restaurant we met Lofty and Michael, who had spent the morning in bed recovering from a chill. Michael was distinctly sceptical at the casual manner in which I tried to pass off the ground-loop. I thought he was secretly revelling in that loathsome I-told-you-so feeling and that he was only being morbid when he said that he had scarcely ever known a ground-loop without some kind of damage.

After lunch we all trooped down to get *"Thursday's Child"* ready for an early departure to Rangoon, keen to be on our way after wasting two whole weeks in Calcutta.

It had to be Michael, of course, who noticed it first – the thing that was to cause us another five weeks' delay and which should have ended the flight then and there if common sense had prevailed. It was almost unnoticeable and, in fact, both Jerry and I missed it before lunch – that slight inclination of the starboard undercarriage leg which almost inevitably betokened a cracked main spar.

CHAPTER 12
CALCUTTA (THREE)

We were another five weeks getting that undercarriage leg repaired, making seven weeks in all, and we might still be there if we hadn't taken the initiative into our own hands.

The engineer who inspected this damage for the Insurance Company was an airframe licensed engineer, but he couldn't repair the job and sign it out from the insurance angle too, so we went to a nearby firm and asked them to repair it. They told us we would have to wait five days until the arrival of a special man who was on his way from England. Meanwhile, we stripped the leg from the ship and uncovered the main spar, to which the leg was attached by four bolts. These bolts had caused the box spar to split as they turned with the force of the skid.

Days went by, impatient, angry, bad-tempered days, before the special engineer arrived. Then he did arrive; he knew all about the job but he wasn't qualified to sign it out, and the only man on the field who *could* sign it out was the insurance agent, who could not mend it himself. It was all madly complicated and ended up with one firm taking on the job and another firm signing it out. It sounds like a morning's work put like that, but in reality it covered a month of talking and walking and worry.

We were almost desperate: time slid by and although we would go up to the airfield every day, it didn't do any good and Lofty suggested that, as we were only driving ourselves mad, we should spend a week or thereabouts in the Swimming Club. We did, too, for a while. We would get up in the morning, have breakfast and then catch the streetcar down to Chowringee, where we would get a rickshaw to the Club. The streetcars were very smart-looking but terribly crowded. I was still wearing my little short shorts and overshirt and to my intense embarrassment the women would look at my knees with something approaching to horror, whilst the men nearly got up and cheered. The streetcars were in two sections, the first coach being for first-class passengers and the rear one for the rest. Four seats in each coach were reserved for ladies and Mike invariably seemed to choose one of these until some sari-clad damsel gave him a dirty look.

We often went by rickshaw round the town and it would amaze and appal me the way the scrawny Indian boy would run you, sweating his soul out, from one end of Calcutta to another, for a few annas. We had to learn to speak a little Hindustani and it would amuse me when we asked the rickshaw wallah: "Do you know where so and so is?" or "Can you take me to so and so?" and he'd say: "Yes, Sahib" long before you had finished your sentence!

Mike and I really got on each other's nerves at this time. We would snap at each other for no reason whatsoever and once we had a really major row. He said he wasn't going to the Club one day. I said "You can't leave me there alone, all by myself." Mike said nothing but when we got to the door he handed me enough money for my lunch, just enough and said: "I'll pick you up here at five."

I was really mad.

"OK," I thought, "to hell with you!" and made eyes at a handsome stranger at the next table. I made a date for that night with him and when at 5.30 Mike hadn't turned up, I went back on the streetcar alone, really mad. I discovered him in his bedroom fast asleep and so I crept out again, changed and washed, and just before I went for my date (Charles said he was going to pick me up in a cab at the gate) said airily: "Spending the evening out – shan't be very late," and sauntered off.

Mike had supper alone with Lofty and when by ten o'clock I hadn't come in, nor by eleven o'clock, the two of them really got worried. They thought I must have been raped by a Sikh taxi driver or murdered in some silent alley and they took the truck out, driving it uselessly around for an hour or so before they returned, worried and exasperated, to the flat.

Lofty was tired and went to bed but Mike, nearly sick with worry, restlessly paced the room. Eventually he got the mattress that I slept on (there were only two beds and Mike and Lofty had these, because I can sleep anywhere on anything) and put it just inside the door, so that as I entered the flat, I should have to step over him. About four o'clock I stepped quietly over him, for he had just dropped off to sleep, but he woke instantly and in a voice, dry and brittle with anger said: "Good morning, Dikki."

The hair stood up at the back of my neck. Together we dragged the mattress into my room. He didn't say a word, until when everything was tidy, he straightened himself and said: "Where have you been?"

I told him truthfully: "The Saturday Club."

He asked me who with and I told him that, too. I was scared, quite candidly, and I really did think he was going to hit me, but with an effort he controlled himself, turned abruptly and walked back to his own room.

The next morning (why do I always have hangovers?) we sat in the *gharri* outside the hangar, where he lectured me until the tears dripped off the end of my nose. He made me cancel the next date I had with Charles and I promised never to be naughty again. I was very douce and contrite for at least three days after that.

The days drifted by. Lofty's lease on the flat ended and he went to stay with friends, whilst we repaired to a crummy little hotel in a side-street off Chowringee. Oh, the food! I've never eaten such mysterious and nauseous combinations in all my life. Run by Armenians and housing impoverished whites (like ourselves) and middle-class Indians, the food, I suppose, catered for their tastes. Onions and garlic formed a large amount of the flavouring and mysterious lumps of minced meat wrapped in vine leaves and secured with a toothpick were among the food offered. What, I often wondered, was inside?

We used to walk up to the BOAC head office every morning and get a lift down to the airfield in one of their personnel buses. The traffic in Calcutta is indescribably chaotic. It is as crowded as London, only everyone walks twice as slowly and twice as aimlessly. Many of the natives have no homes and all seem to have nowhere to go. They charge straight across the roads, looking to neither left nor right. The only way to drive is to be an expert in the art of cutting-in. Rickshaws and bullock carts sway and surge across the roads. Dogs, goats and sacred cows saunter where they want to and how more people are not killed utterly defeats me. In the course of my stay – and Lofty was a good driver – we damaged only two dogs, and a man who walked into the side of the car.

When, as is sometimes unavoidable, an Indian is run over, I was warned: "Don't stop. If you do, a crowd will form, they will swear you did it purposely, that you had a life-long feud with the man and probably break up your car." They put their feet on your running-board and rock the car until the whole thing is tipped over and then, as likely as not, set fire to it.

Actually this very thing nearly happened to Lofty and Mike on their way back from the airport one evening. Lofty, who was driving, had just swerved violently to miss a rickshaw that had attempted a swift dart across the road and was still hurling invective at it over his right shoulder. A sudden yell from Mike cut it short and he trod on the brakes just too late to avoid a second rickshaw wallah determined at all costs to cross the street, no doubt trusting in Allah and the Sahib's good brakes. Unhappily both failed him and his three Indian passengers were ejected violently into the road, whilst he and the rickshaw were propelled some five yards along in front of Lofty's bumpers. All four picked themselves up but Lofty's kindness of heart was greater than his wisdom and he stopped the truck and jumped out to offer his help. No sooner had he appeared than a crowd began to form, curious at first and probably glad to have some form of diversion, until a stout Bengalese – with horn-rimmed glasses, half an education and a large topee – began to harangue them.

It's funny about those topees; very few Europeans seem to wear them nowadays but many Indians, like our friend, no doubt feel that it raises their social status.

Anyway, it soon became obvious that his words were having an effect on the rapidly-growing crowd and Mike started the engine for a quick getaway. Even old Lofty must have realized that the position was getting serious when the crowd would not let the rickshaw wallah accept his very adequate financial compensation. Giving the situation up as hopeless, he was just turning to make a dive for the truck when the police arrived on the scene.

Then followed a motley procession to the nearest police station, Lofty and Mike leading with their covered truck full of Himalayan Aviation Indian mechanics; the rotund wearer of the horn-rimmed spectacles and the topee following closely behind looking like some dark skinned and voluble Pied Piper.

The Police Station was incredibly small and its floor was so thickly packed with destitute or delinquent Indians that it was difficult to find anywhere to put one's foot. This actually turned out be a blessing as it was a physical impossibility for more than a very few of the 'Pied Piper's' followers to squeeze in. Many of those who did manage it soon got fed up with waiting and, when the time eventually came to give eye-witness statements, that of their topeed leader had to stand alone against the signed evidence of Mike, Lofty and every one of Lofty's mechanics, who stood by him and swore that the accident was not his fault.

By this time the 'Pied Piper' realized that discretion was the better part of valour and when offered a 'ride' home by Lofty's mechanics, he wisely refused!

CHAPTER 13
CALCUTTA (FOUR)

A very interesting story was told me at the airfield: The first Aeronca Sedan aeroplane had been received at Dum Dum and, as the pilot was taxying past the control tower, an Indian waved him to stop and delivered a message from one of the men in the tower. "Would he wait a moment so that one of the officers could come on the flight too?"

The Indian, having delivered the message, stepped backwards into the prop and had his head cut off. The body lay on the ground, and the head several yards away. The pilot stepped out and, with his usual *sang froid*, turned to the body and said: "Say, bud, are you hurt bad?"

He was accused of murdering the man, of having placed his ship on purpose to kill the Indian. He got off, of course, when his case went to Court but it does show the limits to which these things are sometimes taken. Life, I suppose, is often very dull for the Indian and maybe that is why, when they do start a little lynching, they really go to town. I heard some vivid and gory descriptions of the last lot of fighting in Calcutta following partition and when all was over, apparently they tidily popped all the bodies down the sewers and then wondered why the drains didn't work.

Oh, but the poverty! Never having been East before, the sad aged faces distressed me. The shapeless coolie women, bundled in dirty white cotton, bitter-eyed and broken with work, seemed to me a most terrible thing. Apparently they do the work of the home, as well as bear children, and work in the fields. The women – even the grandmothers, I was told – are used sexually by all the males in the family. How they survive beats the hell out of me. The refuse and the filth is tipped into the ditch, which runs in front of the three-walled shack, and then little spindle-legged naked children play in it.

There were so many things to watch that were so utterly new to me. The devout Hindu, bowing down and touching with his head the tools of his trade – the carpenter a piece of wood, the typist his typewriter, the bank clerk a pile of *rupee* notes (I had to wait five minutes to change a traveller's cheque whilst the cashier did this once). And the cab driver would decorate his cab most beautifully with flowers at religious festivals. Apropos of cabs, I would get great pleasure in choosing a cab from the middle of the rank for the sheer pleasure of watching the driver go backwards and forwards and backwards and forwards with the vehicle until a big enough gap had been made to drive out.

One thing in India I hated to see were the beggars sitting along the sidewalk showing their sores and whining. There was one I remember particularly who had no legs from the knees down and walked on all fours like an animal. Little skinny children too, who ran after me, crying that they had no mothers and fathers. They probably had, so I didn't mind that so much, and anyway, nor had I, so what? The size of the newborn babies impressed me because they were so very, very weeny – just a brown sausage with drumsticks – and being a woman I noticed how much smaller the 'first size' in clothing was for a child as compared to England; they were more like dolls' clothes.

One day at the airfield, whilst the split in the main spar was being repaired by means of a block glued on behind, we suddenly spotted that the metal attachment plate of the leg was definitely twisted. We should have noticed this before, so we sent off a frantic wire to England for a new leg; we thought that while we were about it we might as well have a whole new leg, for that leg was the one which was low. Of course then there was nothing we could do but sit down and wait. I know that I was frightfully tensed up at the time and, one morning while I was having lunch at the Swimming Club, Lofty spoke to me sharply and I just burst into tears.

To add to our misery we were having dreadful cables from Tokyo with dire warnings about the weather over the North Pacific. At least three copies arrived at different times of the following:

"To Mrs Morrow-Tait:
Received following message from Rangoon quote following is text of telegram from Tokyo concerning Morrow-Tait flight begins in view of delay in progress of flight I have reassessed position for prevailing season stop as a result I must suggest that the appropriate competent authority bring the following points to Mrs Morrow-Tait's notice whereas leg of flight from Chitose Hokkaido to Shemya Aleutions was fairly practicable at end of August when her clearance for Japan and North Pacific was originally requested possibility of flying this leg is diminishing very rapidly as year wears on stop weather conditions prevailing between Hokkaido and Shemya in first week of October as provided by HQ US Far Eastern sources in Tokyo (A) hours of daylight are becoming progressively shorter. For the tenth of October hours of daylight between Hokkaido and Shemya are anticipated to be 0615 to 1715 (B) The icing conditions on this route average four thousand feet on favourable days lowering to two thousand feet during adverse weather and the icing is extremely heavy (C) Prevalent weather conditions for the route during the period include an average of six days of sunshine for the entire month of October (D) It is forecast that there will be only two periods of three days in which favourable flying weather for light planes will exist stop Mrs Morrow-Tait will have to remain at Chitose awaiting one of these periods and there is a gamble that this forecast was right (E) Severe icing, turbulent precipitation and strong winds up to one hundred knots are common during adverse weather (F) In the event of a forced landing at sea during the autumn months in that latitude chances of survival are extremely limited stop in view of limited safety margin provided by Proctor IV for flight in the conditions likely to be encountered I consider it

necessary to recommend that the flight be postponed indefinitely with a view to later attempt being made in late spring next year when the chances of success should be reasonable ends Bowker Unquote."

CHAPTER 14
INTERLUDE IN A PALACE

At this juncture fate took a hand to raise us a little from the pit of depression. One night in the "300" Club I was introduced to Mahabir (His Honour Major General Mahabir Shumshere Jung Sahadur Rana, to give him his full title) and his friend Warris (the Murchidzada of Murshidabad – and, incidentally, a direct descendant of the infamous Indian prince responsible for the "Black Hole of Calcutta"). They liked us and asked if we would care to go and stay with them at a friend's, the Maharajah of Cooch Behar. We thought it would be a darned good idea, though we worded our acceptance somewhat differently. We could do nothing until the arrival of the new undercarriage leg and thought a change away from Calcutta would do us a lot of good, and, anyway, we might get some shooting in. They arranged to pick us up at the weekend and fly us by Dakota, for Mahabir owned Himalayan Aviation, the airline that Lofty worked for. We packed our bags, wishing our clothes were smarter and younger and drove down with Mahabir and his party to the waiting Dakota. That was the first time in my life I'd ever been in a big aircraft and I didn't like being a passenger a bit. I can quite understand how people can get airsick, for personally it always gives me a headache. Added to which the ship was well loaded and I nearly sweated blood on take-off willing the sluggish ship off the deck.

The journey to Cooch Behar seemed to me to take a long time, for the windows of the Dakota were covered over with orange plastic stuff to keep the sun's rays out and there was nothing to do but to sit and talk; as I was sitting next to Mike and at this time we felt we'd said everything, and some things more than once, it was a bit tedious.

In Calcutta we had discussed practically everything under the sun to while away the evenings, for we hadn't enough money to go to the movies or go places, except as guests. Our stories had sunk to a rather low plane, and were getting less and less funny. Mike had even attempted a practical joke. He came into my room one afternoon when I was having a nap, tiptoed to the wash basin, and got half a tumblerful of water which he poured over me. I awoke smartly, madder'n' hell, and gave him a straight left. Then he got mad, handing out a friendly uppercut which, dazed with sleep, I took on the chin. I fell straight back with the impact, tearing some skin off my right shoulder against the wall. I still carry the scar.

However, the last half hour of the flight I spent in the cockpit and so I could watch the little State and the Palace as it all came into view. We made a circuit over the Palace so the Maharajah could get into his car and go to meet us, and so we hadn't long to wait after we had touched down before he arrived. I don't know what type of person I expected but the arrival of two young, good-looking men in a sports car, one of them clad in blue jeans, cowboy boots and coloured shirt, completely flabbergasted me. Both were introduced with long and complicated names, to which I answered politely but feeling none the less quite certain that neither of these could be a king.

At luncheon in the palace, though, I discovered that the taller of the two men, the one who had been wearing cowboy clothes, was HH the Maharajah of Cooch Behar. They called him Bahaiya which is, I believe, brother and his companion was 'Budh,' his cousin; Budh's full title was Iskumar Gautham Narayan (Gautham after Buddha), hence the nickname. The other members of the party comprised Mahabir and his girl friend, Warris and Captain Kimpton, the senior pilot of Himalayan Aviation who was, like Bahaiya and Budh, an old Cambridge man.

I shan't ever forget the stay at the Maharajah's palace. Life was very spacious and picturesque and so utterly out of this world that it might have been a dream. Only I can still see vividly the luxuriously furnished rooms and hear my heels tapping on the stone verandas. A small square of grass entirely surrounded by palace buildings was at night covered by insects and made a noise like a machine shop so that you almost had to raise your voice to be heard above it. Insects were a trouble there, more so than in the town of Calcutta and if you didn't keep a letter or a book over the top of your beer, an over-eager bearer whipped it away as it probably contained some minute particle of insect life. I wonder what became of those half-drunk beers?

Bahaiya had an Indian cook, whom he had sent to France to be trained and, brother, could he ever cook? Mike and I tried hard not to appear greedy but it's rather revealing, I think, that a few days after our arrival back in Calcutta we both had bilious attacks.

The afternoon was spent in sleeping, until about seven, when we got up, bathed, changed and started another drinking session, on hard liquor this time; this went on until about eleven, when we knocked off for dinner, which was very ceremonial and after which we resumed our various occupations; four o'clock was usually the time the last of the party retired to bed. These were usually Mahabir and his friend, Baronov. The latter owned a gin distillery (the sole industry of Cooch Behar) and was reputed to be a former officer of the Imperial Guard of Russia. This, however, did not save him from Mahabir who kept him playing at liar dice or gin rummy until he won; this could quite easily be until 6 am if "the Baron" had soaked him to start with.

Mike and I didn't quite fit in with this programme. We liked to get up for breakfast in the dining room and go and do something in the morning and again, though we might have a nap in the afternoon, we still couldn't waste all that time, when there were things to be seen and done. The result was, too, that we went to bed earlier than the rest.

In all fairness it must be said that the life of sociable idleness and drinking was part of Bahaiya's magnificent hospitality to his guests and gives little idea of the business of state which went on underneath, nor of the serious side of his guests' lives. Both the Maharajah and his cousin were "on the water wagon" during our stay at Cooch Behar and, whilst his guests were still recovering from the night before, Bahaiya would be up at 5.30 am and riding or driving through his State. On these rides, any of his subjects with a grievance could approach him and he would settle it right away or send for the man to bring his case to the Palace. Cooch Behar was a small State but prosperous and the people looked better fed and contented than any others we saw in India.

It was difficult to realise that Mahabir had any other side to his character than the jovial, fun-loving one we saw. Consequently it was a shock to find that he was the owner of engineering works, factories and cinemas all over Bengal. This was even more astonishing in view of his background, for he was a member of the ruling family of Nepal ("General" was a courtesy title in the Nepalese Royal military hierachy) and had left his country due to family disagreements. In a comparatively short space of time he had multiplied his fortune until it would have been the envy of any of the traditional American millionaires.

One morning we spent visiting the elephants. We went by car along a dusty track. Budh took us, because Bahaiya was busy with affairs of state. First we saw an elephant which was chained by itself in the shade of some trees. We took a photograph of him but the picture looked more like "Puzzle, find the elephant!" than an animal study. Then we watched the elephants having their daily scrub in the river. The *mahout* would scrub each elephant with a half brick which, though it sounds kinda rough, gave the elephants great pleasure, as you could see by their evident enjoyment as they wallowed in the water to their *mahout's* command. We watched this for a while and then went along to the stable where they were kept. We watched them being fed on rice folded into leaves. There were big elephants and little elephants, many born in captivity. Their foreheads were painted, though the paint had faded somewhat, and we were pointed out the leader and the histories of each one but I am afraid that to me an elephant is an elephant, except in the case of pink ones.

Budh gave a demonstration of how to climb one. You stand up and, reaching as high as you can, catch hold of the elephant's ears. Then you gently kick its trunk, so that it curls it out a little making a step for you. You put your foot in the trunk and the elephant gives you a rapid boost up, so that you land on its forehead on your tummy. You then wriggle round and put a leg behind each ear. I gave an undignified performance of this after a little encouragement from the rest of the party because, supposing I hadn't, I should have regretted it so.

It gave me a tremendous thrill to ride around on an elephant. It surprised me how very prickly they were. They have long stiff bristles, like a hog's only bigger, sticking out over their body and, wearing only cotton shorts and a shirt, I noticed it quite a bit. I walked it around, pretending I was a Maharajah (you kick the ears as you would a rudder bar) and then in due course the *mahout* said the magic word and I held on for grim death whilst the animal doubled under his front legs and then his back legs so that I could slide off comfortably to the ground. I walked over to the party standing there (none of the others had dared to do it!) feeling I had undergone the greatest experience in my life and I told Michael confidentially that I would save up all my money and buy an elephant. Michael was sceptical, however, and pointed out that it would be hard to keep in a flat, to say nothing of the gazelle and the half a dozen lizards I'd already vowed to possess.

I had asked several times whether there would be the possibility of a leopard shoot, which they had mentioned earlier, but unfortunately there had not been a kill recently in the district. However, one afternoon we did go out, about twenty of us, two on each elephant. It seemed a very dangerous game. There was one gun to each elephant and the front person on the elephant nursed the rifle across his knees, holding on to it with one hand and the pad with the other to keep his balance. As we were all in line, your gun would frequently be pointing at the next person and it needed only to be caught in a branch . . . . Brrhh!

The elephants lined up along the road and all dipped into the marshy jungle at the same time. The ground was wet and sloshy and the tall, reedy grasses and lush undergrowth reached high above the elephants' shoulders.

"Not much chance for us if the engine quits over Burma," Mike called over his shoulder to me.

I agreed, singing: "Bingle, bangle, bungle, I'm so happy in the jungle."

Our elephant pushed over light trees like a bulldozer and it was in one of these little trees that a hornets' nest hung. They zoomed down like fighters. Mike got stung on his starboard ear (maybe they couldn't see him so well, he was wearing khaki) but I was wearing a bright yellow shirt over my brown linen slacks. I was stung on my arms and my hands, and squashed many inside my shirt, getting stung there too, as I squealed and batted them off. I think the elephant got stung, too, on his trunk, but after pirouetting wildly around the *mahout* led him out of range. I had seven stings and they were sore, and after about ten minutes a rash started, like nettlerash only unbearably irritable, from the crown of my head to my knees. I scratched madly and frantically at first but it only made things worse.

I told Michael: "Mike, I feel dreadful."

Mike got worried. He said: "I'll see if I can see the Maharajah," for he was way down at the end of the line.

We spoke to the people on either side of us, who said:"Coo, doesn't she look awful?" and Mike turned himself round to see. He was horrified. My mouth had swollen out like an ape's and my eyes were half closed with the puffiness of my cheeks. Later on I moaned once or twice without meaning to and I don't remember an awful lot what happened during the rest of the shoot, except that I seemed to go through years of pain.

Everything ends, however – a consoling, though at times disquieting thought – and the elephants walked back to the cars. We were given ladders to climb down the elephants. I don't remember how I got down. I slithered down, half fainting. Mike had got the Maharajah by then who sent me straight back in the car with Mike to the palace and a doctor was sent for.

I took my clothes off and lay stretched out on the bed, semi-conscious and moaning occasionally. I didn't mean to and I was afraid that someone might hear, but it did seem to help. I remember I heard a knock on the door and drowsily answered "Come in." It was one of the bearers; he stood there shocked and then backed out, paused a moment and then knocked on the door again, as if he had been over-eager on his cue. By this time, though, I had got under a sheet. I dimly remember the doctor coming and his giving me a shot of adrenalin.

Mike told me afterwards that he had said that the Indians often die if they get stung by these tropical hornets and Mike thought: "Oh Lord, how shall I explain it away to Morrow if she dies?"

The doc then handed Mike some ammonia and some bicarbonate of soda. He said: "Dab the stings with the ammonia and make a solution of the bicarbonate of soda and paint the rash with it," and then departed, leaving Mike to cope as best he could.

Apparently there seemed to be no women servants in the Palace, which resulted, of course, in my getting very much less attention than Michael, who was in the bachelors' quarters. Here every morning the bearer would come in to run the bath and lay Mike's clothes out and even dress him, much to Mike's intense annoyance when daily his wild grab for his trousers was foiled.

In about thirty hours the pain had gone, and I was able to get up to watch the ceremonial procession. There was a religious festival, a Puja, and this was the culmination of nine days' festivities. Bahaiya headed the parade in all his regal finery and glorious emeralds, looking like an Arabian Nights prince, seated on an elephant in a silver howdah. The elephants had all been redecorated for the occasion in blue and gold and red. Budh followed next, almost as magnificent, and then a whole procession behind with a leaden effigy of the goddess Djurga, behind whom there followed important state officials.

We sat and watched the procession from a balcony at the Law Courts. I was too weak to stand for long and afterwards sat in a pavilion by the river's edge, whither the goddess was dragged. There at sunset, stripped of her finery, she was thrown into the river. It was very, very impressive: the hustle and the bustle of the crowds in their very best clothes and the hush which stole over, stilling their chatter, as the sun sunk finally behind the hill when the goddess was tipped jerkily into the muddy, swirling water.

Mike and I, after we had changed for dinner, stood on the balcony over the great hall, looking down on Bahaiya seated in his ceremonial clothes under a silver canopy. He was smoking a big silver hookah, which burbled contentedly in the silence, whilst rows of state officials, one after another, rose noiselessly from their cross-legged position on the floor, walked bowing to the throne, and touched his hands as a vow of allegiance.

These things may never happen again. Times are changing in India and the small rulers are dying out. I am very glad that I saw those things when I did.

UPPER: The palace, Cooch Behar.
LOWER: Religious festival in Cooch Behar.

UPPER: *"Thursday's Child"* at Haneda Airport, Tokyo (see Ch. 17).
LOWER: Dikki and Michael are greeted at Haneda by the Assistant Air Attaché, Flight Lieutenant "Tinker" Bell (see Ch. 17).

CHAPTER 15
CALCUTTA (FIVE)

After a week's stay at the Palace, we had to get back because the undercarriage leg might even now be waiting for us; so the next Dakota which landed at Cooch Behar, though it was really going to Hasimara, picked us up to make a roundabout journey to Calcutta. Hasimara was a plantation and we were going to pick up some chests of tea. On our arrival, however, these were not yet ready as they had to be loaded onto the lorry and the lorry driven down to the airfield. However, a friend of the two pilots had seen us arrive and picked us up in his car and took us back to his home. His wife had just come out to join him and the house was not very settled. For all that, we sat out there on the verandah and had an English tea, with scones and honey and the baby cooing in the pram besides us, whilst all around, crowding on to the little house, steamed the Indian jungle.

It wasn't until after dark that the tea was piled into the Dakota. There were 5,000 lb of it and it all had to be handled by the crew and us, as it was after working hours for the natives. Then the truck drove down to the end of the runway and turned its lights on for the Dakota, so that quite a reasonable take-off could be made. Mike dozed while I chattered to one of the pilots, Bobby Gray, and then we both dozed, arriving in Calcutta sleepy and thirsty. We made our way to the bar, where after prolonged negotiations we got a lift back to the hotel. My, my, how humdrum it looked.

The next day we made our way up to the airfield bright and early but no undercarriage leg had appeared, and we were just as far from leaving as we ever were. Everything had gone wrong. We had an awful feeling of anticlimax and I felt most horribly sick with a bilious attack. I went to bed that afternoon and most of the next day, when Mike came home early, complaining that he too felt sick. We neither of us ate food for a day and a half, after which we were as good as new but very much off the food at the hotel.

Day after day passed, each one with no signs of the undercarriage leg at the BOAC goods depot. No one in England evidently gave a darn about us or maybe they were sending our spare part on the six-week sea voyage! A fat look of good that would be; by the time it arrived the weather over the Pacific and Atlantic would have been impossible and we should just have to go home and listen to everyone saying "I told you so."

It rapidly became evident that it we didn't do something to help ourselves, no one else would. The small metal bracket that was causing the hold-up was only very slightly twisted but engineers at the airport asserted very positively that it could not be straightened without breaking. Eventually Mike decided that even if it did break we should be no worse off as we certainly couldn't use it as it was. So one Saturday morning he placed it in a vice and a little pressure with a massive wrench soon straightened it.

He then brought it back to the hotel where we scraped off all the paint with my knife and a metal ruler and inspected it for cracks or strains in the metal. No blemish was visible at all, so we joyfully cleaned it up and swept the scrapings under the only mat, which portrayed the Taj Mahal upside down.

The next morning, a Sunday, we took the part to a paint spray firm on the airfield and got them to dope it up all shiny silver. We paid them on the spot and took it back to the hotel, making plans and chortling over our secret. On the Monday morning, as arranged, Mike walked joyfully up to the hangar waving the part, and explained volubly that it had just come from England and had been waiting for us at the Swimming Club.

The men said: "Oh, that's fine," and tested it on a metal trueing plate. Then they turned and looked at each other.

"This won't do," they said.

It was a little out of true – twenty-thousandths of an inch. I thought that was a darned good guess on Michael's part. We trued it down to the last thousandth but they were still not happy and refused to fit it.

"Is this a new part?" they asked, "or is this the same part straightened out?"

"Why, it's a new part, of course."

"Well, where's the old part?"

We had got that one lined up. We said that Mike had tried to straighten out the old part but had broken it and had in despair given the bits to a friend at the Calcutta Swimming Club as a souvenir of our desperation.

It ended up by Michael and myself refitting the repaired bracket. *"Thursday's Child"* had been up on trestles for five weeks gathering dust in a corner of the hangar and, inexperienced as we were, the task of reassembling her seemed pretty grim in the heat. However, in the course of two or three days the oil tank was replaced, the undercarriage leg fitted and the wings reassembled, besides numerous odd jobs like cleaning and replacing plugs, checking the tyres and various requirements of the periodic inspection sheet.

Then the Aeronautical Inspection Department woke up to the fact that I had had an accident and that "major damage" had been sustained. The Inspector there and the Insurance Inspector decided that they wouldn't let us go until we could prove to their satisfaction that our resuscitated undercarriage attachment bracket was a new part. It really all hung on the Insurance Inspector – quite a nice man who constantly chewed betel nut. The other Inspector was prepared to take his word.

Either we had to produce the broken pieces of the old part or the papers which would have accompanied the new part. Personally they said they did not believe it was a new part; they indicated as tactfully as possible that they had heard it was the old one straightened out. I tried all ways to get them to let us go on but they wouldn't and I just didn't know what to do. I sauntered along in the hot sunshine, kicking at the stones in anger and lost in thought.

I found a place in the main hall of the airport terminal and sat down dejectedly with my eyes shut, just thinking. I looked up as a man passed and noticed that he was a member of one of the airline companies. He smiled at me and then he stopped and chatted to me; soon I explained my troubles and asked him if he could help me. Could he, I begged, provide me with any evidence that this part had come by air?

He thought a while and said doubtfully: "Well, I could type out a manifest," and darted off behind the scenes, to come back in a few minutes with a manifest in his hand. It described the part, stated which aircraft it had arrived on, who piloted the ship, how much it weighed and when it arrived.

"This is the best I can do," he said, "but you should really have the Customs stamp on it."

He handed it over to me.

"For the love of God," he said, "don't let it out of your possession. Destroy it there and then rather than let anyone else have it, please." I assured him most fervently and thanked him profusely. I could have kissed him, only I didn't know him well enough and anyway it was a bit public just there.

As I wandered down to Customs, I wondered just how I should get the papers stamped; in fact the more I thought about it, the harder it seemed. I knew that the Customs men, though friendly, wouldn't help me, having just got their country to themselves, and I hadn't the money to bribe them. However, I chatted to them and they gave me a sweet lime to suck as I sat on the counter. Then I wandered into the Holy of Holies, the Chief's room, and played with the things on the table. Suddenly I noticed that the large stamp, the only stamp in fact, that was used on incoming goods, was just in front of me. I picked it up, toying with it as I thought and with elaborate idleness stamped everything in sight; the blotting paper, an old envelope I had in my hand, the inside part of my left wrist ... and the manifest. One of the Customs men jokingly initialled my arm and dated it, so I knew that that was all I had to do, thanked them kindly for the lime and went to the fuel representative's office, where I copied down the initial and the other date on the manifest.

I fixed up to meet the Insurance Inspector that night in a hotel off Chowringee. We had a couple of brandies and then I produced my manifest, having explained that it was found at the Swimming Club. I can still feel that sickening feeling as he picked it up and peered at the document. My knees really were turned to water.

I could have counted a hundred while he looked, and after a while he said, grudgingly: "Well, it seems all right."

Then he asked to keep it but I said: "No, we want to get out tomorrow and on our way and this is my only chance of denying all the rumours regarding this attachment plate."

On my suggestion and after a little persuasion, he agreed to write a little note, which he did there and then, to the AID Inspector because he had already told me he probably wouldn't be in until after midday, as his father was dying. I thanked him and said goodnight and walked back to the hotel in a state somewhere between ecstasy and exhaustion.

Next morning we were all packed up to go and took our bags up to the ship. It was utterly imperative to get out before midday and before our sins were discovered. For not only had we forged a document but we had added another two fuel tanks, making an extra 150 lb weight, without permission from anybody. We wanted to get off before the two Inspectors got together and started talking and checking up.

Mike and I took the plugs out again and cleaned them the next morning, sweating profusely in the Indian sunshine. Then I walked the mile (oh that endless mile! I must have walked it dozens of times in the course of our stay there) from the hangar to the Admin buildings. I had to organise some fuel, for every drop we had had been stolen. We had put a wire through to Delhi the night before for a further fuel permit but the fuel company at Dum Dum wouldn't allow us one drop, not even enough to run up the engine, until the order came through. Whilst I was worrying out this, I discovered we were being charged 450 *rupees* for aerodrome fees, despite the fact that the ship had been cared for in a private hangar. I swore so roundly at the Aerodrome Manager about this that no doubt he thought me dangerous, for he reduced it to 45 *rupees*.

When at last the fuel had been taken to the ship and the refuelling completed, and the engine run up, we found we had a leak in the fuel system. Oh what a flap we were in! It had been one of those frantic days anyhow, and Mike had done a lot of exotic cursing after he had folded the wings forward again and locked them carefully with safety wire only to discover that, with full span, he couldn't get it out of the hangar door. But it was nothing to what he said when he discovered there was a leak in the fuel system! Fortunately it was only in the priming line and we were able to start the engine without danger. It went first press of the starter, too, after five weeks' idleness and ran perfectly, which says something for Jerry's work on it.

At this point some unexpected expert help appeared in the form of Mr Bannerjee, the chief engineer of an Indian airline. He told us to taxy up to the aerodrome, where he would get our leak fixed. Away we went for the last time up the dusty, stony mile, stopping every so often to avoid hitting water buffaloes, piles of rocks and individuals taking a lunchtime stroll. Having safely negotiated the road we taxied past the control tower and parked the ship as far away as possible so that no Nosey Parker would poke his head in and see our two homemade fuel tasks. Mr Bannerjee was as good as his word and, with his two European assistants, got to work on our priming line. It was finally fixed by sunset and our benefactor insisted on giving us dinner before we said goodnight. We went to bed right after leaving him and slept once again in the VIP quarters.

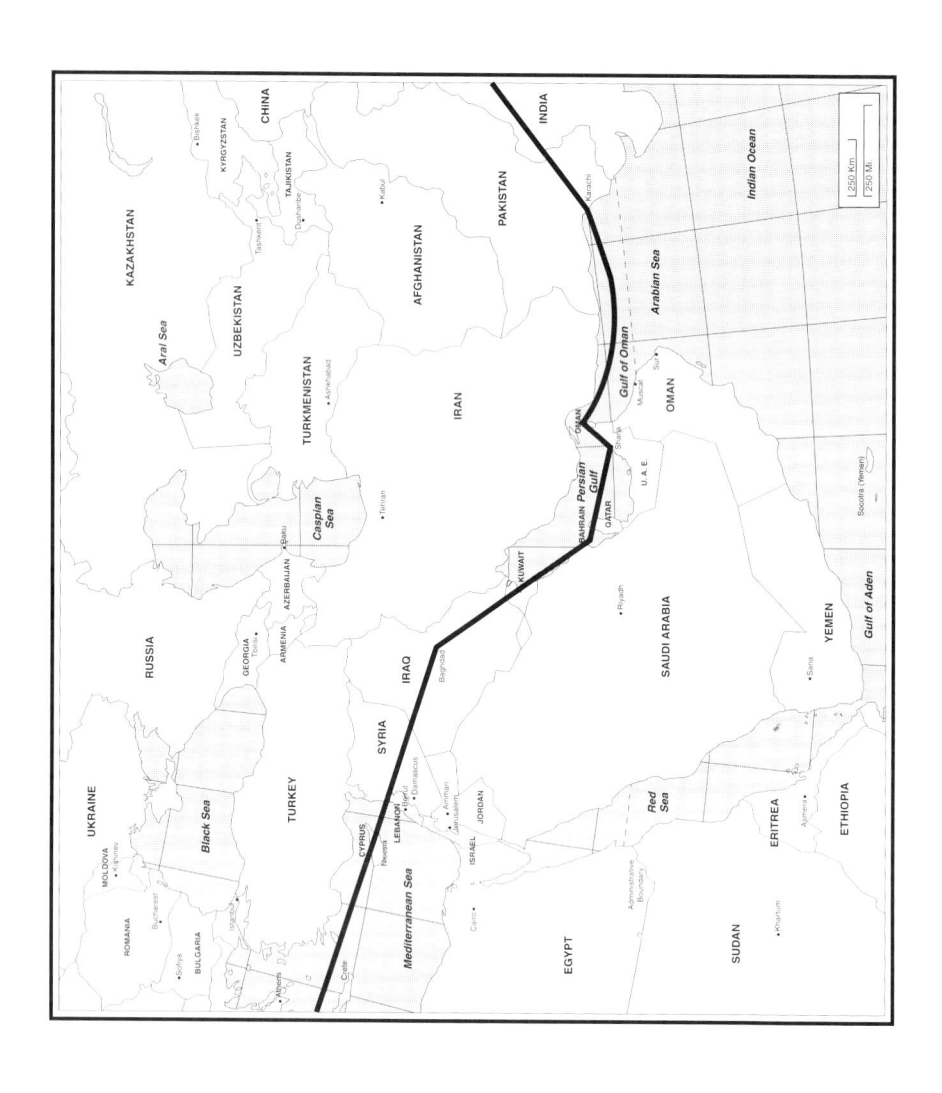

CHAPTER 16
CALCUTTA–RANGOON–VIENTIANE –HONG KONG–OKINAWA

We took off into the deep blue star-speckled sky at three next morning. How glad we were to leave Calcutta! The frantic endeavour to get out reminded me somewhat of the Red Queen when she took Alice's hand and ran like hell in order to stay still. Several times we thought we should have to turn round and go back to England. We even thought we might have to abandon the ship there. Isn't it more often the thought of what one's enemies might say if one quit, rather than what one's friends would say if one went on, that keeps one going on long after it's humanly possible? I could see, and I kept on seeing, what people would say; the sort of I-told-you-so attitude. I wonder what made Mike go on? I never asked him.

I felt excited and happy as I saw the runway lights far down below and we headed on course for Rangoon. Free at last, I thought, always assuming our sins didn't catch up with us. Busy as I was with the instruments, I could still find time to marvel at the Sunderbunds in the River Ganges delta, wet and meandering beneath us. There was much big game, I had been told, down there and I wished I could have had a chance to shoot something. How strange it is, that over-civilised as we are in some ways, how very much on the surface that sophistication lies. We still want to hunt, to kill and brag about it, the same as all mankind has done since the first Stone Age man took a pot-shot with a flint-tipped spear.

Dawn broke as we flew over the Bay of Bengal and at one period the sun was obscured by a cumulo-nimbus cloud and we gazed entranced as it stood awesome and symbolic with its anvil-shaped outline marked out in fire. We couldn't understand at the time why there should be so many cu-nims over the middle of the sea but we discovered afterwards that this was due to the inter-tropical front, which was now on its way southwards. The monsoon followed the sun, going south in winter and north in summer. We'd met this inter-tropical front in the north of India and it had overtaken us whilst we were in Calcutta. It is the very centre of the most turbulent part of the monsoon but we were lucky in that chance had cut a path through it exactly on our course so that, though big cumulo-nimbus masses had formed on either side, we could press on at our own altitude without any danger. We were a little perturbed by the coughs the engine gave every so often and I kept worrying about the water content in our fuel tanks. Calcutta is a very wet place and, with the tanks being empty, condensation might have resulted. We had no means of draining the cabin tanks and I binded about this several times to Mikey, but it was one of those things we could do nothing about, it just couldn't be helped.

We avoided the turbulence over the Arakan Range by dicing directly across the Bay of Bengal, turning inland near Bassein round the southern end of the mountains.

As we crossed the Irrawaddy, Mike remarked: "To the north is Mandalay, to the south Rangoon."

I was thrilled. The very names were romance on the tongue and the casualness with which he told me, as though he had commented on Highgate and Clapham, amused and fascinated me.

"*By the old Mulmein pagoda,
Looking eastward to the sea,
There's a Burma girl a-sitting
And I know she thinks of me.*"

I sang joyously and lustily but not even Michael could hear. We were on our way to new lands. What could be lovelier?

We touched down at Mingaladon Airport after 4½ hours' flying, for a quick breakfast and refuelling. We were the guests of the RAF again, God bless 'em, and whilst Mike had a quick look at the fuel strainer, I endeavoured to make a flight plan out for an airfield in French Indo-China which, according to the French airline pilot who had suggested we landed there, was called Vientiane, and which was marked on Mike's French map as that. Nobody, however, seemed to have the remotest idea where it was, though I guess if we had called it Wien Chan, which was the Chinese way of putting it, they might have recognised it, but we didn't know that at the time.

We had rather an exciting take-off from Rangoon. I had opened the throttle and we were trundling along the runway, when she suddenly forked off to the right as the tail came up. I suppose it was a gust of wind she turned towards. I held her down on the wire mesh runway until she reached the side, then gently eased the stick back. She just mushed through the air, flying in a half-hearted manner a few feet from the ground. I'm sure the control tower was surprised; I must confess I was, myself.

We flew over a lot of jungle that afternoon, besides two 7,000 ft mountain ranges, and if the engine had quit and we had had any trouble there wouldn't have been a single spot we could have landed on. We'd seen a bit of jungle in India and we had no desire to land anywhere near it. We had water bottles with us and an American parachutist's jungle kit with an absolutely wizard machete. It was a glorious weapon, looking every inch a knife and once or twice I had waved it around feeling all tough and Commando.

We didn't climb over the cu-nims nor beneath them but in and out between them. This gave the journey plenty of interest to me. It was like an obstacle race and I really enjoyed whizzing round, not quite touching them, though God knows how Mike ever managed to plot a course. Eventually the clouds got too thick, even though it was evening, and at one point we had to climb up to 9,000 ft to be quite sure of clearing the mountains' peaks. Not, of course, that we could have climbed much higher even if we had wanted to.

As the sun was sinking, I trimmed the ship in a downward glide and we started looking for the Mekong River, which should appear any minute flowing in from the north. Sure enough, there it was a few minutes later, a broad silver streak cutting the dark green, about five miles away on our port beam. As we drew level, it turned abruptly eastwards and we flew along parallel, occasionally losing sight of it as it meandered behind a hill. We were looking for a certain bend, which due to Michael's good navigation duly appeared straight ahead. On closer inspection we could see a small town but, horrors, no airfield! Had we been misled by the handsome Frenchman? We flew round & round the town in ever-increasing circles searching for an airfield, and it was quite a while before Mike said: "Got it." The runway was of hard earth but due to the rains it had sprouted green blades of grass, giving it a light green sheen, a remarkably smart bit of camouflage!

We were greeted by the Commandant, who was very charming and very kind. He had had no previous warning from Rangoon about our arrival but we got fuel OK and our ship was pushed into the bamboo hangar, which had neatly woven walls. He drove us back along a winding dusty track in a Jeep. I am afraid I dropped a brick for, as we were chugging along, I noticed we were on the left-hand side of the road.

"Oh!" I said brightly and in French, "I thought you drove on the right."

I felt awfully silly when I was told they did and he wasn't.

We stayed the night in the Commandant's house with his wife and family. They were very short of water and one was only permitted to slightly sluice oneself from a pitcher of purchased water. Vientiane, we found, was very French, both in language and customs, for we were taken to an incredibly French café that night, only the food was much worse than you would ever get in France. Maybe it was because I was tired but I must confess I suffered agonies of indigestion that night after some mysterious and highly seasoned food had been consumed, together with a bottle of wine. Very vivid to me, too, is the impression I still have of the people in that little café. There were two French soldiers going home on leave, both of them with French Indo-Chinese wives clutching babies on their knees. The thought of what their mothers would say when they brought back to their French village these barefoot and draped women worried me for weeks. These Indo-Chinese women had never seen civilisation such as in France, nor worn European clothes and shoes. What would they do in civilisation amidst traffic, rations and local political issues? I wonder just how they did get on.

We had breakfast at six in the morning (oh God, this early rising!) and were taken by Jeep back to the field. We had seen to the refuelling the night before. As we were taxying out someone rushed up brandishing a slip of paper containing the latest met. report and by seven o'clock we were airborne on our way to Hong Kong, 700 miles eastward across Annam and the China Sea.

After climbing through a thin layer of scattered cumulus, we found it necessary to fly in cu. clouds over a 6,000 ft-high gap in the mountains of Annam. As we had 9,000 ft to the north and 7,500 ft to the south, it was not my idea of fun and games but we levelled off at 7,500 ft and were soon out of harm's way in the clear with the coast on the horizon ahead. This side of the range we came down to 6,000 ft, economical cruising. There was a lot of cloud that day and a fair amount of drift, and as we progressed conditions got bumpier and bumpier. Instead of ground shrouded in soft swirls of mist as at the start, there were churning seas with whitecaps to watch. It was hard work flying that day too. I had never been so tossed around in my life. We were worried enough as it was with the makeshift repair on the main spar and when the wings flapped up and down like a crow, there was cause to be anxious.

The latter part of the flight seemed unending. We were flying low now along the China coast, over seas smashing onto the rocky islands beneath. The lower we got, the wetter it looked. We were at about 800 ft when Mike turned to me and called: "We'd better go down a bit more, we don't want the wings to drop off."

I didn't hear what he said. I misheard it as: "The wings are going to drop off." If they had been about to do so, he would not have appeared more perturbed, and for one horrid moment a streak of fear ran through me and my armpits pricked. He repeated his remarks and I dropped down to 500 ft. Behind some of the islands little fishing junks sheltered in fleets with their batwing sails furled. They looked so like what the real thing is supposed to look like that they might have been toys.

Mike offered to take over several times but being perfectly convinced that nobody could fly that ship as well as I could I wouldn't let him. Every time we came behind an island or over one, the beating we were getting was so tremendous it beat the paint off the spats, and I wondered how we would ever stand it and how the ship hadn't disintegrated into matchwood underneath us. Everything ends, however; a very pleasant and comforting thought, that, for though the lovely things end and the happiness too, so does sorrow, so does pain and so does weariness. It wouldn't be worth while going on if it weren't for that.

Hong Kong duly appeared and I did two left-hand circuits of the field. It is an awkward airfield with mountains on three sides of it. I remember having to exert nearly all my strength to get that ship to turn in the turbulent conditions. I was reprimanded after landing, not only for having done two left-hand circuits when the field was a right-hand one, but having landed on the wrong runway which, though incidentally more into wind, was not the one indicated. I thought that both errors on one landing was rather choice! There again, the signals had been placed near the back door of the control tower so the guy who had to change the signals wouldn't have far to go, even if this meant we never saw them. We learned from Met. on our arrival that our troubles had been due apparently to an unforecast typhoon passing through the China Sea to the east of our route.

At this time we noticed that our revs weren't any too high and so we consulted a big red-faced English engineer, who kindly dived into the engine and fiddled around. Mike and I were bitterly tired and we almost creaked with old age. He lent against the mainplane, whilst I sat listlessly in the cockpit idly watching the engineer.

The fuel representative and his wife cared for us as if they were old friends. Mike slept the whole way back from the airfield to their lovely little house high on the hills. But though I drowsed, I had one eye open to watch the people of this new city and I noticed how much better fed and dressed they were than those in Calcutta. A couple of cold beers in tall thin glasses helped us a little but I can't remember another time on the trip when I was more tired. I remember sitting clutching my beer, trying to stop the tears that rolled down my face from my aching eyes. Mike had been to Met. and had had a long discussion with the met. men about the Pacific weather. We were warned it was bad, yet again, and were urged to go back.

"What should we do?" he asked me.

I couldn't care less.

After a bath in brown water, which I enjoyed with a celluloid swan, we sat down to a beautifully cooked meal but I could scarcely tackle it. The soup I swallowed gratefully but the lobster laid me low. I felt terribly sick and went to bed as soon as I politely could. God, was I tired!

We were to have gone to Shanghai the next day, but as there were bad headwinds our best plan seemed to be to set course for Okinawa, via Formosa. In this way we would have very largely a light wind and be over the sea where it would be less bumpy. The Tower was horrified.

"Oh! you can't do that. You've got to give 36 hours' notice before you land in Okinawa. It's a military base."

We were threatened with everything, including shooting at dawn, but since speed was utterly essential and we had to get to the Pacific as soon as possible, they finally promised to try and get us cleared, meanwhile releasing us at our own risk.

The runway for take-off had a mountain at the end and was short enough anyhow, so I did an aircraft carrier take-off: sitting on the first inch of runway with brakes full on, opening the throttle full, and then letting go. She made it easier than we expected, and as soon as we had made any height I swung out over the bay and out to sea through a gap in the islands.

We climbed through scattered cu. clouds to our 6,000 ft and then there began a very tedious flight. Maybe it was because I was tired still, or maybe because I was eager to get on, but how boring this flight and the next turned out to be. Those seat tanks we had had installed were no aids to comfort, for though I sat on a leather cushion, there was underneath me a strap from front to back over the tank. You would think that under the cushion that strap wouldn't worry me but after the first couple of hours I'd start to fidget, sitting first one side and then the other. First my instep on the rudder bar and then my toes, till *rigor mortis* would set in in the lower limbs and I'd lose all sense of feeling.

We flew a straight course for Formosa and then out across the East China Sea. There was scattered cumulus most of the way but as we neared our destination they thinned out and we had no trouble in finding the island. Actually, though, we were peering out on all sides looking for it when we unexpectedly found it bang underneath, on track. I thought that a pretty good piece of navigation on Mike's part after several hours at sea.

I'd carefully asked before leaving Hong Kong which airfield I was to land on and had been told: "First on the left as you go in." After sighting the field, we circled and landed, only to be told to land in another field further up the island as the General wanted to see me. My heart sank as I thought of the 36 hours' notice we should have given but apparently he wasn't going to row me, he only wanted to be nice.

I was most impressed on looking around after landing. What plump, pink faces these men had, after the gaunt brown ones of Calcutta. I don't know why it should have impressed me so much here. Of course Americans always look so terribly well-fed. Mike had really been looking forward to landing on American stations because of the food, and that night we were not disappointed when we had the traditional steak and ice cream. I almost got up and sang the *Star Spangled Banner,* I could think of nothing more American. And I had my first *Coca-Cola.*

I spent the night in the 'visiting Generals' quarters,' I think. It was all very nice and civilised. Mike just got ordinary field officers' quarters, but the loss was mine, for he had *the* towel, a point which unfortunately escaped my notice until after I had had a shower and I had to run round the room and 'hurrh' on myself to dry.

CHAPTER 17
OKINAWA–ITAZUKE–TOKYO–CHITOSE

After a good night's rest (the weather was quite a lot cooler now) we got up early and entered into the prolonged negotiations, unfortunately necessary, before take-off. We were to have had an escort of Mustangs but, to our intense amazement, the flight was cancelled due to what they called bad weather, but what we thought were just ordinary conditions. They warned us very solemnly and seriously: "No Air Sea Rescue, you know," and probably thought me very foolhardy to care so very little about this. After a lot of thanks and best wishes on both sides, and clutching firmly the gift of a bottle of Scotch and a pack of candies, we climbed into the ship.

It was well daylight and after the climb the sun was shining and, flying northwards along the Riyuku Islands, I could see sunken vessels, some partly submerged and one broken in two complete halves, lying like a child's toys in the blue, blue sea. That bitter struggle seemed so far off now; those bloody days when the Yanks were fighting and burning the Japanese, foot by foot, from Okinawa.

After three hours, heavy frontal clouds as forecast caused us to descend quickly through a clear gap to 1,800 ft. The weather beneath the cloud was stormy and as we reached the Southern Island of Japan it became bumpier. Between mountains we followed railways to Fukuoka. We circled round Itazuke airfield several times, wondering if it was the right one. You never can tell and as far as I can remember it was not marked on our map. Mike called up on the RT and I entered the pattern and went round and round waiting for permission to come in. After a while I thought it was about time and came in, and just before we touched down, Mike obtained clearance. We taxied to the Tower, climbed out and stretched our aching bodies. All this sitting for hours and days on end had almost produced bed sores and I was awfully glad that flight was over, I was so appallingly stiff.

We were whisked away to VIP quarters some way from the actual Base, where we received lavish hospitality. Driving across the country a little, I noticed how much better fed the average Japanese looks in comparison with the Indian. Everywhere we noticed intense cultivation, every inch of land being utilised and the many coloured fields marked by little ditches. This was particularly noticeable from the air, where it looked very orderly and industrious. There seemed to be no motor transport in possession of the Japanese, all the cars being American.

That evening, whilst absorbing liquor after a good solid meal, we were rather hurt by the attitude of a certain Colonel in the Mess, whose disparaging remarks about Sunday morning flyers and the trouble we had caused and also how Japan was a front line of defence, nearly in the state of emergency etc. etc. rose to a crescendo. We realised, however, that the gentleman was slightly 'in his cups' and took it in turns to make non-committal replies.

Of all the dinner table etiquettes, I found the American most hard to grasp. In other countries, you tackle one, perhaps two, plates at a time but Americans make it frightfully complicated as they have a plate for bread, one for salad, and maybe an extra one for peas, or corn in the cob, all satellites to the big oval-shaped plate planted in front of you. The first time this happened to me, the soup and salad got served together and, being most confused, I had to talk furiously to the officer on my left so that everyone else got tired of waiting and started first. I had to do this several times, until I got the hang of the order and weapons for the food.

Itazuke was quite cold, or we considered it such, and I changed from my shorts into grey flannels and a sweater for flying the next day. Breakfast was served luxuriously in our quarters, though due to my unreliable insides I was unable to eat anything. Whilst I was drinking coffee one of the officers came in with a big box, a present for me. Would I take it now or should they send it? He opened the box and there was a beautiful Japanese *geisha*, about 13 inches high. I had seen her on a table whilst passing through the Mess, had touched her hair and had commented on her great beauty and asked what it was for. They told me it was a bingo prize, which at that time conveyed less than nothing to me. How funny, when I think of it now, when I've seen bingo played from Fairbanks, Alaska to Buffalo NY and Goose Bay, Labrador.

The cooler climate, needless to say, had its effect on the engine, which by this time needed a little coaxing to start. We paid our debts, checked Met. and filled in the long form which is considered necessary for a flight, then shook hands and took off for Tokyo.

We had to climb and circle the airfield at the same time because of the high mountains all round. These mountains were covered with trees but soon we left them behind us and flew between the islands of the Inland Sea at about 6,000 ft, I for one admiring the Japanese landscape. The neat little islands and the even neater volcanic mountains made me think instantly of the homely willow pattern. After a short time, we flew over Hiroshima, where we circled in the sunlight, eating *Babe Ruth* candy bars (I was getting hungry now). We both took turns holding the stick so that we could lean out and see as much as possible of this 'atom bomb' town. Candidly, I was much disappointed. Of course I guess you couldn't see much detail from that altitude. The land was obviously flat and very tidy but we could make out wooden huts and what we took to be a few steel girders standing. The streets were still plainly marked out and it looked more or less as though the bomb blast had sheared all the buildings off at the foundations.

The rice fields we noticed were quite a lot under water, bordering and forming an actual part of the almost land-locked Arai Bay. Fujiyama was soon visible in the distance on our port, projecting through the layer of clouds beneath us. 60 miles off Tokyo we let down through the cloud over the sea. Then we had to follow the coast at 1,000 ft instead of over land, because of the hills. Presently we passed low over the Naval Dockyards of Yokohama; a few moments later Haneda (Tokyo airfield) was in sight and we called for permission to land.

We had only one microphone so Mike did all the calling up, whilst I circled the field, often giggling helplessly at his agonised grimaces, because the VHF radio which we carried had unfortunately no volume control. Either you couldn't hear anything at all or else it blew you to pieces. Haneda Tower told us to land on a runway not into wind as repairs were being carried out at the end of the one that *was* lying into the wind. However I demurred at this, due to the great likelihood of our ground-looping, so Mike asked if we could land on the one under repair. Lord, *we* didn't take much room to land on.

They said we could if we came in short. Mike did not complain about the approach, even when we were just skidding over the housetops, but when I brought her across the river at just about the height of the runway the other side, his nerve failed him and he slapped on a lot of throttle. I was righteously indignant and immediately pulled it back. Such interference! I think we touched down on the first three feet of runway for all that, which was exactly what I wanted to do.

We were greeted by the British Air Attaché, among others, who looked after us. We had maintenance to get done there, so after consultation we decided to stay two nights. We had a distinct tailwheel wobble and there were several other minor problems. The junior Air Attaché was a charming lad by the name of F/Lt. 'Tinker' Bell and he ran us round in his car, took us to the hotel and arranged maintenance so that I could sleep that afternoon.

We had reached Tokyo in five days from Calcutta, working and flying every day from before dawn until after dark without a break; I was getting a bit tired by now, not 'surface-tired,' but with the kind of tiredness that makes even your sleep feel sub-standard. Mike and I had a quiet dinner that night, incidentally a very good meal at the Marranouchi Hotel, which is run by the Australians, and went to bed early. I was highly amused by the taps in the washbasin, one of which was marked on the top with a squiggle and the other one with a squiggle-squiggle. It was very difficult to choose which one was 'Hot.' The baths, too, were wide and short and made of mosaic tiling. There's nothing like studying another nation's customs in your bath.

The next morning we trotted up to Haneda to supervise the refuelling and check the ship over. The wind was whistling across the field and I was glad when we were taken back in the car to change for an Ambassadorial luncheon. Clothing, due to the chilliness of the weather, was becoming quite a problem for me and I'm sure those at the luncheon must have been mildly surprised at my green cotton dress covered by Mike's sports jacket, a little on the large side, which completed the ensemble. His Excellency, to whom I had related the tale of how I was given a bottle of whisky at

Okinawa and how I tried to change it for a bottle of brandy in Itazuke, only to be pressed to keep both, presented me after lunch with another bottle of brandy and another bottle of whisky. Did I really strike him as being that kind of person, Mike complained! He doesn't appreciate good liquor the same as I do and said he was "flipping well not going to fly in an airborne bar." So we gave a bottle of Scotch to 'Tinker' Bell when having dinner with him that night.

The next day, all ready in the morning, we checked Met. for the umpteenth time (we were really getting in a flap about the Pacific crossing) and decided that it looked like being good that night for the great flight. So we set off at 9.50 the next morning, after having swung the propeller to get her started – due to an oversight, the radio had been left on all night and the battery was drained. It was quite an exciting take-off. "Thursday's Child" again took it into her head to go off on to the side of the runway and, though I left it until the last moment to ease the stick back, how we missed one of those stripey huts that house the GCA Unit God only knows. I noticed a few minutes later when we had gained 1,000 ft that my left leg was jumping badly. I honestly didn't think we would make that.

We had been told to call a couple of airfields on our way north, which of course we couldn't do as our radio refused to work (the generator not charging properly) but we were not unduly perturbed. However, an airfield halfway along, called Mizawa, was distinctly worried at this unidentified aircraft coming over. They sent up two Mustangs, who flew round us making frantic and quite unintelligible signals from their cockpit. I first thought we must have left our undercart behind at Tokyo but later realized that it could be they were wanting us to land, so down we came, cursing them heartily for the delay.

Standing by the control tower was General Partridge, who happened to be passing through. He said: "What are you doing here? You should be at Chitose!"

We explained between clenched teeth that we were only too eager to go to Chitose, that it was our chief aim and desire to get there but that his nasty little fighters had forced us down to Mizawa. He thought it was quite a joke and tried to persuade us that Mizawa was a far better starting point for the Aleutians than Chitose. Actually he was quite right, but we decided to press on for Chitose which was 100 miles nearer Shemya as the crow flew, not realizing that military regulations made a devious route necessary. As it turned out, the flight from Mizawa would have been better from the weather point of view as well. We were allowed to take off again after handshakes and kind wishes for our success.

We nearly had another of those hair-raising swings to the right on take-off but I was ready for it this time and caught it before it developed. It was only 140 miles to Chitose, on the North Island of Japan, and we made it in an hour in spite of rough weather, which tossed us around quite a bit. We raced northwards at 500 ft above the waves, which were whipped white by the strong following wind. So this was the cold, grey Pacific? It looked appallingly wet and cruel. I wasn't enamoured at the thought of 10 hours of it.

CHAPTER 18
CHITOSE – WAITING

We slipped into Chitose in the early afternoon and went straight up to the Met. office. I was getting to understand the weather charts quite a bit now. Once they were found it looked like being good for our crossing that night, but we also heard that we must wait for a B-17 Flying Fortress to escort us and that we were forbidden to go without it. The reasoning: it is much less trouble and much cheaper if a ship is flown along with us so that if we get lost they can drop us a boat, or if we crash into the water and out of sight, they will know at least that we are dead and will not need to waste thousands of dollars looking for us.

We were a little surprised at all this concern for our welfare because in England not only were we told that there would be absolutely no offer of an escort, but that there was no Air Sea Rescue either. We waited impatiently, trying consciously to relax, for that B-17 to come in. It didn't come and didn't come until way after midnight, by which time, of course, it was too late for us to get off. We were just hopping mad. Here we had been told in frantic wires from Tokyo that the weather would be OK for crossing, once in a blue moon, and then when we tried to cross, with quite reasonable weather, we couldn't go because their unasked-for escort had not appeared. Added to which, time would slide by until the next good day came along, if ever, by which time we would be too old to handle a ship.

The result of this delay was that we had to sit around very much on tenterhooks, had two false alarms, and a lot of nattering to one another, before the real opportunity came. We wanted a good tailwind, cloud tops below 6,000 ft – our best cruising level, so we couldn't get iced up – and a clear sky above, to take astro-shots.

During the five days we spent at Chitose we studied closely the island, its inhabitants and the American Air Force. Chitose, on the Island of Hokkaido, is almost entirely moorland and mountains with birch forests and swamps. It doesn't get very hot in the summer, although it is in the same latitude as the South of France, and about this time, the end of October, the temperature is around 34°F with a frost at night. The people we saw were still wearing the traditional costume and the women were shapeless in quilted *kimonos*. Rice and Indian corn and other vegetables are grown around the place and they catch a lot of salmon in the most unsporting way, by trapping them as they swim upstream.

Mike and I were tense and quarrelsome a lot of the time and I thought Mike horribly possessive about my ship for he wouldn't let me look inside the engine and potter like he did. I spent a lot of time getting mad at him over this and the madder I got, the less he said, which made me madder still. If you are going to have a quarrel you might as well have a good one, but he would close up like the proverbial clam.

One day, in a huff, I left him alone and sauntered down to the village with one of the wives on the station. We pottered round the village shops, chattering and generally having much fun, slightly perturbed though by a little Japanese man who had followed us all the morning at a respectful distance of 50 yards like a detective or something. However, he eventually introduced himself. He was a reporter, apparently, and asked us if we would care to take tea with some friends of his.

We said we would be delighted, and soon we were shown over quite a charming and apparently very symbolic Japanese garden, then we left our shoes in the porch and stepped into the house. The floor was of woven straw and we were given cushions on which we perched politely and in pain. We were also given little rests for our arms, and I greatly admired the portable charcoal fire in a china pot. The walls really *were* made of paper, just like I'd been told, and one side of the room had an alcove in the wall, which was the centre spot of the room, much as a mantelpiece is in England, and there hung a scroll and another beautiful *geisha* girl doll under a glass case. This was produced for me to touch and admire and I was taught how to write my name in Japanese characters, which I copied with infinite pains.

My hostess brought in tea in handleless cups, cakes – pink and green – and slices of raw apple – peeled – which we tasted delicately. It was all incredibly polite and complimentary and much time was spent in bowing, which I found a most infectious habit. I was tickled pink when I saw two men bowing who hit their heads together by mistake, for the vision of the two frog footmen in *Alice in Wonderland* rose before my eyes with appalling clarity. I was offered a gift: would I like a *geisha* girl or a *kimono*? I said I had already got a *geisha* girl, or rather that she was being sent home for me (it's never come yet) and I said I would love a *kimono* (that's never come either).

We had to get back for lunch, so my friend and I rose and, bowing our way out, slipped on our shoes and beat it, giggling like schoolgirls when we had got out of earshot and the tension was relaxed. Fancy having to live all one's life in that over-elaborate atmosphere. Perhaps they don't, though, amongst themselves.

When I came back to the base and found Mike, I was terribly disappointed that he hadn't even noticed my absence but had gone out with the colonel to look at the salmon traps. Oh the heartlessness of men!

Apart from a jolly Fancy Dress party on Hallowe'en when Michael got behindhand with his Tom Collins's and I swiped all the cherries out of them (I found it a huge joke because it made him hopping mad) there was nothing much of any significance which occurred at Chitose. There was nothing at all to do. We went out one afternoon with the rifle but the woods were silent and desolate as though a curse was on them. I was most interested, though, in the Japanese hot baths – there were men's and women's baths at the Base but normally in Japan they are communal. First you have a shower to get the dirt off, after which you ease yourself into a large pool of scalding water where you stand motionless, every ripple being agony, until the heat colours your skin to raw meat-red; then you struggle out into your clothes. I was always too exhausted to dry myself (and anyway I always felt it might be dangerous because my skin might peel off in the same way as after scalding peaches or tomatoes) and with heart pounding I would labour up the stairs to lie prostrate on my bed. I could only stand about a quarter of an hour but some of the old hands stay in for ages.

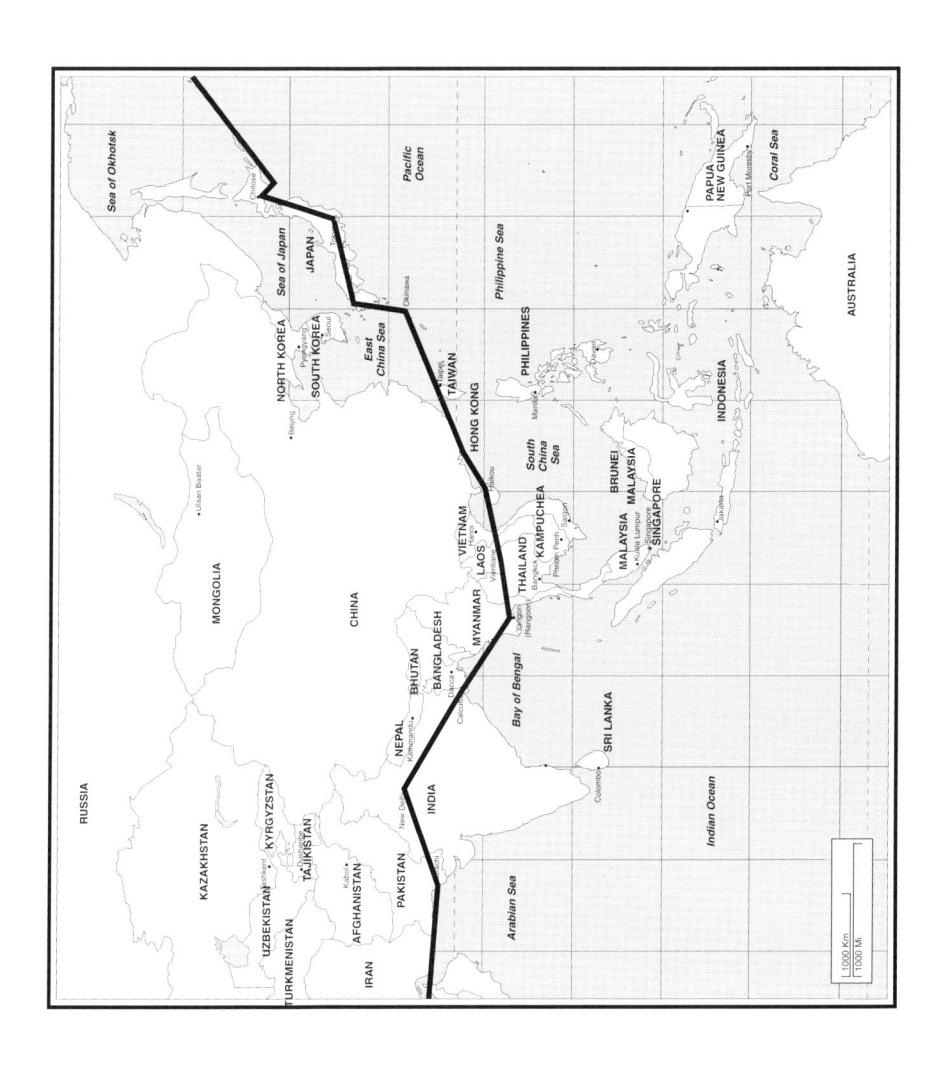

766　　FLIGHT

June 30th, 1949   767

NORTH PACIFIC NAVIGATION . . .

Navigator's chart used on the over-water (Hokkaido-Shemya) section of the North Pacific flight, showing approximate conditions encountered, together with the actual synoptic situation during the flight. Note the position lines plotted as "spokes" radiating from Shemya.

SHEMYA ISLAND.
E.T.A. 2215 G.M.T.

G.M.T.	L.H.A.	AZ.+90°	ALT.
2051	311	222	10° 04'
2107	315	226	11° 48'
2123	319	229	13° 26'
2139	323	233	14° 56'
2155	327	237	16° 18'
2211	331	241	17° 34'
2227	335	244	18° 41'
2243	339	248	19° 38'
2259	343	252	20° 27'
2315	347	257	21° 06'

CHAPTER 19
THE NORTH PACIFIC

The first two attempts at making the Pacific crossing were cancelled due to adverse weather conditions, but on the night of the 3rd of November the forecast was as good as it was ever likely to be, so we decided to press on. We were quite pals with the crew of the B-17 by now and before taking off we discussed it thoroughly and got ourselves clued up. They were to take our luggage and our spares (any help in lightening the ship was a good thing) and were to fly a zig-zag course carefully calculated by Mike and their navigator so that they would just keep behind us and not go too far to either side. Their call-sign was *"Jukebox Special"* and we were to call them every 30 minutes. They would also help us with the navigation as much as they could.

They took off first into the dark blustering night; we finished our fuelling up, did an engine run-up and then filled up the tank we'd drawn the fuel from when doing the check. You couldn't have got a teaspoonful more in. I was shivering: of course it was cold, but I noticed Mike's voice was impatient and rasping and maybe he swore unnecessarily violently when he dropped his torch into the guts of the ship and demanded another from a nearby GI. Rain was falling as we taxied down to the runway (requiem for the dying?). Even though the runway was long enough for a B-17, we were so heavily loaded that as a precaution I held the brakes on until the throttle was well and truly opened, when we lumbered off between the avenue of lights.

I don't mind admitting I was pretty damn scared as, chattering instructions to myself in a fury of concentration, we climbed shakily into the stormy weather. We entered the cloud base at 1,500 ft though it took us long enough to get up there. Strangely enough my weakest moment was soon after take-off, when, struggling upwards, the ship was suddenly tossed into a dive. The only instrument which registered this instantly was the sensitive climb-and-dive gauge, the others being more slow to react, and I was confused. There was a sudden helpless moment when my brain refused to function and my hands to co-ordinate. We just dived and I thought sadly: "Is this it, so soon?" as we plunged into what felt like a dimly lighted well – an illusion created by the cockpit walls.

"Michael?" I wailed, and he grabbed the control column.

"OK," he said, "look where you are going."

I was OK then, sane, calm and normal.

After half an hour our escort was unable to hear us, so Michael said. We wondered what it was; I could see Michael pick up the microphone every few minutes: "*'Thursday's Child'* to *'Juke Box Special,' 'Thursday's Child'* to *'Juke Box Special.'* Are you receiving? Over." "*'Juke Box Special'* from *'Thursday's Child,' 'Juke Box Special'* from *'Thursday's Child,'* do you read me, over?"

It was useless . . . Our generator gone again and now, of all times. We had only just gained about 2,000 ft and were in rain and scattered low cloud. To make matters worse, we kept glimpsing lights down below miles away to the south. As we were supposed to be flying eastwards along the south coast of Hokkaido these lights meant that we were being blown inland towards the mountains. Mike altered course to starboard; still the lights twinkled dimly and fleetingly through the clouds scudding beneath us. Another alteration followed and then another, until we were heading far to the south of our intended track.

After an hour the cabin lights were getting dimmer as the battery slowly discharged and by this time all contact with the escort was lost. Mike called my attention to what had happened and said that we could either go on and risk it, risk finding an airfield on a small lonely island two miles by four, or turn back. I thought it out hard. It would be difficult, too, if we did turn back, for the weather was bumpy and because we had an outward tailwind it would take us at least an hour and a half to get back again, by which time the flares at Chitose would be out, and the whole airfield in darkness. In any case we would have to use up seven hours of fuel before we would be light enough to land safely.

I took a deep breath and said: "Yes, we'll go on."

If we did quit, I didn't think I'd ever manage it again. I felt that I'd already aged years, and my youth declined even further as the compass light bulb fell out and was lost in the bottom of the cabin. Presently we altered course sharply to the north-east; at least we were heading towards the Aleutians now instead of the Central Pacific. We levelled off at 6,000 ft and soon passed over a flashing light.

"That should be Kogoshi Light on the southern tip of Hokkaido," Mike yelled in my ear; "we ought to be clear of the mountains by now."

We had only covered a hundred miles of our route (as the crow flies) in an hour and a half. It had been a hard decision, Mike told me later, whether to keep our original flight-planned course and risk hitting the mountains or whether to waste 15 minutes of our precious fuel on steering a 'dog-leg' out to sea.

The clouds above us thinned out except for a veil of cirrus, which didn't stop Mike getting out his sextant and taking star shots. We got a good fix and made an alteration on the compass to avoid hitting the peaks of the Kurile Islands which were a bare 10 miles off instead of the intended 50 (regulation range from Russian territory). After this, Mike turned round on his seat and after a lot of superhuman effort unscrewed the filler cap on the fuel tank behind him and wobble-pumped 20 gallons from the seat tanks into the cabin tanks. He took so long over the filler cap that I was suddenly smitten with the appalling idea that he was never going to get it off and that we were going to run out of fuel whilst there was still some in the tank which we couldn't use.

Oh, I thought up enough scares that night to drive me to insanity; perhaps they did. Come to think of it, I don't think I've ever been the same since.

Whilst Michael was thus employed, ice started forming on the windshield so we came down to 3,000 ft, flying in broken clouds. We were getting carburettor icing, too, so I switched on to hot air and soon the speed went up a bit. This was just as well because the aircraft had been in a climbing attitude and still losing height!

After 7½ hours from our take-off we were still in cloud. Time lost all meaning. It was time, yet no time, and I noticed the hands on the clock, in vague surprise that they ever moved at all. The clouds beneath us thinned out into broken cumulus and we skipped the tops at 4,000 ft. The overcast, too, started clearing above and just before dawn Mike took four more star shots after an agonising wait while he fiddled with the sextant with my nail file to make the light in it work.

After 10½ hours the dawn broke and the familiar cockpit took shape again in the grey early morning light. I looked at Michael and noticed that his knees were trembling; poor Mike, here I had dragged him halfway round the world to drown in the cold grey waters of the North Pacific. I watched his face, scowling in the repose of concentration, his hair towsled and his eyelids blue with fatigue. I felt infinitely sorry for him, almost aching with compassion.

I touched his arm.

"Have some coffee, Mike," I said, somewhat inadequately.

We had a cup of black coffee apiece but the packet of Fig Newton biscuits above the instrument panel was left unopened. I took two Benzedrine tablets and maybe that is why I caught myself saying idly: "A flying ship gathers no ice – an icing ship gathers no flies – a flying ship gathers no ice," and so on, much as Alice said: "Do cats eat bats, do bats eat cats?"

As I watched the dawn rise, my mind wandered back to those wonderful dawns we used to watch, my two sisters and myself, whilst driving in the old *Chenard et Walcker* to Wales for our summer holidays. We used to get up at 4 am but were not allowed to speak to Mummy until after breakfast, which we always had at Market Harborough; for Mummy had a weak heart and couldn't bear the early morning. I mused over the funny excited feeling induced by the crisp rustling sound that clean clothes make (those horrible cotton linings like running shorts) and having eaten a four o'clock snack (in haste with our loins girded) out of unfamiliar kitchen spoons.

So many, many years between, and that was England and this was the Pacific Ocean.

The sun spread over the horizon and I felt a little happier. "Silly child," I said to myself, "you're no aboriginal savage afraid of the dark and bold by day."

Soon the clouds pressed up under the wings, making me instinctively climb the ship, though I knew that we had to come down through a hole in the clouds and to get higher was only wasting fuel. Underneath, it was dark and stormy and all around us stretched unending the grey inhospitable Pacific Ocean, wearing whitecaps. We peered this way and that looking for Shemya. My feet and legs were numb. I hadn't moved them for hours. On we went, peering and hoping; low storm clouds drove us down to 500 feet (an excellent view of the water) and, as each low cloud came sweeping over, it would get darker and you could hardly see the whitecaps through the driving snow; then it would lift and for a few minutes the sun would brighten the water and under each low cloud in the distance we would see make-believe islands.

Fuel was getting low: we had already flown for 12 of our 13½ hours' endurance and I sat furtively trying a ditching procedure. What a hope! Firstly, we had no safety straps – they would not fit over the fuel tanks on which we sat; secondly, we had fixed landing gear and would be almost bound to somersault as we touched the water. We had only a non-provisioned dinghy apiece and two red rockets which lay beside the Fig Newtons on the ledge above the instrument panel. We would never have ditched it, yet I tried to think we could.

After a while Michael turned to me: "If something doesn't turn up within half an hour," he said, "I shall be distinctly perturbed."

He smiled.

I nodded brightly.

"Yes, so shall I," and then I thought over what he'd said.

According to the fuel gauges we had roughly three quarters of an hour's flying left. I prayed passionately and then I stopped and remembered another snatch of poetry.

"If on a Spring night I went by
And God were standing there,
What is the prayer that I would cry
To Him? This is the prayer:
Oh Lord of courage grave,
Oh Master of this night of spring!
Make firm in me a heart too brave
To ask Thee anything."

I wasn't much good at praying, so I stopped, and just hoped that if I did have to die, I shouldn't do anything that Michael would be ashamed of.

Still no island appeared and I felt sicker and sicker and sicker.

"Look!" said Mike for the fiftieth time, "I think that's an island over there, under that cloud."

He pointed to the front left where another grey shadow lay on the surface of water.

"Oh no!" I said firmly. I at least wasn't going to kid myself. "That's not an island, that's just another bit of cloud."

A few moments elapsed and Mike could not suppress the eagerness in his voice as he pointed again and exclaimed: "It is, I'm sure it is."

I said: "No, no," a little wildly. "Things like that don't happen outside books."

But as we lurched forward, dropping another 100 ft as the last tank but one drained and we switched on to the last 10 gallons (in the centre-section tank) the island formed and became real and stood there, suddenly free of clouds, peaked and jagged, white and glorious in the sunlight: more wonderful than the pearly gates of heaven, far, far more wonderful.

"That's Agattu," said Mike after consulting his map. "Yes, you can just see Shemya behind it."

I know my eyes were smarting and there was a lump in my throat as we sailed past Agattu in the clear bright sunshine – all the clouds had gone now – to the little low island of Shemya. There was the long runway and the bright snow made my eyes sore as I watched the ground. Yes, there was the runway.

"Oh! Mike, look," I cried, "there's the B-17."

It was just taxying up to the end of the runway ready to take off and search for us.

I circled the field and came in rather low, touching down at the very beginning of the runway. The ship rolled on to a halt.

I turned to Michael and with unusual enthusiasm said passionately and fervently: "Oh! Michael, you're a *wonderful* navigator."

Mike blinked and looked slightly surprised. He wasn't used to such impassioned outbursts. I gave him a big hug and a kiss, opened the throttle and taxied behind the "Follow Me" Jeep to the tarmac outside Operations. I climbed out on the solid cold ground.

This was Shemya, this was real dry land and we'd flown the Pacific. My God! We were wonderful and we were alive.

I smiled politely into the cameras, too full of assorted happiness to say anything. The humming of the engine in my ears was sheer magic. As I walked into Operations, my eye caught a little notice painted up: "Shemya Air Force Base. Elevation 20 ft." It was true, it wasn't a dream. Oh thank you, God!

The rest of that day is rather hazy. It's not surprising really, for we had flown for 13¼ hours and according to Michael's log and the gauge in the panel, we had five gallons left in the ship.

I remember somebody asking me, after the papers had been settled at Operations: "What would you like? Sleep or food, hot shower or what?" and I remember hearing my voice ring round the room as I emphatically stated: "I'd just love a drink."

There was a dead silence and the CO, a perfectly charming type called Freddy Armstrong, said: "Sure, come round to my house and we'll have a drink."

UPPER: Major Freddy Armstrong, Base Commander at Shemya, the Aleutian Islands.
LOWER: Typical scenery off the Aleutian Islands – not a good place to have to make a forced landing.

Dikki and Michael sitting on the overload fuel tanks specially fitted for their winter flight across the North Pacific, which took over 13 hours non-stop for nearly 1,800 miles: cramped quarters indeed.

CHAPTER 20

THE ALEUTIAN ISLANDS

The American Air Force were very kind to us, and the first thing they did was to give us suitable clothing. We each got issued with nice warm parkas, which were very necessary, for the next day the wind rose and it snowed and rained (the fierce kind of rain that makes you think that a box of pins or Lilliputian arrows are being fired at your face) and we should have been frozen without them. For seven days the wind was so strong that it was impossible to get the aircraft out of the hangar. The only time we did was to check the engine, or rather we attempted to, but since it took six men, three on each wing, to hold the aircraft down, we gave up in despair.

The strain of the flight did take its toll. For instance, Mike's hair fell out by the handful, and after a few hours of intense admiration for each other, we were soon snarly and growly again. Enforced idleness, the inability to entertain ourselves out-of-doors and our eagerness to be on our way caused us to snap at each other and get disgruntled with things. Besides which Mike elected himself to teach me the noble art of table tennis, which had hitherto passed me by.

Mike's method of teaching was such that you hit the ball and whenever you did anything wrong, he would say: "Ah! my point, you shouldn't have done that."

So I got mad and kept saying: "Why in the blazes didn't you tell me before?"

Damn it, I didn't mind losing but, when he always found some convenient rule which invariably ended in him reaching 21 when I was only 10, it was enough to make anyone burn with resentment. I still feel angry when I think of it. However, I doggedly played on, and one happy day in Anchorage, I actually beat someone.

With the exception of an occasional transient airline hostess there were no women on the island, which possibly may have accounted for a drunken type who broke into my room, waking me up in the middle of the night. Nothing makes me madder than being woken, particularly to be breathed over by whisky. I was a bit hampered by the fact that, not wearing pyjamas, I couldn't very easily get out of bed. The man made wild clutches at me and touched my shoulders, blithering something about "so smooth, so firm" which I always understood to be part of a slogan for a certain brand of American cigarettes. As I am not the screaming type, he probably thought he was making great headway but when he attempted to get into my bed, I took one wild leap out the other side and, clad in nothing but outraged dignity, snatched on my parka and my flying boots and stalked out into the snow. I must have looked quaint but I never stopped to think as I pounded up the steps to Michael's hut. I stumped down the hall and opened

Michael's door, knocking over the chair which was tilted under the knob (a cautious type, Mike).

"Wassa matter?" called Mike.

"There's a drunken man in my bed and I'm going to sleep in one of the rooms here."

Mike grunted and went back to sleep again. He didn't seem in the least perturbed and I curled up in a vacant room.

I was woken next morning by Mike.

"You'd better get out of here, you know. These are officers' quarters, even if there aren't any here."

It was about 7 o'clock and fortunately still fairly dark. I slipped out stealthily, looking all ways at the same time, realizing that dressed as I was, just in parka and boots, I created quite a striking sight for that time of the morning. Fortunately no one saw me and the man had gone from my room.

Major Armstrong drove us around the island and we took some lovely photographs of the sea, two of them on one plate, but the rest in a more normal form. He made us put our 'paddy-paws' in, to feel how cold it was. We did and it was.

"That's why I want you to have an escort," he said.

We couldn't do anything about it; if he said so, it was so. For after all, he was 'king of the castle.' We used to spend the evenings in his house, sitting on the table drinking or leaning against the little bar. We used to talk all night, gazing intermittently at the very striking copy behind the bar of *A Hangover*, painted by the former CO.

After a week, during which we studied the weather very closely, the winds dropped, likewise the snow, sufficiently for us to press on to Adak. "Dry and dusty down the Chain" (The Aleutian Chain of Islands) I was told, and certainly it was a great improvement on the weather hitherto. The Aleutian Chain is where all the weather begins and winds are reported at as much as 120 miles an hour. We set off, accompanied by our B-17, rather later in the day. It was not the B-17 which had escorted us from Chitose; that one had gone home to Tokyo and, incidentally, ran into some icing troubles. I believe the deicing boots on the tail did not work and they spun from 12,000 ft down to 4,000 ft. They dropped the lifeboat attached to the belly of the ship but apparently otherwise caused little damage. I never knew a B-17 could spin, and come to think of it, I don't suppose the crew did either.

We followed the Airways route along the Chain, flying through snow showers which brought us down very low over the sea. Much of the time we couldn't see the Fortress and later we were requested to fly over Ilak Island where we were to meet a Catalina flying boat (or PBY as they are called). Mike mistook this for Ulak Island and we kept circling around that until he realised his error. We picked up the PBY later on and the Fortress left us, flying on to Adak. The PBY had very much the same speed as ourselves and could fly with us. It's 'ever so chummy' flying next to something like that, and at any time you want you can wave.

The Fortress called back, advising the eastern route to the aerodrome; the clouds were too low to fly through the Pass. But the PBY advised a trial of the Pass at any rate, as there was a low ceiling over the Bay, too. Adak was as spectacular and inaccessible as any storybook pirate's hideout. Chosen as the site for an American airfield after the bombing of Dutch Harbour, it was the base from which the Japanese were finally blasted out of Kiska and Attu. With high mountains rising sheer to north and south of the camp and active volcanoes guarding the pass to the west and the bay to the east, Adak must have been almost impregnable. And there was the weather, too, with its summer fog and winter low clouds and blizzards. The US Air Force lost more planes in the Aleutians through weather than through enemy action.

If they thought the conditions were good on our flight, I'd hate to be caught when it was bad. How those airline pilots do it day after day beats me. I really take my hat off to them. Seven landings out of ten they do by the aid of GCA and the casualty rate is now practically nil. *[GCA (Ground Controlled Approach) was still fairly new in those days – an approach and landing system in which an aircraft is monitored both in azimuth and altitude on ground radar and the pilot follows instructions which should bring him down over the runway and enable him to complete a visual landing. – M.T.]*

The flight was only 3½ hours from Shemya to Adak but I sure was glad when it was over, for we were pretty well tossed around and I do like to be higher than 500 ft above a stormy sea for you're so soon in it if something goes wrong. As on the Vientiane–Hong Kong run I did all the flying when the weather was bad, Mike not even taking over for the hourly 5 or 10 minutes. I prefer it that way somehow, for I find that I cannot relax when it's bumpy and always keep watching the instruments. Actually, on the long flight across the Pacific, Mike may have done about half an hour in all, no more. It would have been useless him doing more and in any case he was far too busy at his own job most of the time.

We followed the PBY skimming through the Pass and as we circled Adak Mike put out a call asking for men to steady the wings when taxying. As it happened, we didn't need it but just as I was touching down, a sudden gust caught one wing and we ballooned up again, landing safely but a bit skew-whiff on the runway. Taxying was difficult in that weather but we managed safely and put the ship away in a heated hangar.

Then I lost Michael. All the afternoon I looked for him. We had split up and I got sent to the nurses' quarters while he was put with visiting officers; but he wasn't in his billet, and nobody seemed to know anything about him so eventually I folded up and had a nap. The nurses were very kind to me and one, as I complained of the cold, made me the gift of a very serviceable garment – a T-shirt which stretched halfway down to my knees, bearing the immortal words "Army Technical Schools, Sioux Falls." I was suffering again from feeling sick and every meal I ate I regretted. I was dosed with peppermint and thus armed was driven to the General's residence, where I tried to tackle a steak of gargantuan proportions which, though appealing to the eyes, created troubles within and yet again I had to make my excuses and go to bed early.

The next morning we met our escorting pals in the weather office, where we were told that it was again good. We were following the weather along the Chain. Whilst the Catalina and the Fortress were waiting lined up on the tarmac with engines running, we were delayed 20 minutes whilst they made out our little bill. We were rather amused: 20 minutes fuel used up by two ships would cost a lot more than our humble little cheque; still, that is the way of the Air Force.

CHAPTER 21
ADAK–COLD BAY–ANCHORAGE

The weather was really cold by now and we were having quite some trouble in starting the ship each day. The battery was low so we used to use a trolley-acc and, as its plug never fitted our socket, we used to have a special contraption composed of two brass screws with a piece of wire. All very Heath Robinson but still serviceable.

The Aleutian Chain is very largely volcanic and each volcano that appeared would stir Michael to fresh spasms of excitement and he would give me the personal history of each one, taking frantic photographs at the same time, persistently opening the window and letting the cold air stream into the none-too-warm cabin, until I wished he would drop the darned camera over the side. I never met a man so enthusiastic over a few beastly volcanoes, mostly extinct, each one looking exactly like the last. The brilliant sunshine on the tundra was a hollow mockery. My feet froze, my legs froze and it slowly crept up.

We passed over the north shore of Unimak Island and soon found Randall Field on Cold Bay. I was very glad to land and climb out of the cockpit, for *rigor mortis* had almost set in my lower limbs, and I creaked as I stretched them. Cold Bay is built up on a flat marshy area of tundra, surrounded by volcanoes and mountains. The thing I was interested in on the flight were the Kodiak bears, which are common and often wander onto the airfield. They weigh upwards of 1,200 lb and stand over 10 ft high on their hind legs.

I prayed fervently that night in our very comfortable VIP quarters that the weather would become utterly ghastly and we could spend a pleasant week there hunting. They were very nice quarters we were in, too, with two blazing furnaces, scalding hot water in the shower and the washbasins and a nice little kitchen complete with electric irons and cans of beer in the icebox.

I created a flap and panic all round by insisting I had lost my glasses. I can't do anything without them and I only take them off to be sociable. What I mean is that when I'm not using my eyes for anything in particular, eating, talking and walking about the place, I don't wear them, having been well drilled in the age-old rhyme: "Men seldom make passes at girls who wear glasses." Of course after everyone had been informed of their loss and people had gone out and got cars to look in my aircraft for them, I found them in one of the innumerable pockets of my parka.

I was beginning to get confused with these American Bases. They were all built much to the same plan but just a little bit different and I would remember seeing, say, a safety pin, on the window sill in my room and go to get it because I needed it, only to find it must have been in the last place, not this.

The next day, after a lot of cursing, we eventually got the aircraft to start. We reduced the procedure to a fine art, a few turns of the prop by hand, so many primes from inside the cockpit, so many primes from outside under the engine cowling, which Mike could operate, then I'd press the button and Mike would prime furiously at the same time. Unfortunately the weather was CAVU and gone were all my hopes of a bear skin.

Michael was still as enthusiastic as ever over the volcanoes; Pavlov was smoking and I suppose the scenery was magnificent, though of course it depended on where you looked. The terrain that passed under the wings was just flat tundra, coarse grass and low bushes, speckled by frozen lakes, and black sand on the beaches, but over on our right the peaks, snow-white and impressive, glistened in the sunlight. Michael took another photograph, this time of Veniaminof volcano, pointing out to me how the top had once upon a time collapsed or been blown off and another perfect little volcano had formed inside. This, too, was active and looked most peculiar, puffing smoke from the middle of the old ice-bound crater.

We had a little trouble flying through Iliamna Pass, which had volcanoes on both sides, for the cloud base was down to 1,600 ft. However, it cleared up and Michael asked me to fly along the west coast of Cook Inlet in order to take photographs of Iliamna Volcano and Mount Redoubt, both over 10,000 ft high. I was bitterly cold; why oh why didn't Michael quit this photographing business and get down home? As the mountains were all my side, I had to take the photographs this time. I already felt frozen solid to my waist and now my hands froze too. Soon after passing over Kenai emergency landing ground, the Catalina escort reported back that our destination, Elmendorf Field, the Anchorage military base, had fog right down on the deck and visibility down to a quarter of a mile. Merrill Field, the civil airport, would be OK if we could reach it within an hour. They suggested that we should land at Kenai but we had already passed it and as Merrill Field was only half an hour away, it seemed well worth a try. When we got there the fog covered both airfields from about 500 ft downwards to the ground.

We attempted to approach along the coast just over the water and sneak inland when level with Merrill. We had been anxiously watching the sun as it almost imperceptibly sank behind Mount Redout. After we had been vainly circling for half an hour, the last glow had vanished in the south-west and we were left in darkness with the flat white top of the fog beneath us and the snowy peaks of the Cugach Range projecting a few miles to the east.

Now we could see occasional blurred neon signs as we flew over Anchorage city and at one time a row of lights marking a road; but there was no sign of either airfield and when we did attempt a closer investigation, the red light on a water tower flashed past well above the level of the port wing!

Eventually Mike managed to contact Elmendorf GCA. This was just as well, with our fuel getting low, but it would be the first blind landing I had done. The first time we went round, half the runway lights had gone out but they brought us down bang over the runway, which gave us a lot more confidence. It was not an easy procedure to do in the first place on that aircraft, for Michael would receive the compass heading by RT, set the compass – which was over my side and had no light, – and then I'd have to try and steer the heading given; added to which, when we were still about four miles from the runway they insisted on telling us: "Gear down and locked (our undercarriage was fixed, anyhow) and flaps half down"; as these could only be regulated in two positions, 'up' or 'down,' the whole thing was appallingly confusing. On our second attempt, all the runway lights were out and the windshield iced as we came in through the fog. The first intimation that we were over the airfield came when the red light on a hangar roof whizzed by close above the starboard wing. We missed the trees at the far end of the field by a hair's breadth. The third time was eventually successful despite the fuel cutting whilst I was struggling with the flaps, trying to get them down at too great a speed. However, there was just a driblet in one of the other tanks and I switched over with my numbed fingers while Mike took the stick, without its spoiling the glide path angle any.

We were both flying it at this time; I had almost reached a state where I didn't care how I came down as long as this bitter cold would end. We knew that there was ice on the runway and I'm surprised now that we didn't run into trouble for, as we touched, Mike held the stick forward to do a wheel landing whilst I endeavoured to pull it back to do a three-pointer. We bounced, of course, but nothing very much and anyway we were down and safe.

I taxied the aircraft to the tower but after that I remember no more. I was suffering from brain icing, I think. Apparently I got out, shook hands politely with everybody, made a few bright comments about GCA for the newspapers, did a broadcast, collected my bags from the PBY, was driven to the hotel, bathed, changed and went out with Michael to dinner in a party. It wasn't until I had had a couple of brandies that I remembered things again. Brother, was it cold! We were installed in an appallingly expensive hotel where we had a double room each, with two double beds in it, looking out on Mount McKinley across the bay. It was six bucks a night each. Maybe you don't think that's a lot, but I do.

CHAPTER 22
ANCHORAGE

I think Alaska is a very fascinating place. It has the American gadgets and the American amenities without the hurry and the way of life that is found in the States. It's a place of its own and it grows on one. Anchorage itself is very largely a boom town due to the proximity of Elmendorf, the big US Air Force Base. Fishing – as the inlet is free of ice even in the middle of November – and some mining are the main permanent occupations. Flying is a very large and a very prosperous trade out there, as the only ways one can go 'outside' are by air or the long, twisting tedious Alcan Highway. *[The Alcan (Alaskan–Canadian) Highway is also referred to these days simply as the Alaskan Highway. – M.T.]*

Merrill Civil Airport has handled as many as 90 aircraft within an hour and I suppose that is why they are building the great municipal airport. Everyone seems to own a plane in Alaska, very often with skis or floats for convenience in hunting trips. The temperature was only really a few degrees below zero but as three weeks ago we were wearing tropical kit and scorching in the sunshine I found the change almost unbearable.

The next day after our arrival, we taxied our ship from the transient aircraft hangar to that of the Tenth Rescue Squadron, who spent a lot of time and trouble on us. They whipped out the two emergency tanks we had built up in Calcutta and replaced these with seats from an old Norseman aircraft. They also loaned us an MF receiver so that we could fly across America on the radio range. On paper we had planned a flight to White Horse but, as the weather was very unpredictable due to a depression in the Alaskan Gulf, we decided that the next hop would be to Northway only.

It took us nine days before we did set off, due to the fact that every time we took the ship out of the heated hangar, did a run-up and then left it while we went to the tower or refuelled, condensation would take place in the electrical leads, creating a quite impossible mag. drop. This happened three times and each time we had to wheel it back into the hangar, take off the plugs and hang up the leads to dry. Oh how we cursed. For over a week either the aircraft or the weather was no good. If we were unlucky it was the aircraft and we dragged all our worldly belongings down to the field before we found it; on luckier days we found out at 5 am when Mike rang up the Met. office. One of these dismal, early morning conversations about the probability of blizzards *en route* was livened up by being interrupted by a minor earthquake, our third since leaving England.

This was my first visit to US Territories and the American way of life, and what I saw I liked, bitterly cold though it felt to me.

I was still terribly nervous of going about by myself. I always have been so and to go on buses alone to me is sheer martyrdom. I found this much more so with the different American system, where you pay your fare into a machine right by the driver. Of course the first time I got on I didn't pay and just pressed on down to the end of the bus, and when I saw other people surrendering coins into the voracious maw of this quaint gadget and realised my mistake I blushed crimson for 10 minutes. Then, summoning up courage, I asked the man beside me how much the journey cost (from the airfield to the town).

"Two 'bits,'" he told me shortly.

"Thank you," I returned politely, and thought hard.

"Now they have 5 cent pieces and they're called nickels, and 10 cent pieces and they're little things and they're called dimes, but what the hell is a 'bit'?"

After thinking very hard I then gave up, turned to my companion and asked simply: "What is a 'bit'?"

It took him a while to cotton on to the fact that I was referring to our brief conversation of 15 minutes before and he was highly amused to think that somebody didn't know that 25 cents was 'two bits,' but then why should they, I asked myself.

There were many little things like that that moved me to mirth or wonder: the toothpicks so prominently displayed on the café table or conveniently posted beside the telephone; light switches, which switch 'up' to go 'on.' instead of 'down.' There were the traditional hot cakes and syrup to be tried (and even these were expensive in Anchorage) and little things to be memorised, like looking left when you stepped off the sidewalk, not right, and that to stand on the "pavement" was to be in the middle of the road. Then there was getting accustomed to the peculiar way that so many Americans have of saying when you thank them, either "You're welcome" or the completely out-of-place "You bet."

Table manners I first thought most extraordinary and yet now I've only just got back to using a knife and squishing things up in front of a fork held in the left hand as all the English do. Salt is always disguised in a pepper pot and the only way to obtain any is by the sprinkling method. Mustard, I found, was nearly extinct but salt was most predominant. I was impressed, too, at the way even grown men drank soft drinks out of bottles, which the Englishman condemns so utterly, as did Chesterton in his *Song of Right and Wrong*:

"*As for all the windy waters,*
They were rained like tempests down
When good drink had been dishonoured
By the Tipplers of the Town;
When red wine had brought red ruin
And the death-dance of our times,
Heaven sent us soda-water
As a torment for our crimes."

We were shown around Anchorage and we walked quite a bit. One afternoon we were taken up to the two Lakes joined together, where planes operate on skis in the winter and on floats in the summer. We were given a flight in a Piper Cub ski-plane, flown over Cook Inlet and Fire Island and had the sights of Anchorage pointed out to us. I found it huge fun to sit and look, instead of having to concentrate on the flying, and we were flown low over the woods to look for moose. We saw several and then we were lucky enough to see two moose in combat in a clearing in the wood. Three times we came over whilst Michael took frantic photographs. The last time we came so low they broke it up for good and all, but it was an unforgettable sight.

The second night we were given a dinner in our honour in Anchorage's smartest night club. This was a subterranean joint and a microphone had been fixed up for speeches from the important citizens. I was very impressed and I was presented with two books by the Aleut author Nutchuk, a book of Alaskan recipes (which has since proved most useful) and a lovely piece of Alaskan jade. I was very thrilled but by and large this was not my best evening. I was wearing the *sari* which had been given me in India, six yards of sky-blue material like thin georgette, edged with gold, worn of course in the traditional way. This was referred to by the compère as "a safari" (which, as far as I remember, is a hunting expedition). I had scarcely recovered from this when I had to get up and speak. Unfortunately I had moved my feet whilst sitting so that, as I rose, my shoes were on the hem of the sari, pulling all the folds undone. (They're only held by being tucked in at the waist over, in this case, Mike's blue pyjama bottoms with the legs turned up, for I had no petticoat). Grabbing furiously at the tucks unripping like a parachute, I made a somewhat embarrassed and hasty speech.

As soon as the others had finished, I made a dive for the cloakroom. I had the choice of two arches, one with the word "ALEUT" and the other "ALEUTTE." How was I to know which was the little girls' room? I dived into the nearest and had already started fixing myself before I noticed the other occupant. He emitted a muffled exclamation, whereupon I beat a hasty retreat, blushing to my toes.

There was a little shop below the hotel where Alaskan-made gifts could be bought and Michael and I pottered around there quite a bit looking at the furs, the gloves and the quaint garments. There were some quite wonderful parkas, which would look delightful in Anchorage but were really not quite the thing, I thought, for Cambridge. I was very lucky, however, in being given a beautiful pair of *mukluks* (Eskimo boots) the soles being made of walrus hide and the tops of thick reindeer skin. Mine almost neighed when I stroked them. I was also given a pair of little white ones for my daughter.

"Thursday's Child" at Elmendorf Air Force Base, Anchorage, with the Alaskan mountain range as a backdrop.

A Press interview for Dikki at Anchorage, Alaska, shortly after she landed there in ice crystal fog.
Photo: Mac's Foto Service, Anchorage.

Flying through "Sheep Mountain" Pass, Alaska; this photo was taken just a few minutes before engine trouble necessitated a forced landing on the Alcan Highway.

UPPER: *"Thursday's Child"* is discovered by a road patrol vehicle shortly after the forced landing.
LOWER: *"Thursday's Child"* the next day after a snowfall.

CHAPTER 23

ANCHORAGE–TANACROSS

During the last three days of our stay we were carrying our bags to and fro expecting to leave any moment. The last night, as we intended to get off early and we were tired of the expense and time involved in staying in the town, we slept on couches in the pilots' lounge: a very uncomfortable night, as the couches were not long enough and *rigor mortis* set in by dawn. First we shut all the windows and got too hot and then opened too many and got too cold.

We left on the 21st November at about 8.30 in the morning, feeling rather chilly and half-hearted as we climbed up into the bumpy sky. We were followed by the Tenth Rescue ship, a Beechcraft AT–7. Our ship was behaving very badly that day, but as we were flying through Sheep Mountain Pass, a very narrow pass, barely wide enough to turn in and with high mountains on either side which shut out the sun, we presumed it was down-draughts which made the speed so low. It's perfectly true, as Michael will bear me out, the aircraft did sometimes fly well and sometimes badly, though I've often wondered why. We were only indicating 85 knots and I had difficulty in maintaining height as the climbing and gliding speed was 80 knots. The rest of the instruments read normal and I exhausted myself with will power, willing the ship to better flying, but we pressed on pretty well following along on the radio range.

We flew over Gulkana and I remember wishing that this was our landing field. I was getting bitterly cold by now; my feet had died ages ago and the numbness was creeping up my thighs. Mike took his eternal photographs, Mt Sandford (16,000 ft) and Mt Drum. The engine coughed several times as we flew over this desolate country with its meandering road and endless trees and scrub. I was sweating with anxiety (a cold sweat, of course!) but the instruments were reading OK and there was still no drop in boost or revs. But it wasn't right, there was just no power. We lost more height, flying only 1,000 ft. above the ground as we came into the Mentasta Pass. It was slightly overcast and we wanted to keep away from anything like a cloud.

I had read up a little booklet in Anchorage entitled *Ice Formation on Aircraft* and I had really got the wind up about it. The engine was coughing again now and I was quite sick with worry as I willed her along. The instruments were still reading normal but the ship had no push in her at all and seemed steadily to be losing power. I looked at Mike once or twice, wondering dumbly if he knew how afraid I felt and then hoping heartily that he didn't.

He seemed quite unperturbed, gaily pointing to the fir trees on the steep mountainsides and babbling: "Look at all the pretty Christmas trees."

Jeeze, I could have murdered him, but I contented myself with an absolutely filthy look and said nothing. We flew along in a tunnel composed of the high mountain walls and a ceiling of clouds, and my heart was beating fast as I weighed up the situation.

There beneath us and getting steadily closer was the corkscrew Eagle Highway, twisting and turning, climbing and diving its way to join the Alcan Highway. There wouldn't be the chance of a snowball in hell if we landed on that. The rest of the ground was covered by low trees and occasionally we could see a lake. A lake wouldn't have been too bad, but this was only November 21st and would the ice hold? I worried and I worried trying to inch the ship up into level flight. The carburettor heat was on, I put that on before entering the valley, but the engine kept coughing and we were obviously sinking quite fast.

I turned to Michael. "Do your straps up, Mike (this was the first time we had had them since Calcutta) and put out a call to the escort ship." Mike snapped the belt to cover his parka and grabbed the microphone whilst I flew on, praying for something to land on. When Mike had completed the call out to the AT-7 that we were in trouble but would hope to make Northway, he took over whilst I did my straps up. By this time, we had come to the end of the Mentasta Pass and just around the corner the Highway stretched straight and inviting, if you could ever call a highway that. At any rate it was a lot more comfortable to land on than that rugged mountain pass. We had only a few hundred feet by now so I lined her up and let her sink down between trees and undergrowth which skirted the road. The engine was popping and puffing and though we tried it first in rich mixture and then in lean, it seemed to make no difference. We were only a few feet from the ground when I finally cut the throttle and endeavoured to do a three-point landing on this white strip of snow.

I touched down surprisingly neatly and was just beginning to praise God when the starboard wing hit one of the wooden posts that the highway patrol put up so that the snow plough can see the road when it is all covered over. The ship immediately swung into the undergrowth. Mike grabbed the handbrakes which lie between the seats and I switched off the engine. The trees rushed towards us in one brief horrifying moment; there was crashing and splintering, the strain of the safety strap around my waist, then – silence. Silence more profound than any church, more complete than any night. I think we probably swore next, mechanically, till Michael and I noticed that there was smoke or something rising from the engine. I got ready to pull the red handle below the panel but Michael handed me the little pump fire extinguisher and I got out, walking cautiously round the ship, weapon in hand, ready to extinguish anything that flamed. No, it was just steam, so I relaxed and climbed smartly back into the ship.

It was cold. It was about 30 degrees below zero and the coldest I'd met yet; Anchorage, being on the water, though more raw due to the damp, was actually less cold, being at that time only at about zero. I'd been cold enough sitting in the ship for it had no means of heating and though Michael always said he thought it was a warm aeroplane, I had other feelings on the subject. My feet really were cold at this time and whilst Michael was putting out another call to the Beechcraft, I debated on what I should do. The ship told us they were going to fly over low and drop us food, sleeping bags, clothing and anything else we wanted and advised Michael to build a fire.

With the enthusiasm of a blooming Boy Scout, Mike immediately went rushing hither and thither excitedly gathering twigs, seized by an uncontrollable frenzy to build a fire. I had a sneaking suspicion he was getting an enormous kick out of this but I must confess the quiet part of my mind stood back and cheered as the rescue ship with trained precision dropped an exciting-looking bundle from 30 ft which, incidentally, missed hitting us by inches. We rushed to it and began undoing things but were a bit nonplussed to discover a bundle of clothing apparently made to fit a 8 ft giant and in which there was one pair of everything. I rooted for socks. I had already two pairs inside my fleece-lined flying boots but as soon as I handled this chilly knitwear, my feminine mind immediately registered the thought that, as it was not aired, I'd be worse off if I wore *them* than I was before. I had another worry; I knew that what I most wanted if I was going to spend the night out there was an article of feminine gear which though so necessary to me at that time of the month would certainly not be found in this heterogeneous collection of men's clothing.

Michael had now come to a halt for he had discovered that the matches in the parachute pack were of the safety variety and wouldn't strike on anything. Being a smoker I could produce matches and was all keen and ready and prepared to 'hurhh' on the fire – or "fan it with me 'at" as the saying goes – when a road patrol car came along. Oh, was I glad to see it! I had no desire to spend the night out there. We tidied up the road, rolled up the bundle, collected our log and such paraphernalia as we thought necessary and packed into the car. I think it was less than 15 miles away, the little post of Tanacross, from which the Civil Aeronautics Administration (CAA) were informed immediately.

Whilst trundling back we met the crew of the Beechcraft who had landed at Tanacross Field, and so went back to the scene of the crime again. There we all stood round and inspected everything. Tail, fuselage and engine appeared to have survived unharmed but the wings were in poor shape. Both the undercarriage legs had folded up flat under the belly of the ship, pointing towards the starboard wing. Strangely enough the one which had been repaired in Calcutta was less bent than the other. The starboard wingtip was missing about 18 inches, this having been sheared off clean by the road marker. Both wings, of course, had been torn by fir trees and the fabric pierced by brambles and stumps. The main spars looked OK otherwise, though of course the centre section would be quite u/s. We measured the distance across the road between the posts as roughly 30 ft so an accident was inevitable, our wingspan being over 39 ft.

We went back to the road patrol place at Tanacross, which was also a radio post for sending and receiving messages. There at last in front of a fire, or rather at a distance of about six feet away, I took off my boots and fingered my numbed feet. They were absolutely dead white and the process of thawing really hurt. The conversation chattered on about me whilst I sat there, quite oblivious to anything but the fact that here had come a very definite stop to the flight. The ship could be repaired, I thought, but where? And how was it going to get transported and who was going to pay for it? I felt blank with the misery inside me; everywhere I looked there seemed just no way out. I could have cried, but I thought to myself: "I'm a big girl now and anyway it doesn't help any."

We spent the night with John Lynn, a CAA official, and his wife. They were very good to us and talked about everything else under the sun except aeroplanes, a kindly piece of tact for which I was really grateful. Late that night we tuned in on John's radio for the BBC Overseas programme and heard the report that I had crashed in Alaska but was unhurt. This my husband heard on my little bedside radio in Cambridge when he turned on the 8 o'clock news next morning, my birthday.

CHAPTER 24
FAIRBANKS, ALASKA

There are nine families out in the wilds of Tanacross; all have beautiful little cottages heated by oil, and with every convenience, even down to the inevitable American kitchen, so ideally fitted. The temperature next day was 35 degrees below zero but the weather was sunny, so we all piled into cars, complete with cameras, and went out to the ship again. A light spattering of snow had fallen and poor little *"Thursday's Child"* looked very bleak and unhappy. Everyone stood around and peered, staring at my beautiful little aircraft lying crumpled there, with that blank curiosity that people show when they all lean peering at a still shape lying under a coat after a car smash.

I turned away blindly to one of the cars, stumbling in the snow, opened the door and climbed in and sat down. "This is my birthday," I said; "today I'm 25," and because I felt bitterly sorry and, I must confess, sorry for myself, I wept. Soon with a clattering and chattering, when all the cameras had frozen, and everyone had seen enough, they trooped back to the vehicles and piled in. Mike leaned over and squeezed my hand sympathetically and grinned. He's got a nice grin.

That afternoon I wrote out a report and, after another setback had occurred, when the breakdown equipment located at Tok Junction only two miles from our ship was refused us by the Alaska Road Commission at Fairbanks, we were flown in the Beechcraft by Chas Weir, the pilot, to Ladd Field, Fairbanks.

At Fairbanks I was overwhelmed with reporters and radio men. The effort of being gay and valiant was proving a bit of a strain by now and made my face ache, for I was photographed on an Army cot, first "smiling bravely" and then, in case the editor didn't like it, there was another taken of me looking picturesquely downcast. I was put in the nurses' quarters, where I changed, not that I had anything much to change into really, for I remember full well having to make the acquaintance of General Gaffney's wife clad in Army pants and my T-shirt bearing the legend *US Army Air Force – Technical School – Sioux Falls.*

We spent I think it was five days in Fairbanks, during which things were a bit mixed in my mind. I know that we went to a lot of places and we tried to get a lot of things done, but without much avail. Captain Accas, the liaison officer, shepherded us around with great care and Mike and I were sent in to be interviewed by General Gaffney. I can still remember every detail of that scene, for while we were waiting until he was free we stood outside the door staring at a map and I was suddenly and vividly transported back again to my childhood where, studying a map of Cambridge, I would await the ever too frequent 'interviews' with my headmistress at school. This was a bad thing because I diminished visibly in size before even entering the room, and resulted in a sudden spate of schoolgirl jingles much to Captain Acca's surprise and delight, such as:

"Aunty, if it caused no pain
When falling from that willow tree,
Could you do it once again
'Cos my friend here didn't see."

and:

"I sat next to the Duchess at tea.
She chattered most kindly to me,
But her rumblings abdominal
Were something phenomenal –
And everyone thought it was me."

General Gaffney wanted to know what we were going to do next. Mike said he was going back to England as, unless he got back for his University Term at the beginning of January, his Government grant would cease and he would have to leave the University. After all, he had already missed the October term and it would mean that he would have to work pretty darn hard to catch up again if he was going to get a Degree in June.

General Gaffney turned to me. "What are you going to do?"

I said I was going to stay, that I wasn't going to leave the ship and that somehow or other I was going to get it fixed up again.

He told me not to be silly. He said I had already left the ship.

"Only by orders, sir," I interposed.

"How are you going to get it mended?" he asked me.

I replied that I hoped to get assistance in Canada if I could get the ship to Edmonton.

"How are you going to get it there?" he demanded.

I said that I hoped he would help me to do that.

He told me that he couldn't and that I'd better go home with Michael. The trip was over, he said, and I must accept defeat.

I was damned if I would! I didn't say so, needless to say, but remained quite adamant though the General commanded and cajoled and argued with me in his endeavour to get me to go back with Mike. He nattered for quite a while, during which time I became more and more stubborn, and when he asked me: "And what made you start this trip in the first place?" I had got to the state where I just answered, childishly: "Because I wanted to."

He turned to one of his officers standing beside him (there seemed to be hordes of people around). "How old is your daughter?"

"Five, sir," replied the man.

"They don't change," said the General.

A murmur of merriment went round the room whilst I blushed as crimson as only a redhead can.

I had my first Thanksgiving dinner there and the food was so good and there was so much of it that I ate and ate and ate until I could scarcely move. Wonderful feeling!

Fairbanks lies about 100 miles south of the Arctic circle on the banks of the Chena River. The population is about 7,000 and it was originally a gold-boom town. There was only one main 'drag' as far as I remember, though the bright lights in the shops which lined it showed Christmas presents of all kinds but at high prices. Everything, of course, had to be brought up by ship and rail through Seward and Whittier, by air from Seattle or along the Alcan Highway. The cost of transport is so enormous that prices in Fairbanks, as elsewhere in Alaska, are twice as much – and sometimes even more – than those in Canada. There is a certain amount of farming done but there again the farm products are exceptionally high in price because the farmer has to cover himself for the long winter, the growing season being short, three to four months only. Apparently, though, the products are very luxurious and I was told that cabbages – and I quote – "frequently exceed 20 lb in weight." But who the hell wants a cabbage 20 lb in weight?

One of Fairbanks' main industries is apparently night clubs and liquor stores, in fact the town is reputed to have more liquor stores per head than any other town in North America. I don't expect they have much else to do, poor devils, in the winter, for even if you're one of those types that don't drink until the sun goes down, this gives you a pretty wide scope, the sun rising about 11 am and going to bed at 1.30 pm.

I had several offers to go and sing in night clubs, which I politely refused, partly because I was not staying there very long (as the General said he would ship us to Edmonton at the end of the week) and partly out of tact because he had taken, so I heard, very stringent measures to prevent the corruption of youth in these dens of iniquity.

I was asked to speak after dinner to a group of business women and candidly I confess I was scared stiff. The critical hostility in women's eyes invariably unnerves me, and a whole bunch of them – ye gods! I borrowed Michael's best trousers (RCAF officer's tropical worsted) and thus clad tried to make the best of it. To my surprise I enjoyed myself immensely, the only blot in my copybook being when I stepped behind a car which suddenly started up, blowing carbon at me through the exhaust all over Michael's beautiful trousers. I felt so ashamed and so apologetic, because he'd given me strict injunctions to keep them clean and I had teased him too often about the way he spills his food on things.

Ladd Field, Fairbanks, is a big US Air Force Base with a big Mess Hall, in which I was most surprised to see the officers' wives and children feeding. There were shops and houses on the camp and even a beauty parlour and an awful lot of people. Prefabricated houses are imported there at great cost from the States because, of course, accommodation is scarce. It is difficult to build in a climate that runs to 60 degrees below and what they do is erect a marquee and run machines which give out hot air into them.

Meanwhile, I was outraged to find that behind my back Michael had sent a cable to my husband in Cambridge, asking whether he should bring me back to Cambridge with him. He kept unobtrusively haunting the Post Office waiting for a reply, which inevitably I received first. The reply was typical of Morrow: "Let her do as she feels," and as neither hell nor high water would make me turn, having once put my hand to the plough, this was just as well.

I wonder what have happened, though, if he had said: "Come back." I was going through a phase of dogged determination and, sometimes sitting looking back on it now, I wonder what would have happened if I *had* gone back home. Would I have just folded my mind up and put away all thought of the flight, or would I have nursed the dream till it grew to a canker? That the flight could have been done if I'd only been allowed to stay? There is, of course, very often a time when it is wisest to cut your losses and go back by bus. I had put so much money into this, though, as well as work and hope and, after all, I'd done three quarters of the flight round the globe, so to me at that time there was only one way out. I was so certain the ship could be repaired.

I contacted a contractor named Al Ghezzi, the young owner of a fleet of trucks which ran between Fairbanks, Anchorage, and right down to Seattle, the whole length and more of the Alcan Highway. Having since found him a most elusive person, I realize now that I must have been very very lucky when I put through a call at random, suggesting that he truck my ship down to Edmonton for the advertisement – and not only that, but finding him interested. Over a few drinks late that night, we settled it in a bar and arranged to see another man the next morning, who would lend me a hand by crating it up. Just a few wooden cradles would be necessary to stop the aircraft from being damaged any more by rattling around inside the truck.

I was impressed when I saw the trucks the next morning though I was later to become very familiar with the orange 'car' with its bunk behind and little chimney and the huge long silver box such as you never see in England. We had a little talk with an aircraft firm about the crating of the ship and that, too, was promised to be done for free. I felt on top of the world. I'd show General Dale Gaffney that I wasn't the nitwit he thought I was.

When I saw him the next day and told him of my progress, he too said he would help. He'd get the aircraft brought into Fairbanks but to Weeks Field it would have to be, as the Air Force Base was overcrowded as it was. We then saw the officer who would be in charge of the party, who would partially dismantle the ship, and briefed him thoroughly, clinching matters by handing over the booklet on the Proctor. We then sat back on our haunches and smiled, Mike and I. We realised it would be a wee while before the actual aircraft arrived in Edmonton as the Alcan Highway crossed the Big Smoky River and, until this had frozen over thick enough, transport would be at a temporary standstill.

I found Fairbanks the most incredible place for static electricity and many times when making my bed I would emit little yelps when my hand came in contact with the metal bedstead. I also broke my glasses there, but, praise be to God, just before leaving England, I had got a spare pair, so that was all right.

We were told that we would be flown down to Edmonton in a B-17 Flying Fortress bomber any day now and we were to have our kit packed. This of course we did, and after a few days, during which we were issued with the most appalling underwear I've ever seen in my life but which it was compulsory to wear, we were all set to go. I made many protests that I wouldn't be seen dead in a khaki vest that reached me from neck to wrist and halfway down to my knees and an absolutely hideous pair of khaki "Long Johns," but having been threatened that if I didn't put them on, I'd have them put on for me, I finally agreed. I was wearing the same underclothes that I'd worn in the tropics; over that I wore a T-shirt, then my thick Army vest and then a very heavy navy sweater, which was my own. Then long Army underpants, khaki trousers, a parka, two pairs of gloves, two pairs of socks and my fleece-lined flying boots. For all that, I've never been so cold in all my life. I hadn't got acclimatised yet and the journey in the B-17 (they couldn't turn the heat on until we were airborne) lies recorded in my memory as the coldest incident in my life. I had even 'goose-flesh' across my shoulders. I parked myself in the Bomber's cubby-hole underneath the cockpit and there, with the hot air vent in the small of my back, I read magazines and chatted by means of a microphone to one of the crew.

We landed at Fort Nelson where we had a quick cup of coffee while the ship was being refuelled, and then pressed on to Edmonton. I slept the last bit as I was by this time warm at last, and my first comment on landing and stepping out of the ship was: "Coo, it ain't 'arf 'ot!" And so it was – by comparison.

There were quite a few reporters, for which for the first time I was very glad, for I realised I needed every inch of publicity there was. This was about 4 o'clock in the morning, when I didn't feel at my brightest and best, but I tried awfully hard to appear so. We were allowed to stay on the camp that night and I was very glad of the white hospital bed.

Our first call next morning was on the CO at the Base, thanking him for the hospitality, of course, and asking for help. We found that the RCAF could not help us and so we tried the civilian firms, also on the same airfield. Northwest Industries, God bless them, said they would try to lend a hand, and anyhow would handle the ship on its arrival. Mike, we decided, would call in at Toronto, where there was a firm who, we understood, made Proctors, and try to organise some parts. It was all very difficult, because we didn't really know for sure how damaged the ship was and no firm would promise to repair damage that might come to thousands of dollars.

CHAPTER 25
CHRISTMAS IN EDMONTON

Immediately on our arrival, Mike went sick, for whilst walking around his room in his stockinged feet at Fairbanks, he had run a splinter into his foot which promptly became septic; he had to be dosed with penicillin and sulphur and put to bed in the hospital. Oh, they were miserable days. I knew he was going soon and I couldn't ask him to stay, though there was nothing I wanted more. To be stuck in a strange country, with not much money, no friends and a packet of flying trouble wasn't really much joy. How I wish Michael had been able to stay, yet it was quite impossible; he had to get his Degree and I knew that, and every time the words begging him to stay rushed to my lips I swallowed them back. I'd mucked up his life enough as it was, I thought, by stealing one term already.

We went down to the town (*"I always make my journeys the Yellow Cab way"*) and bought a ticket for Mike to the East Coast, and on the 30th November I waved him goodbye. He was off to Montreal, where we had planned to spend my birthday. I'd been looking forward childishly to seeing Mike's Montreal where he had lived whilst in Atlantic Transport Command, and I wanted to have dinner at the Royal St. Lawrence Yacht Club where in his wealthier youth he had been the proud owner of a little craft he used to sail there, and I wanted to have dinner, to dine and to dance at the Normandie Roof. I was disappointed out of all proportion about that, and after waving a sad goodbye the tears froze on my cheeks as I trudged back through the snow to my quarters.

My only consolation was the little compact Walther PPK automatic that I carried with me from that day in my parka pocket. It had belonged to an SS officer, I was told, who had now no further use for it. The feel of its weight in my pocket gave me a pleasant feeling of being grown-up and it is a very comforting thing to have, like hugging your Teddy Bear when the nursery lights have been switched out.

That afternoon I had to do a radio test for a broadcast. I wore *the* dress, the one and only dress, and *the* pair of shoes that Michael had bought me as a birthday present before going. The dress was bright green and I wore it and I wore it and I wore it for weeks and weeks and weeks. I would wear my Army pants in the morning, and then in the evening this green woollen dress. Oh how I thought of those days back in England when, even at school, I hated wearing the same dress two days running. Oh womankind, is there anything more distressing than just one dress?

Not knowing any current dance music for the radio programme, I sang *Comin' Thro' The Rye*, copying as best I could the gramophone record we have at home sung by Madame Adelina Patti. It was one I knew well and had recorded myself, which was a good thing because I was utterly consumed with nervousness, having never sung in public before, and of course I swore blindly I had. This singing racket started way back when a reporter asked me what was my hobby. I had said "Singing" because I had just made some gramophone records for my husband in case I should get killed; four folk songs and *The Jewel Song* from *Faust*. It had delighted me no end to see the mystification on my baby daughter's face as she instantly recognised my voice and the songs I sang round the flat; she would point to the radiogram and say "Mummy!" and then turn and watch me, sitting motionless in a chair.

Whilst I was living at the Camp, I was asked if I would care to see over the local oilfields which had been recently discovered. Edmonton was very much of a boom town, I suppose, in that money could be made in a very short time. That evening, though, one of the men who showed me round brought me back to have dinner with his wife, whom I liked instantly. She asked me if I would care to stay with them for a wee while and I accepted gratefully. I did so need a friend and the last thing I wanted, now Mike had gone, was to mope away my time in a cheap hotel. The next day I took up my residence with Yvonne and Whitey Wilson, complete with a very bad cold. I stayed with them two weeks, which gave me time to turn round and take stock of this strange country in which I suddenly found myself. The currency I was *au fait* with, and the food by now, but there were complicated things like streetcars, cafés and table manners which had yet to be sorted out. This didn't take me long, however, though understanding the people certainly did.

I had by this time, to my intense surprise, acquired a manager called Frank Eckersley. He said he would contact firms for advertising and get me to do shows and give lectures. We talked things over at great length and with childlike faith in the future – which, however, didn't build up the castles we had planned. I did do a show or two here and there, simple little things, and I didn't get on too badly, much to my surprise.

There was one show in a night club just before Christmas where, clad in one of the two plaid shirts I'd frightened out of the Advertising Manager of the local Hudson Bay Company (H.B.C. – here before Christ), my Army pants and the inevitable flying boots, I had to pretend I was someone from the Wild and Woolly West singing *Don't Fence Me In* and things like that. To my mind, though, that evening is far more memorable for the agonies of fear I went through: sheer common-or-garden funk, when, after the show was over (the show didn't scare me any) the girls changed into their party dresses, or 'formals' as they called them, to dance with their boy friends. I, having no 'formals' and having to catch a night train to Calgary to give a lecture, had only the clothes I stood up in – shirt, pants and boots. I must have paced and sweated behind the scenes for about half an hour before I could summon up enough courage to sneak out behind the band. Actually, as soon as I was out there, people came rushing up and were very charming and all the rest of it, and they never never knew the terror I had been through.

The train journey to Calgary that same night struck me as huge fun; I'd never before been on a train where you slept. I had a top bunk and apparently I had met the Army type across the gangway, though I didn't remember meeting him in the least. He was going home on leave for Christmas and our animated conversation brought forth the heads of sundry other Army types also going on leave, and a packet of *Lifesavers* from a woman further down, who had heard me say I was hungry. The whole thing was most friendly. When we all retired to our bunks for the night, I found great difficulty in removing my trousers in a horizontal position. Excited, I slept badly, hugging my Walther, but Calgary struck me as a rather pleasant town when I arrived there, though it was smaller than Edmonton.

Here I was very nicely looked after by a flyer with the unenterprising name of Bill Smith. I spent the day in the hotel, where I let myself go by having a facial and a shoe-shine. Then Bill drove me round the town a little, invited me to dinner with his wife, fortified me with a Martini and led me like a lamb to the slaughter to the Flying Club, where I spoke for about an hour and a half on the flight, my first attempt at public lecturing. I guess I blithered a hideous amount of rot, but everyone was very nice about it. In all these speaking engagements I stressed, as I had to, my financial difficulties. I was hard up and I said so and people were very good really, often saying: "Well, send me a copy of your book and I'll give you twenty bucks."

Still, *"Thursday's Child"* did not arrive. I saw innumerable people to try to back me, and after a while I left Yvonne's home (for I couldn't be a guest for ever) for a small and crummy hotel in the back streets. This was all my money would run to, for I had to buy that vital necessity – at any rate to me, who had warmed my limbs that summer in tropical sunshine – a warm coat.

Apparently living in cheap hotels was rather a foolish thing to do. There was a lot of pounding on my door, and what I hadn't realized was that they were red light hotels (so many people may have acquired a very erroneous impression). I was most appallingly lonely in them. One is never lonely at home, however many days are spent in solitude, nor is one alone on a high mountain, but oh God, the loneliness of being in a crowd! I longed for friendship more than anything and in this mistaken search I came across some very queer types. I went wherever I wanted, there was no one to say "No," and I was just so clueless it wasn't true. I didn't care who I met or where I went so long as I could find a person or persons who would help me finish the trip. That was my second big mistake.

For a week after leaving Yvonne's home I stayed at the YWCA in a tiny cold room with a bed, a dressing table, a weeny radiator and, of course, the eternal Gideons' Bible. I once heard a story of how a man left a $5 bill in a Gideons' Bible with his name and address, asking the finder to contact him. It was found somewhere in the middle thirties, a period of about 14 years later! I had nothing else to read and, you know, religion apart, there are certainly good parts in the Bible from the literary point of view. There's one chapter of Isaiah, Chapter 40 I think it is, which is really beautiful oratory and makes you rather want to get up and shout about it.

Maybe it was reading the Bible so much that influenced me but after we had flown the Pacific I became aware of simple things such as I never had before. When I grew up – in other words, after Mummy died – when I was 17, and I learned to know adult misery, I also learned to know when I was happy. So many people in this world can only recognise happiness when it has gone, and spend so much time looking backwards that they never see it around them until that, too, has gone. I was lucky in that I could look about and say quite often: "I am happy." In fact, it became a habit. Then, when I had crossed the Pacific I again cried: "I am happy," I also added gratefully: "And I'm alive." Then the ordinary pleasures of being alive – fresh air, blue skies, crisp white snow, the smell of woollen clothes and the roughness of towels to the face – became so much more valuable because they might not have been.

They became so important that I wanted to thank God – not just dutifully and in a hurry, but clearly and loudly. I wanted to shake the people hurrying down the street scowling at their toes, and tell them to look up and be glad. I had been christened into the Church of England and had been through all the subsequent ceremonies, politely but untouched, for I found it too cold and unemotional, so I turned to the Catholic Church for help. I had been to Masses said in many countries and I liked and understood it more than my own Church. Say I "got religion" if you like – perhaps I did – but I'm glad.

I used to hear other peoples' radios from my little room playing carols, for it was almost Christmas, and I was unbearably homesick. I'd never been away from home before in my life. I was trying to save my money, too, at this time because I thought I should probably need it, as I looked like being there quite a while. However the YWCA could only keep me for a week so I had to move out and find somewhere equally as cheap. For a month I wandered, in and out of hotels, where a room was between $1.25 & $1.75.

Needless to say, I worked my way down, for I found that I had to buy firstly a coat, and then, to save myself from going stark staring mad, a tiny radio set. I would get up about tennish, read a bit maybe in bed and maybe stroll around the town for a while, if there was nobody I had to see or no business I could possibly make for myself. Maybe I would buy a bag of oranges or apples and would eat one or two of these for lunch and maybe a piece of chocolate. I'd tuck the rest of the food away until next day and spend the afternoon lying on my bed listening to the radio, playing endless and soul-destroying games of solitaire. In the evening, as often as I could, I went out, donning my only dress and trying to kid myself into believing that I didn't care. But there were many nights too, when I eked out the evening till I was really very hungry, about eightish, when I'd go out to some café, quite often a Chinese one, and brood over a solitary meal, picking out the cheapest items on the menu. Edmonton wasn't too expensive really; you could get turkey and cranberry sauce followed by ice cream for 75 cents, and it wasn't a stingy dish either, there were plenty of vegetables with it.

Later I took a job as a model to the University Art School, where I would sit for hours thinking of nothing very much but enjoying seeing human beings move around me, talking and friendly, neither hostile nor "on the make." I got a few dollars for this but what I really did it for was the company and the pleasure of having something to do and somewhere to go at a set hour. It's very pathetic now when I look back on it but oh, I'd much rather be far too busy than have nothing to do.

I became more & more hard up. I also became more & more disgusted with the people I met and everything became blacker and blacker. I thought it would be absolutely the end to spend Christmas Day alone, but Mr & Mrs White of one of the fuel companies took pity on me and asked me to a Christmas dinner at their home and, God bless 'em, they gave me a Christmas present, a pair of stockings. I really enjoyed the Christmas happiness of their two children and themselves and late that night they drove me round the town whilst I watched wide-eyed the lovely display of lights on the Christmas trees outside people's doors. So utterly different from England, for in the more residential parts light bloomed on every tree, like some nocturnal Christmas blossom. I had dinner several times with Professor Rowan, a well-known zoologist, and his family at his home. It was so nice to feed in people's homes instead of cafés, though I rarely had the chance.

There were unpleasant parts, too. There was a night I went to a party and then, when the evening closed, somebody said: "Oh! go with 'old so-and-so,' he'll give you a lift." I'd scarcely spoken to "old so-and-so," but everyone seemed very friendly about everything so I accepted the lift home for it was snowing and I had to take care of *the* shoes. Unfortunately "so-and-so" was more drunk than he appeared, which I didn't realize to start off with. He said we would just stop in at the office to pick up a bottle of rum and I couldn't very well stop him. In the office, he located his rum after a while and was annoyed with me because I wouldn't take my coat off or drink any. I don't care for it particularly and I didn't want to drink with him. He then appeared to have attacks of DTs and insisted on me going out into another office with him to meet "a Norwegian pilot friend." By the time we'd gone to this office, he'd forgotten about his non-existent friend. He told me to wait there while he made a private phone call. I waited there a while and then wandered back. He was getting a bit mad by now and demanded where I had been and then insisted I must have had someone in the other room with me. I, too, was getting quite perturbed and tried to beat it. He grabbed me by the coat and pulled me back twice. The third time I got as far as the darkened outer office, where he struggled with me and then started putting his hands around my throat. There's something singularly nasty, I always feel, about anyone's hands on your throat, even in fun, and this wasn't in fun. I'd got my Walther in my pocket and loaded, but shooting people is a messy business and entails a lot of explanation, so the rage and fear that flared up inside me was just translated into a right hook. I'm no frail woman and I've hit people before. He fell over straight backwards, to my great surprise, hitting himself with a loud crack against a table. I didn't even look round: I just beat it, pretty Goddam quick.

CHAPTER 26
THE END OF THE PROCTOR

I didn't go out for about a week after that until my nerves had settled back to their normal place, and it wasn't until one night when I was having a quiet and solitary supper at one of the cafés that I met a man I'd met in Anchorage, who flew F-80 jets in the American Air Force. Isn't it funny how some people haunt you? Have you ever taken a train up to town, only to find that you are dining at the next table to a face you'd seen very often in your own home town? It was the same with Tom McCabe. We met first in England, then again in Anchorage and now once more in Edmonton. "There must be something in this, let's go and have a drink." He was on his way flying an F-80 between Great Falls, Montana and Anchorage, Alaska and had had engine trouble at Edmonton. This conveniently lasted for a couple of weeks so we spent many cheerful evenings talking and eating, to say nothing of playing dice, until his ship was repaired and he had to go.

That gave me an idea – his going, I mean. Maybe I could bum a ride from the US Air Force from Edmonton to Alaska and see how my ship was progressing?

After Tom had gone, and feeling very lonely again, I tried so hard to persuade the US Air Force to give me a lift but they wouldn't play. I sauntered disgruntled back from the base and bummed a ride in a truck into town. Whilst chatting to the truck driver, I told him how I wanted to go north.

He said: "Sure you can. You can go by truck, hitch-hiking the whole way."

I got it all lined up and was introduced to the appropriate truck driver with a swiftness that made me gasp, tucked away 14 hours' sleep in one fell swoop and, on January 24th, set out for Anchorage.

Of course one of these strokes of Fate intervened. I hadn't gone more than 60 miles from Edmonton when my truck driver stopped on the road to chat to another driver in the same firm; he heard that my aircraft was already nearly in Edmonton and it must have passed us while we were having some lunch. I quickly changed trucks, dashing back to Edmonton in another one, as fast as wheels could take us.

When I got there, the aircraft was parked outside the trucking office. I scrambled up the side and peeped over and oh, was this my lovely aeroplane? This snowy crumpled wreckage, scattered at the bottom of the truck. Well, perhaps it's just the way it's lying. I tried to cheer myself up and failed miserably, for there was fear and worry and anger in my heart. How could they do this to me? I soon found my friend, Gordon Best, and we arranged for the truck to be emptied. He stood by, shaking his head, as they decanted the silvery remains on to the hangar floor. I blinked hard and tried very much not to cry as piece after piece came tumbling out.

The fuselage that I had left lying in the snow there nearly unscathed, with not even the plexiglass cracked, now looked as though a great axe had cut her in half along the CG line. The instrument panel was crumpled and torn. All the perspex was missing, as well as the engine cowling, the compass, the clock, the makers' nameplate, my RAC Club badge and practically everything else worthwhile. This would never, never fly again, not this mutilated mess. *[The fuselage must have been dropped when being transferred from one lorry to another, and obviously the souvenir hunters had also been busy. – M.T.]*

Tongue-tied I stood, wrestling with anger and despair. God! I'll get them for this, I thought. It has been handled by three Companies, I told myself. Yes, but what about the Insurance? You're alone in a big strange country, Dikki. I sighed.

The next day I put frantic phone calls through to New York, giving the Press the gen, and then arranged with a photographer for six bucks to take two big pictures as evidence. Then late that night I set off again for Alaska in another truck with pure vengeance in my heart and damn-all in my pocket book.

We left about 9 o'clock at night; it was snowing and it snowed all the way till my eyes were conjuring up visions in the snowflakes we went through. At about 2 am the truck driver stopped his vehicle in the little town of Smith (oh, exotic name!). There in a very primitive hotel did we stay. There was only one cold tap and that was in the kitchen and the hot water came off the stove, so I washed there in the kitchen sink. I was given the best room, which was distinguished from the others by having a chimney coming through the floor and the ceiling, giving precious warmth to the little wooden room. The bed was remarkable for the vivid blue, pink and mauve check flannelette sheets. I was tired too and slept soundly.

The next morning after a few coffees we pressed on again. The truck, I must say, was fairly warm, for all Canadian vehicles are heated, some better than others though. We drove all day over endless bumpy roads, stopping for dinner at a cheap greasy café and then driving on through endless forests, up countless hills, down and round and up again. We had a couple of beers at a place with the delightful name of High Prairie, picking up another passenger, and went on that night to the little town of Grand Prairie where a flat tyre caused us to halt again. This was about midnight, so we stayed at the hotel there. It was a very nice and, to me, positively luxurious hotel. I only just stopped myself from exclaiming in delight as the man showed me the room: "Why, there's a carpet on the floor!" I can remember little of that room but the blue fitted carpet, which impressed me immensely but there was, too, a wash basin with real hot water. What a luxury, but then, of course, it was two bucks 50.

Onwards again next morning after the flat tyre had been fixed, up appalling hills and down their equally appalling other sides, and being fed with tales of smashes, overturns, skids, and brake drums which "go." I learnt a lot about that highway for it has a life quite of its own. You've got to have your wits about you for death is all around for anyone who is careless, or grows tired at the wheel, or who is forgetful and drowses in his cab with the engine still ticking over so that the heater works, and forgets to open a window. Come of think of it, that's an easy death, just to sleep your way out of this world.

Dikki makes the front page on arrival at Edmonton. The newspaper caption reads: "Hard-luck flyer broke but happy." Photo: Edmonton Journal.

The end of the Proctor, trucked to Edmonton from the site of the forced landing; it had suffered not only by being further damaged during the road journey but also at the hands of souvenir hunters.

CHAPTER 27

NADIR OF THE FLIGHT

I was dumped at Dawson Creek with my duffel bag and my little leather case full of papers on the 27th January in the afternoon. I checked in at the Dew Drop Inn (God! what a name) but was persuaded later on to go to the town's best hotel, which wasn't anything much either. I rested much of the next day as I felt very, very tired but on Saturday morning I saw the Customs man, who had seen the aircraft coming through, as I wanted to find out how damaged it had been at this point. The rest of the day – early closing – I spent in my room. I did nothing all Sunday, except go to Mass, and I almost despaired of ever being able to converse in the human tongue again after such a long silence.

On Monday I tried to find people and get places but it was a pretty miserable dump, Dawson Creek, and there was absolutely nothing to do in the evenings: they even roll the sidewalks up at six. I tried to get to know a few people in the hotel to talk to me, without much success, and I lapsed into a solid chunk of misery. I was bitterly hard up by now. I had a few travellers' cheques which were cashable only in the States or Alaska but I had nothing for now. I sent a frantic wire back to Edmonton for $20, which was forwarded, happily, but it meant only one meal a day.

By Friday I nearly went berserk. I couldn't get out because I couldn't get a lift out of the wretched town; I wasn't getting anywhere with seeing people and I thought I was going to die right up there in the frozen North and nobody would even notice.

I saw a little poster up saying that there was a dance that night, so I wandered down to find out. I hadn't eaten all day and foolishly tried drinking on an empty stomach, a most unwise thing to do for you don't get high, you just feel sick, at least that's what I found. I was escorted back to my hotel in the middle of the night and, due to an altercation wherein our voices rose too high and loud in the night as to just who and how many were going to spend the night in my room, I was asked to leave the next morning: I was mad. Apparently if I'd just accepted the proposal and made no noise about it, nobody would have cared a twopenny damn, but because I chose to yell blue murder I was out. I moved across the way next day, feeling very forlorn and carrying quite a sizeable hangover.

However, I was cheered by an offer of a lift to Fairbanks but I realised later the next day, after further acquaintance with the driver, it was another of those "either-or" cases. I met somebody else that day, who also promised me a lift but that, too, never turned up. God! would this never, never end? This little place where I was staying now really was a lousy dump. As with so many of these primitive wooden hotels, the heat was in the corridors, emerging from begrimed ventilators, and unless you opened your bedroom door you got precious little heat in your room and I always found that to have my door open was just asking for trouble, so I was torn between the devil and Jack Frost.

Even the radio programmes brassed me off to the wide. There were only two stations I could get and they played nothing but gramophone records of Western stuff. I can never face it even now; the first strains of a tum-tummy Western whirls me back to the white misery of Dawson Creek. There was one particular song which used to drive me mad because I heard it so often and always the same recording: *"Put down them shootin' irons, Pappy, we ain't goin' feudin' any more."* These records were usually request numbers and the man used to read out the little message: "To Dad and Mum from Sis." It's ludicrous now, but when you sit for days & days on end, like the Frog Footman, with nothing in your mind but your own thoughts, and you've thought everything once and some thoughts two or three times, it does save you from the lunacy of solitary confinement.

There were also commercialised religious programmes of a type that I'd never come across before, at the same hour every evening, after a signature tune which began (sung Western-style, of course): *"Have you ever seen Jesus?"*; this was followed by a condemning feminine voice threatening you with all sorts of hells and torments if you didn't turn to Jesus and be saved. The details into which she would delve held me in fascinated horror – she left nothing unsaid. Occasionally, like a fresh draught of air, I would get a gay and light-hearted programme by some strange chance from somewhere in Seattle. It was quite a good radio set, though where it is now I don't know. So much of my kit and my souvenirs got lost in the mail and just disappeared.

I longed for a dog at this time. It was just the kind of companionship I wanted, somebody who would look at you with loving eyes and ask nothing more, but I could scarcely feed myself, let alone an animal. Usually for lunch I'd buy a 10 cent packet of nuts and then spend about 75 cents on a meal in the little Chinese café. There in the evenings I would loiter over my food for as long as was decently possible for though hemmed in by high wooden seats making each table into a cubicle – a thing you never see in England, – I could hear the chatter of other people's voices, and enjoy the sound of other people also absorbing thin chicken noodle soup.

The two Sundays I was there, of course, I attended Mass in the little wooden church. I was highly impressed by their abandoned pious devotion, the last thing you'd expect in that town. The church was always crowded and everyone sat as near as possible to the altar rails, though the whole church was packed five minutes before the beginning of the service. There was no need for a sign such as I read in the States once outside the church: *"Come early and get a back seat."*

I was later to see many strange religious ideas, at least they were strange to me. Being very English, I always considered it 'not nice' to advertise religion as it was something that was a personal thing entirely, and seeing churches lit up with neon signs and great placards always gave me a feeling of vague embarrassment. One day someone pointed to a sign proclaiming *"Jesus saves"* and remarked cynically: "Did you ever know a Jew who didn't?" That convinced me more than ever that advertising was wrong; on the other hand, there is no need for the utter drabness inside a church that is found too often in England. Sure, the architecture is often brilliant but the sheer joy and colour that can be seen in some village churches in Canada or the States is much more appealing to an ordinary person like myself. That and adequate heating.

I was lying writing on my bed on the Monday morning when there was a pounding on my door. I heaved myself up and opened the door to two hulking great Mounties, who fired a series of highly impertinent questions. What was I doing here? Why didn't I get out of the town? Where was my money coming from? I was completely mystified until they practically accused me of prostitution and told me (and I quote) that I was sticking out in the town like a sore thumb and that I must get out, whereupon they abruptly left.

I lay on my bed and wept. Do you ever remember as a child your father accusing you of breaking something when you haven't and being punished for something you hadn't done? That helpless, hopeless feeling of despair when nobody in the world believes you and not even God is listening. I sobbed on my bed for an hour or more until I felt weak and ill. Wasn't there anybody who would help me? Why not ask the priest? I bathed my swollen eyes and powdered a blotchy face. I struggled into my boots and parka, thudded down the worn wooden stairs, out of the rickety wooden door and crossed the road to the little house beside the church. I stumped up the path, my boots crunching in the snow, making the same sort of noise as a person does who is eating celery.

The priest spoke kindly to me; his seemed the first friendly voice in a thousand years. Apparently he knew the sergeant in question and he explained to me that their promotion depended upon the number of arrests. He said he would speak to the man and comforted me with friendly, ordinary words spoken by a man who had faith in better things. I couldn't say thank-you but I think he understood. He said he would try and help me get a lift north, as he knew many of the truckmen and their families. Apparently many men in this town made their money driving along the Alcan Highway.

I saw him again next day and by that time it seemed my luck had changed for I was promised a lift (a *real* promise) to Lower Post within a couple of days.

It was these last three nights that I was pestered by a big tall man, who insisted on pounding on my door. The first time he came, I asked him what he wanted and turned him away angrily when he started waving his pocket book about. Three consecutive nights he pounded under different names and twice I hit him in the face. The third and last time, I lost my temper, picked up my automatic and advanced on the door. I had lost my temper but I didn't lose my head for I quickly slipped the shells out, opened the door and smashed it with as much strength as I could in the face of my unknown persecutor. I registered only the quick impression of a face intensely surprised before I slammed and bolted the door again, pretty damn smartly! I lay on the bed shaking for a while, letting my anger drip away, and then went on packing my kit. They always told me there were wolves in Canada!

CHAPTER 28
ESCAPE FROM DAWSON CREEK

I left at sixish with the man who had offered me the lift. I took him to be a commercial traveller but apparently he owned a shop or café somewhere. As the miles slid under the car and spread themselves between me and Dawson Creek, my heart grew lighter and I sang in a friendly, humming, sort of Winnie-the-Pooh way to myself. There is an obelisk in the middle of Dawson Creek, which announces that it is Mile zero and 1,523 miles from Fairbanks, Alaska. I was really moving up the Alcan Highway at last.

We only did 50 miles that night for we had to make a call at Fort St. John. It was snowing and blowing, a dangerous combination because of drifts, so we decided that we had best park for the night. We drove to a hotel, the coldest hotel of my life, where I went to sleep nearly fully dressed, taking off only my boots and my parka. The hotel was heated by a furnace burning soft coal and the hot air grids blew forth a filmy black dust, which settled on everything. Even the cat made your hands black when you stroked it. I wasn't a very satisfactory companion; I wouldn't drink much and I couldn't play rummy, nor was I of an amorous disposition. Besides which, I had a nasty, sneaking period pain. However, my state of mind had improved considerably over that 50 miles for as I went to take a shower it provoked me to mirth rather than anger.

I do not care for showers. It is a slipshod and haphazard way of ablution, suitable only to the impatient and the insensitive. The shower I had that night was a brute. To begin with, somebody else had been there earlier and the ice was forming in the puddles on the floor! There was a window pane out, as far as I can remember. However, that was merely incidental. As with many showers, the knob labelled 'Hot' brought forth cold and the 'Cold,' after a lengthy period, moderately warm water. The chief trouble was, though, that most of the holes in the nozzle were bunged up and either the water trickled out in a mere drizzle, or those holes which did function produced such a pressure that the water bored holes into my back and chest and shoulders, almost forcing me to my knees. I lost the soap under the rack on which I stood and every time I turned round the shower curtain adhered to me like wet newspaper.

There are other showers, some producing, after turning the 'Cold,' such a scalding supply of hot that I have burst forth with a yell, causing three ludicrous female heads to protrude instantly from three other showers, wearing identical expressions of comic opera-like consternation. Others have a pleasanter temperature but they run icy cold when somebody else turns another tap on. Then again there are the kind that don't have a nozzle but the water comes out in the shape of a ring and you can stand for quite a while in the dead centre of the cascade and keep absolutely bone-dry. There may be, of course, perfect showers, ones which unhesitatingly function and in which the soap tray is located in a reasonably dry corner. I don't say there are, I say there may be. And that being so, I've yet to discover the technique of washing under them. Do you dampen yourself, turn off the shower, soap yourself shiveringly and then try and find the right temperature again to rinse it off, or do you endeavour to soap under this shower, eyes blinded by the torrent and misted by the steam? And anyhow, how do you wash your feet? For you are standing on the soles and if you soap them you slip. I know for I've tried. No, give me a bath. At least you know where the water is when you want it and the heat is evenly distributed over the more sensitive parts of the body.

The next day, through piled up snowdrifts, my companion and I made an effort to press on but the snow caused the exhaust pipe to become dislodged and we had to tie it up with string and go back. I stood around in the garage with him and then went back to the hotel and rebooked our rooms. It was pretty obvious we couldn't go that day so he taught me how to play rummy and we played all the afternoon with a sort of armed neutrality.

One of the girls in the café told me that there were two men staying at the other hotel who were flying up the next day to Anchorage and suggested I should see them. I promptly did this and they told me sure, yeah, they'd take me and they'd give me a call tomorrow morning after they'd called the field and we'd all go together. I waited the next morning, and waited, but they never called me, and when I called the airfield I was told they'd just taken off. I was bitterly disappointed but it had happened before so I just folded away my disappointment and set forth again with my companion of the day before, hardly daring to take my eyes off him in case he too (and he didn't like me now) should vanish. The car wasn't running any too good and consumed oil at a most prodigious rate.

We followed on up the Highway: Charlie Lake, Blueberry, Beaton River, Mason Creek, Thrush, Prophet River, Lum'n Abner trading post, Fort Nelson, Steamboat Mountain – are all vague memories of a gruesome ride. He was, I must say, a good driver but, my God! you *had* to be on a road like that. Bend after bend after bend, tight hairpin bends, too, and you may go up a slope about one in five or a steep skid down the other side. Sometimes there are strips where the road runs almost straight for a mile or more. On either side there are the wild, wild woods where the wolves wander. Those places I've named were the only stops, in fact the only form of civilisation between Mile 49 (Fort St. John) and Mile 387 where we ran out of gas. When the engine coughed and quit I was afraid about how long we should have to stay there alone in the cold night, but we were lucky that time in that a road patrol passed us and took a message to Summit Lake, where a truck went back with some gas for us. Cold and cruel though the Highway is, it is also very fascinating. Living conditions are unbelievably primitive and the only form of sanitation is the-little-hut-at-the-end-of-the-garden. You have to be very determined and firm of purpose to face a trip in weather of 30 or 40 below and execute your mission.

Some time before, I had been told the story of Steamboat Mountain when I was in Anchorage. Apparently a woman was flying out of Alaska, taking her son, aged about 12, back to school in the States. Somehow she followed a cart track instead of the highway and crashed into the side of Steamboat Mountain in cloud conditions. She was killed but her son, so I was told, hung upside down for two days by his legs before he was rescued. I don't think he even had his parka on, but he lived. The story impressed me, as well it should, and I thought of it many times on that last flight out of Anchorage.

After a quick snack at Summit Lake, we went on: Rocky Mountain Autocourt, Racing River, Muncho Lake and Cold River. At Mile 959 the gas gauge registered zero and I'm sure it was nothing but my fervent praying that got us into Lower Post without the engine quitting, at 3.30 am. I was tired. I dragged myself into the nearby hotel, where I snatched a quick sleep, getting up at seven so as to be able to catch the drivers of passing trucks as they stopped for breakfast. I loitered around for a couple of hours dividing my time between the road and the little hall, where hung some beautiful wolf pelts for sale. I did want one but I had no money, hardly enough to pay my hotel bill, let alone food. I had taken a pot-shot at a wolf earlier with my Walther from the car but I'm not much cop with an automatic, as I've never had much practice.

I got a lift about 15 miles up the highway to Watson Lake. There I was dumped in a small wooden café, where I spent the day trying to get a lift, waiting and hoping and wondering however I was going to live. I had nothing left but my silver dollar and about 60 cents. At about 7 o'clock that night, I blew 25 cents on a bowl of soup and as much bread as I could grab from other people's plates. It was my first meal that day and I was hungry.

The people in the café were kind in an unconcerned way. They'd too often seen down-and-outs and they probably didn't trust me anyhow. Men tramped into the café that evening and I played rummy – I'd spent all the day playing solitaire again. I played rummy with a man who had the first two joints of all his fingers missing. He had trouble in dealing the cards. I tried not to look. I suppose that's frostbite, I told myself.

About 9 o'clock that night two lads came through on their way from Washington DC and they said they were going to Anchorage. Could they take me? Would they take me? Please?

"Sure, have you got much kit?"

"No, just one kit bag."

"OK by us."

And so I was piled in, one knee either side of the gear lever. I was happy again.

CHAPTER 29
BACK TO ANCHORAGE

We drove all night. I think they'd driven several nights as well as days, for Bob O'Neal, who owned the car and was driving, was a little slow in his reactions, for I remember noticing (quite an appreciable time before he did) as we approached a bend that it was too sharp a one for the speed we were going. He braked but we ran over the bank and got lodged there at an angle of about 45 degrees. There was nothing else to do, so we slept for a while, waking up at about seven, having slid down the seat till we were both sitting in Bob's lap.

When conditions got too cold, we all piled out and looked around, blinking blearily in the cold clear light of dawn. Bob went round to the back of the car and produced an axe from the boot. He was carting a lot of stuff up to Anchorage to his self-built home, for he had been homesteading near there last year until he and his wife had gone back to Washington that fall. We collected odd bits of timber, chopped them up, and with the aid of a bunch of comics soon had a fire blazing merrily. Then Bob produced a saucepan and some canned beef stew and a can opener and we cooked ourselves a meal, piling on logs at the same time to keep us as warm as possible. When we weren't walking about chopping, we stood on sheets of newspaper, alternatively warming our rears and our fronts.

The land around us was white and desolate. There were a few small trees and stunted bushes and not very far away was a jagged ridge. At least it looked near and we tried guessing its distance and how long it would take to climb. Bob said it would take a whole day from where we stood but I thought less. In any case it would be well-nigh impossible without snowshoes for the snow was deep and deceiving. I had found that out when I had tried to walk off the beaten snow of the road to a trunk of wood at the roadside, for I plunged in way above my knees and after a few staggering paces retired, discreetly deciding that the log was too big.

I was highly amused to see that within three hours the fire had sunk through the snow to the ground, leaving a round, wet hole, at the bottom of which it still burned merrily. We weren't too cold, at least not in the body, but my feet just wouldn't thaw. After several hours a truck came by which, accustomed to such roadside mishaps, immediately stopped and got out some chains, tied these on to the car and yanked us out. It was all part of a day's work up there.

According to Bob, a bit earlier on in the journey a truck had edged him into the side in passing (the roads have a rather steep and high camber), and then it turned round and politely pulled him out again.

On first look there seemed to be little damage done to the car, though we soon found that the radiator had cracked and we only just made Johnny Johns' Lodge at Carcross at Mile 870. There we huddled round the stove all the afternoon waiting for Johnny Johns to arrive back home to tow us into White Horse, where we wanted to get the car repaired as soon as possible. He didn't return until after nightfall, when we had a good meal of moose meat and a few rums with him and then retired to bed. The Lodge, a long low building built of logs, had one long central room with a bar at one end, at which we ate, and a big friendly iron stove the other. I listened to Bob and Johnny Johns talking of hunting goats, caribou, moose and bear, about Huskies and snowshod mountain trips and things so out of my world that they held me spellbound. I'm by no means a city dweller and I know a bit about shooting English game within and without the law, but this was so different. It was here, I think, that I realised that it wasn't only a cold, dismal and uncultured country but it was adventurous and exciting for those who look for it and one's life is much more one's own work than in the overpopulated British Isles.

Johnny was Indian and his wife Eskimo and, as the rum circulated, so mounted my enthusiasm for this romantic Northern country. Good stuff that rum, too, one of those 120 proof jobs that really does put hair on your chest.

The next morning we drove into White Horse, packed tightly into Johnny's truck and towing Bob's car. We checked in at a cheap hotel (at least it was warm), Bob and I and the other guy, whilst we shoved the car into dock for repairs and Johnny took us around. I heard some weird and wonderful Yukon songs over beers that night.

After lunch the next day, when we had spent most of the morning in the garage, we set off for the boundary of Canada and Alaska: Mendenhall Creek, Champagne, Canyon Creek, Haynes Junction, Bear Creak, Burwash Landing, Kluane River, Lake Creek, Dry Creek, Snag etc. We drove all that night and reached the border, where we came to a full stop. We were told that we were not allowed through until 7 o'clock. This was only about 2 o'clock.

"But we've just seen a truck go through," we complained.

"No," they said, "you can't pass through."

We ran the car back down the hill and went to sleep until another truck passed us and got through, when we argued again, threatening to jump the gate, and this time we were permitted through. I was asked a lot of searching questions and then the man said he didn't think they'd let me through anyhow when we got to Tok. I was worried and puzzled: what the hell had I done? We then drove on through the night to Tok, where the American officials, Customs and Immigration have their office.

We got there about 4 am and I was so tired that the rest of the night seemed to me more like a dream. Something had gone wrong with the car again, so Bob extracted the damaged part and we all went into a hotel, where we stood in the men's washroom for three hours, dozing and leaning against the walls. There wasn't anything to sit on (barring the loo) except the cold stone floor and you couldn't sit on that unless you really wanted to freeze. The lights were dim and the place cold and drear. Towards morning we were entertained by watching people come in and shave but, honestly, it was one of the dreariest dawns I've ever seen arrive. I was absolutely squeezed dry of energy. I hadn't had my clothes off or washed for over-long and my eyes felt like baked potatoes.

At 7 o'clock the café opened and we were ready. The cheapest meal for its bulk is the traditional hot-cakes and syrup and those sourdough hot-cakes we had there were the most beautiful I've ever had in my life. Umph-mmm!

The officials were so hot on my track that they breakfasted with me and kept saying enticingly: "You *will* come and see us, won't you?" and rubbed their hands gloatingly.

I said: "Sure, sure," still trying to puzzle it out.

Bob and his pal, Joe I think his name was, went off to a garage again, dropping me with the Immigration Authorities, who told me flatly that I was not allowed into Alaska. I had to show all the money I had and declare how long I wanted to stay for. No, I definitely hadn't got enough money and I certainly couldn't go in. Brother, did I have to talk fast! On the old theory that if you can't convince 'em, confuse 'em, I talked fast and furious, for I was nearly desperate. Here was I, having hitchhiked 2,000 miles up that Alaskan Highway in the middle of winter, and they were trying to turn me back! So believe me, I fought tooth and nail. I talked so fast the man didn't know whether I was coming or going – so I went! He wrote me out the necessary documents and I'd almost got to the state of affectionately inviting him home to England to stay for a holiday when Bob came back and picked me up and we pressed on to Anchorage.

At least that was the idea, but it started to snow and by the time we got to a place called Big Timber (oh, the romance of those names!) the drifts were well across the roads. We dug ourselves out of one drift, although I'm afraid that Bob and his pal did most of that. The wind blew the snow so strongly that it felt like pins thrown at your face and it really hurt. We no sooner dug ourselves out of that drift than we went pounding on into another. We just sat there that time until the snow plough dug us out. Then we decided we had better stay at the sort of primitive hotel there that night.

We consumed a glorious meal whilst the lodge fire was being built up. Several little one-room shacks were dotted round the central building and café, each containing about six beds and an iron stove. There was no privacy. If you wanted to undress, you just had to turn the lights out first but woe betide he (or in this case she) who takes off clothes to get caught next morning by the bright light of day, as I nearly did. Facilities there were negligible. The hut-at-the-end-of-the-garden stood bare and forlorn five snowdrifts down. I really did make an attempt to get there but nobody else seemed to have beaten a track and, since the snow was up to my thighs, I guess I did the same as everyone else.

The next day we set off again and made Palmer just after lunch. Here I said goodbye to Bob, for he lived at Wasilla nearby, whilst I waited for a bus to Anchorage. People turned to look at me as I nipped in for a quick sundae and surely I must have presented a wild and terrible figure, unwashed and smelly, for I'd worn these clothes for over a week, never taking them all off. My parka was crumpled and stained with oil thrown around in the aircraft crash and a lot of hard wear, but they allowed me on the bus and I went into Anchorage. I smiled to myself at the way I was stared at when I checked in at the hotel. It just all depends, doesn't it, on whether you fly your way in, in your own aircraft, or come back bumming rides, flat broke!

CHAPTER 30
ANCHORAGE AGAIN

The hotel was a moderate one for Anchorage (4 bucks a night), and my first move was to soak myself in a big, hot bath and wash my hair. Then I put a call through to the night club proprietor who had wired me an offer of a job when I first crashed. He invited me to a dinner of oyster cocktail, *filet mignon* with mushrooms, strawberry shortcake, black coffee and a b. & B. (brandy & Benedictine). I felt positively human after that, friendly and expansive and at peace with the world, for I had lived the last week on hot-cakes, soup and sandwiches, rather sparsely distributed. So is the human being influenced by the food he eats.

The drinking went on that night to the small hours, for my friend Tom McCabe, knowing I was in town, came and looked for me and found me after about the second guess. The next morning, with a slight hangover, I chugged over to the bank and cashed half my travellers' cheques and, when Bob came in that evening, I repaid him for the meals that he had bought me whilst on the Highway.

Then he delivered to me a stern lecture on my being cocky which, it must be said to my credit, I accepted politely and humbly. But even now, as I look back, I still think he was unjust. I used to be horribly bouncy once upon a time, so people would never know just how small and defenceless I was inside. Now, however, it has evolved into several parts – determination to get what I want, a certain amount of confidence, and the ability to live for the day, for tomorrow you'll surely die. Besides, who was he to talk? He'd quit school and run away to work on various ranches at the age of 11, I think he said, and though he could probably sit on anything with four legs and turn his hands to most practical things, he just didn't seem to realise that there was anything much more to life. He talked for several days in the car, for I must admit I'd never met anyone quite like him in England and as a person he vastly interested me. I loved hearing him talk about a life so different from mine and I tried to picture it for myself. When I tried to explain *my* life, though, where opera, ballet and much-loved books played such an important part, it was dismissed as just "bullshit."

On the Friday (it was now February 18th) a pilot called me up. Would I like to fly down to Seward and back? His name was Don Dorothy and when I first saw him I nearly had kittens. Anchorage at this time had a Fur Festival on, and one of the rules was that every man was told to grow a beard of some sort. Some of the hirsute appendages I saw were, it must be admitted, very far from the real thing, but if you didn't make an attempt, you were taken to a mock court, where you were fined and had to buy your wife a new hat, or some such thing like that. Don, a thick-set man, had grown a wonderful pair of side whiskers right down to his jaw and with his black & red ski-cap, his black & red check overshirt and his pants tucked into his boots, he looked like a cartoon of some 19th Century deer stalker, stepped out from the pages of *Punch*. I'd never seen anything like him in real life. He flew a Norseman and a Waco from Anchorage to Seward and back, flying in and out of the mountains almost every day, even in winter. He had a little house up at the airfield where he would proudly cook me some wonderful meals. He was very kind to me.

He had quite an adventure the day I arrived in Anchorage. It so happened that there were not many passengers to Seward that day so he took the Waco, and there was only one passenger on the return journey, an unusual occurrence. He took off, climbed up and set course for Anchorage and then noticed that his passenger was lying on the seat 'walking' his feet up the walls. Somewhat puzzled, Don asked the man if he was feeling ill. The reply, vague and indistinct, was to the effect that he "felt cold." Don, in his shirtsleeves in the heated cabin, knew this to be untrue but said nothing. Then the man got right up to him and started strangling him, so that Don had to hit out with his fist, but despite his being no lightweight he could not stop the man. Then a pitched battle started, with the aircraft swerving and diving all round the sky. Don, scared for the safety of the craft as well as himself, grabbed the small pump fire extinguisher and laid about him good and well, periodically grabbing at the controls. The man fought hard like the madman he was, and about a dozen heavy dents showed on the metal fire extinguisher before he was laid out, to say nothing of the blood splashed round the cabin. Don, when the man was on the floor, put through a call of "Mayday," stuck the nose down and made for the field PDQ, landing just as the man regained consciousness. What an unnerving hazard to commercial flying!

I saw many people in Anchorage from whom I asked help, though there was none forthcoming. I had originally intended to go to Fairbanks but I discovered that anyway the person I wanted to see, Al Ghezzi, was down in Seattle now.

I daydreamed a lot about the Alcan Highway and all the stories I had heard. That country is one where you can so easily get 'lost,' if you want to disappear. People have flown aircraft up there just to ditch them and make a getaway, whilst others, very many others, have ditched and died without intention in those snow-covered woods. There was also murder committed along the Highway and, if I've got the story right, it makes quite good telling.

It happened that a man and his daughter (aged about 16) were setting out from Alaska to the States, the man having about 2,000 bucks on him. There was also in the car the girl's boy friend, to whom they were giving a lift. Whilst they halted at the roadside, the younger man shot the girl's father with a ·22 and together they dragged him away under some bushes. The girl was apparently quite a willing partner in all this and the two of them went back to the States, where they bought a café and settled down. Nobody would have been any the wiser if it hadn't been that the man got caught for something else and confessed to this murder. He led the cops back up the Highway and pointed out the spot, when they found the body still there, shrunken quite small with the snows and the weather. I wonder, though, if that's the only murder along that Highway.

There are fires that burn all the year round up there, an item of interest that stayed in my mind for quite a while whilst I turned it over and thought about it and, you know, even now I can't see why the darn thing stays alight with three feet of snow over the top, and yet I myself have seen signs of distant smoke. Thousands of trees are destroyed annually through the great forest fires, but then of course there are so many miles of unguarded forests.

As I was only permitted to stay in Alaska two weeks due to my limited funds, March 1st was the deadline date. I frantically flapped round the town, with which I was getting quite familiar by now, seeing people and newspapers, firms and night clubs, trying oh so hard to get some financial backing or an aircraft to fly home on. I went out to dinner some nights and I had many meals in Don Dorothy's little house, otherwise I bought no food at all bar a bag of oranges. For instance, the night after I'd arrived there and dined so well, I coasted entirely, eating nothing the next day and, as is my usual custom, waiting till nightfall before I had my meal the day after.

CHAPTER 31
SOUTH TO SEATTLE

I had set my heart at this time on getting a dog; I decided I had to have some companion or else go crazy and it was with pure delight that I accepted the present of one. It's wrong, I know, to accept "presents from strange men" and I'm positive that his intentions were strictly dishonourable, which might have been difficult, but it so happened that I got the chance of a lift to Seattle before I ever found out.

You see, a couple of days before I left, we chose a little Husky pup. His mother was Siberian Husky, pure white, and his father Alaskan, big and brown. He was a beautiful little thing, with white paws and big blue eyes. Though people jeered at me when I cuddled him, saying that "the maternal instinct will out," I didn't care. Maybe it was true for I was very lonely and there was an empty spot in my heart for just the cuddlesome lump of fluff he was. When I had him he really looked more like a shmoo than anything else and he had never been in a house before. He stayed at Don's place and he would lie on the floor on his fat round tummy with his legs flat out, just cowering the first day. I called him Shemya because it seemed suitable somehow and because Shemya Island was also the beginning of things again. I intended to take him back to England with me and train him to pull Anna in a little cart or, better still, train him as a pack dog with little saddlebags to carry my shopping in. A big Alaskan Husky, you know, would carry as much as 60 lb.

About three days before I left, I cashed a cheque, all that I had in dollars, about 40 odd. That night, while singing in a night club, I put my handbag on the bar while I stood at the microphone. Whilst I was gone, some particularly mean type opened my wallet, took all the money out of it and put it back and I, of course, never noticed my loss until next morning when I almost chewed the carpet in desperation. I'd paid most of my hotel bill, sure, but there were still about four days left and I had literally no money. I was back again to my silver Canadian dollar. I had needed help before but I needed it really badly right then.

I sat down on my bed and tried to think it out sanely. How true, how very true, that old quotation: *"From him that hath not, it shall be taken away."* I walked down to the other end of the town to see the owner of the night club. Not the night club where the money had been stolen, but the one owned by the man who had wired me when he had heard of my crash and with whom I had dined the first night. After repeated visits I found him in and I told him what had happened. He was sitting in an armchair reading a book entitled *Belief*, I think it was. But he just didn't believe my story. That in itself hurt a lot, for I'm not prone to lying, but when he lectured me in believing in myself and explained to me that if I believed I could do something, I could do it, that was just too much. However hard I believed, I just couldn't believe the money back in the wallet and I had to blink hard to keep the tears away as I walked out into the street. He was my only hope because I thought he was a friend of mine and, if he ever reads this, I hope he'll feel just a little ashamed at the anguish and unhappiness he gave me through his disbelief.

Strangely enough, it was the last person that I ever imagined would help me that turned up trumps, God bless him. My pilot pal Don Dorothy paid my hotel bill, fixed up a lift from Anchorage to Seattle on a non-scheduled airline and gave me a few dollars for my pocket, too. He just about saved me. It wasn't as though he was wealthy either. He too had to live (and drink) on quite a small salary and I shan't forget how very, very kind he was.

We dashed around in his car late on Tuesday night, March 1st, rushing hither and thither, then he packed me up and bundled me on the ship with Shemya tucked into the front of my B-15 (US Officers' short fur-lined jacket). I was then shown the ropes, for I was to be a stewardess that night on quite a long flight. We were to take off about 10 pm and land about 8 am next morning. I was excited and I was glad; not that I disliked Anchorage, I'd go back any day, for I think it is a wonderful part of the world and you soon get used to the cold. Anchorage is a very flourishing town due, it must be said, quite a lot to the US Air Force Base but it is very rich in all types of mineral, as well as exotic things like jade (I had a lovely little piece of dark green jade given to me).

It still seems strange to me that you can buy land here, from the Government, which has never ever been used before. That you can build on it with the aid of a Government loan and start your own little farm or whatever you want to do with it. A lot of people dig a hole and build the basement, roof it over temporarily and leave it like that for a year or so, living round the stove in the basement. Then, when they've made some money, they build the ground floor (building materials are expensive), and then rent off the basement. There's a great deal of private enterprise done in this way and due to the housing shortage many people have built their own homes in their spare time.

If for instance they were based at Elmendorf Field, where houses are in much demand and waited for eagerly, their wives could come up and join them. Here at least is a land where, if you are prepared to work hard, you really can get somewhere, but then, of course, opportunities exist in these lesser-populated countries that just aren't there in England. In England too often you train hard and get a humble post in a firm where the only chance of promotion is when one of the senior men die and everyone moves up a step. Out in Canada you aren't waiting for a man to die, but for the new branch to open. I was told that there were more people in Greater London than there are in the whole of Canada. Yes, chum, think that one out!

I had plenty of time to turn things over in my mind on the flight down to Seattle. I was heading for the great USA. I'd never been there before but the mother of a girl friend of mine whom I had known in England lived there. I had written her from Anchorage and her mother had written me back saying that though Beverley was away, she would love me to come and stay there. I didn't even know her, and here I was on my way without her even knowing, with a few dollars in my pocket and a puppy in my arms. Little Shemya slept all the way down, only waking to nibble at a chocolate bar. Oh! how I loved him. I wished I could have slept too for I had had a pretty exciting day, but here I was rushing to and fro with coffee & sandwiches, rugs & papers and oxygen for an old lady who was feeling faint.

We circled round Seattle at about 8.30 the next morning, and out of the cramped cabin windows I could see little glimpses of the sea and the airfield below. No snow! We touched down and taxied to the tower. I handed down the passengers and then pulled myself out, clutching duffel bag and dog and, as I considered I came under the title of crew, entirely missed Customs and Immigration, walked blithely round the corner of the building and hopped into a cab. I gave the driver Mrs Conrad's address at Phinney Avenue and leaned back with a sigh. This was Seattle, oooh. This was the United States, ooh-er. I looked round me, all eyes, and my first impression was that I had stepped back 15 years and this was before the war. There were so many cars on the road; so many little well-kept gardens. It looked so unbelievably peaceful and prosperous but then, of course, there was no snow and the hedges were already starting to look green, for it was spring down here. I opened the window to breathe in great gulps of wet moist air. It seemed utterly wonderful to smell earth and trees again after the cold dead smell of snow. It took me many days to get over the smell, as it did Shemya for, of course, he'd never seen grass before and, as he had only walked on snow, his little claws were as long as a cat's, for they'd never been worn away.

I paid off the cab outside a neat, white-painted house. Why, I thought to myself, it looks just like the American houses you see in magazines. I struggled with my things up the little brick pathway, pausing to sniff once more the green, green grass. I propped my duffel bag against the door and rang the bell. The door was opened onto a thick-carpeted comfortable room and there stood Mr and Mrs Conrad. Mrs Conrad came forward and gave me a hug and a kiss and I was very touched. She was wonderfully kind to me, but nothing was kinder than that first act of friendliness. I needed that more than anything else in the world for it had been such a long time since anyone cared whether I lived or died. I loved her for that. They brought me in, gave me breakfast (and Shemya too), and we chatted about a lot of nothing in a bright, cheerful American kitchen and I told her bits about my journeying.

After a while she said that she was going out to lunch at a women's organisation and would I care to come? So she sent me upstairs to have a long soak in the bath, which I really appreciated, while she pressed my dress, which I appreciated even more. The only trouble was that I had been awake all night and all the day before and just about lunchtime it started snowing. I met a lot of very charming people but when after lunch we stayed around and listened to a talk, the effect of the meal on me caused an irresistible desire to sleep. I forced my eyes open, squinting blearily at the speakers. They must have thought me terribly rude and two or three times I suddenly woke up to find I had been to sleep. For all that though, I never got around to going to bed until bedtime that night, having been awake for about 40 hours.

To begin with in Seattle I just didn't do anything. I just enjoyed the comfort and friendliness of the home, where they made me feel such a welcome guest. I had seen a family photograph before I met them; Beverley had shown it to me in England – just her mother, her father and young Hal, and I remember thinking when I saw it: "Why, how typically American." Somehow they looked very American to my English eyes, if such a thing is possible. Hal went to college during the day and Mr Conrad was out on business. Mrs Conrad was busy a lot in the house, which she kept very beautifully, single-handed, so I was free to wander in and out pretty much as I liked. To make things easier for her, I used to be out for lunch and I'd take a bus into the town just for the pleasure of window-gazing, or else strolled out to the Zoo, just across the common from their house. There Shemya and I would munch something out of a paper bag. It's much more fun going to the Zoo with an inquisitive little dog because the animals take far more notice of you and you feel like a distinguished personage. I went to the Zoo very often, partly because it was pleasant to wander on green grass and talk to the deer and partly because Shemya did so love it.

After a few days of doodling I thought I'd better look around, so to make the necessary contacts I took a bus to the Boeing Aircraft Company, where I had a long natter with Al Hill, one of the advertising men. He was most enthusiastic and encouraging, bless him, and his optimism gave me a bit more faith in myself. He suggested many things, but first, he said, I must let the Press know I was here. He called up the Press right away and down they came. I gave them all the gen I could and prayed fervently it would catch someone's eye: someone who really could do something. Then, of course, it suddenly dawned on me that I hadn't reported in with the Immigration people. Dreadful! I decided I'd go round on Monday for it was then Saturday afternoon, and on Monday I went.

I was interviewed there by a woman who obviously considered me a very unwelcome guest to the States. She announced that I could only stay if somebody would put down 500 dollars and guarantee my good behaviour, when I might be allowed two weeks. I thought it over. I felt sure the Conrads would guarantee the money and my good behaviour but they'd already been so kind I was damned if I was going to ask them. I demurred.

"It's a bit one-sided, isn't it?" I remarked.

The woman was horrified and, looking at me with cold hostility, she told me that I was a highly unsuitable person, that I should not sully the United

States with my presence and that I must be outside the borders within three days. I thought that distinctly unfair. That didn't even give me a sporting chance to get done what I wanted to get done and I said as much but she was adamant.

"OK," I thought, "there's two can play at that game," and demanded to see her boss.

He was at lunch.

OK, I'd wait.

I waited and I saw him and a dear old thing he was, too. I smiled at him sweetly and told him my story. I said I knew I couldn't stay long, I hadn't the money but please would he give me a sporting chance. He gave me three weeks, bless him, and I was very, very grateful. If he hadn't done that, I'd have been in 'jug,' and that's for sure. I'd no more hope of getting out within three days than I had of flying and, anyway, where would I go?

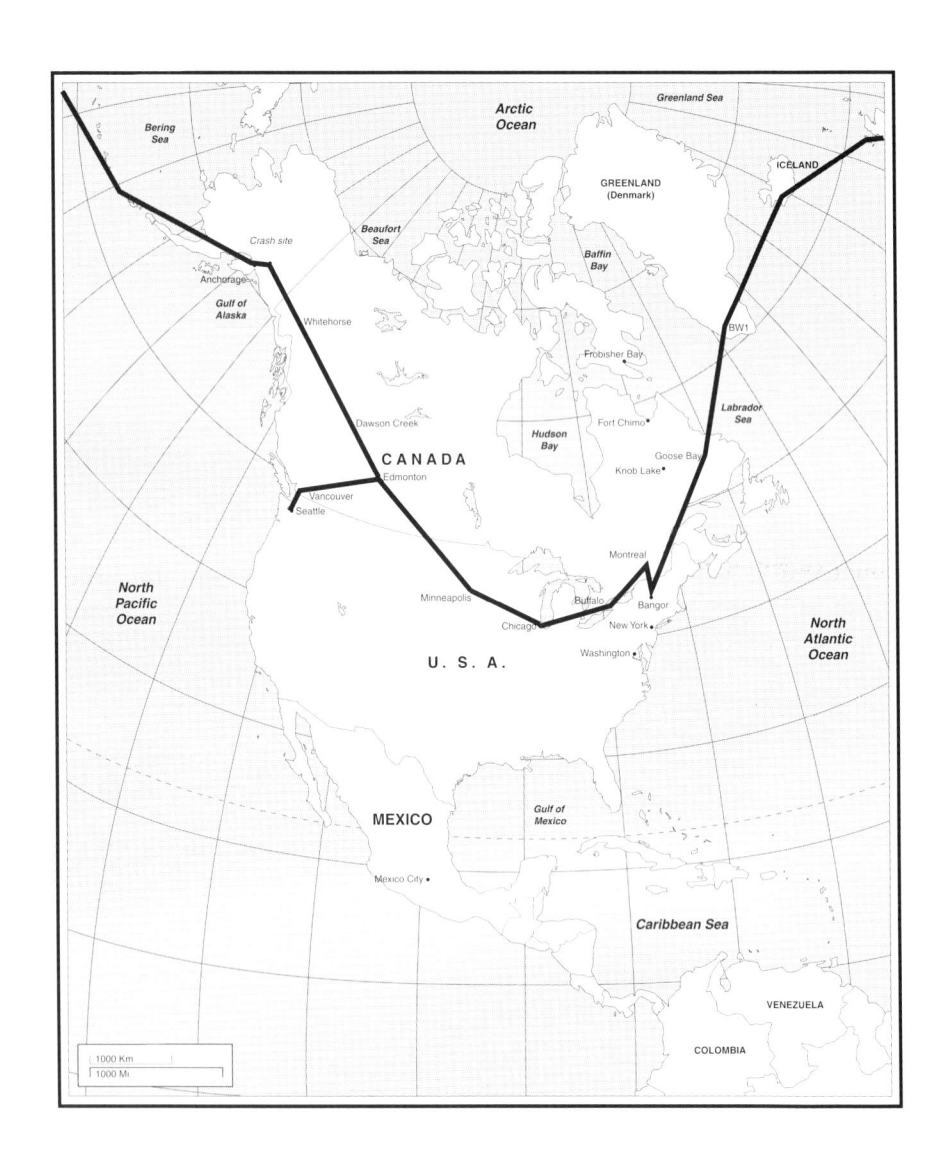

CHAPTER 32

ENTER A NAVIGATOR

Press publicity brought in a spate of calls and letters and invitations. There were some Aviation Dinners which I attended, Associated Air Lines and the Seattle Branch of the AOPA, of which I became a member. These brought me many friends with flying connections and took me to the old Sorrento Hotel to drink quite frequently in the CAVU Room. I just loved to look out high over Seattle and watch the bright lights and the neon signs doubling themselves in the Sound. To one who can scarcely remember those few occasions in childhood when I had the opportunity to see 'the bright lights of London' before the war, just the twinkling of those lights gave me endless pleasure. Really, I thought they were beautiful.

It's strange though, when you come to consider it, how much pleasure human beings get from being in a high place and looking down. Is it because we're always so earthbound and so very near the mud in which we plant our feet? We take up only five or six feet of vertical space on this earth and there is such a lot of wasted room above us. The joy of flying is increased to me a hundredfold because of the houses and the farms, or the seas and the hills, that are beneath me. I could be God when flying, I could lean over this little earth, pick up a house and put it somewhere else, widen a lake, or twist a river another way, because it's all mine. Those little cars that you can see if you fly low enough, just crawling along that model road, they're only toys, they're not real and if I fly really high and look down on the gaily-coloured display spread out so motionless beneath my wings, it could really be only a large-scale map over which I am steering. Only *I* am real, because I can go anywhere I want. I can fly in any attitude, any direction, the air will not mind.

But seriously though, most people will pay the extra sixpence to see the view from a castle tower, and was Hitler so very mad or just human to plant his home high on a hilltop and his special eyrie on the highest crag of all? How very wise it was when, in years gone by, the Japanese common man was forbidden ever to look *down* on his Emperor. How much more God-like to be watched only from below.

I also spoke at a University Flying Club, the *Wing and Rudder*, where I met a very sweet girl, Myrtle Cox, with whom I stayed after a fortnight spent with the Conrads: she and about five other girls at the University and in jobs all were roomed together in a large house. They had huge fun and I thoroughly enjoyed mucking in with them. Myrtle, when she asked me, knew full well my slender financial resources (two dimes and a button, practically) so she and the other girls arranged that I should stay for free and little Shemya, too. We put him in the garage to begin with but he cried like a baby all night so he and I shared a bed in the basement, to our mutual content. He was only a pup, three months old to be precise and he still wasn't house-trained, a fact which used to worry me a lot, but of course he was partly wild for every Husky has, or should have, wolf bred in at every third generation, and Shemya had.

I remember one occasion when Myrtle and I walked into a frightfully superior shop with fitted carpets. As we walked in, our feet sinking luxuriously to the ankles in the pile, four shopwalkers moved forward graciously to greet us, whereupon Shemya promptly made a puddle on the carpet. It was quite ludicrous the way the expressions froze on their faces as they all moved off in other directions pretending they were doing something entirely different. Myrtle and I retreated through a side door out into the street again, where we stood helpless with laughter.

Just before I left Mrs Conrad's I had several calls which I was not there to receive, from an Englishman, a Mr John Mackennan Ellis, so after a while I made an effort and called him back.

"My God! What an English accent!" was my first reaction to his voice. It sounded too terrible to be true. He wanted to be my navigator.

"But I haven't got an aeroplane yet," I exclaimed. I stalled him off with a "Maybe" and a "We'll see" and "Sure, he could ring me Saturday." We had a little chat though and he told me that he knew the Consul.

"H'm," I thought, "that might be handy," so I took his phone number. He did call me on Saturday. Would I have lunch with him? My slender financial state found me reluctant to turn down an offer of food so I said: "Yes, I should be delighted."

I knew exactly what he would be like. Terribly English, I could tell from his voice. Thirtish, rather prim and rather pompous.

When he called for me I saw I'd never been more mistaken in my life. He was tall, quite young (why, he couldn't be much older than me) and nice-looking in a rather shy and English way. I studied his profile covertly whilst he was driving. During lunch I was even more impressed. Why, he was even quite charming and we found we had a lot in common. I smiled at him happily.

Normally he was called Jack Ellis and we soon became firm friends. He had just acquired a dilapidated old Packard and had had it only a week. He just couldn't manage it properly first of all and, whilst parking the car for lunch that day on one of Seattle's many steep hills, had got into tremendous difficulties. He had to edge the car between two other cars, also parked at the kerb, and at each attempt at going forward and back he kept hooking his bumper on the bumper of the car in front and at the back, until he had created such a narrow aperture it was impossible to get a car in. Backing was never his strong point. The same thing happened one night when we tried to stop for a beer somewhere and when we thought we had finally got ourselves settled, I got out only to discover the front wheel was on the pavement.

CHAPTER 33
BUYING AND FLYING A BT-13

One night at the Sorrento somebody advised me to go and see Dr Campbell, a dentist, who owned four aircraft, a Cub, a BT-13, an AT-6 and a twin-engined Cessna.
"He'd probably give you one."
"Likely," I thought, but it won't hurt to try. If you don't ask, you don't get, though privately I thought if you *do* ask, you don't get either. Besides which, the more people who knew about me the better. There was a little rhyme I read somewhere:

"The man who has the goods to sell
And goes and whispers down a well,
Isn't so apt to collar the dollars
As a man who climbs a tree and hollers."

I searched all the telephone directories and finally cornered him and arranged that he should pick me up and take me to his home. I somehow worked myself up to an abnormal state of nervousness, rather unlike me, and I remember thinking afterwards how cruel it was of the Doc to make me sit across the room from him, lonely in a chair, and talk to himself and his wife on the sofa the other side.

I don't mind talking. I can talk with the best of them, but when you are made to expound and you can hear your own words dropping into empty space until they falter and fade away, while the other guy just listens and watches, it's a bit tough. How I ever came through the ordeal and left any impressions at all favourable, I don't know, but somehow or other, he thought I was worth helping. Oh! I'm so glad he did.

I had told him that I had received the offer of a BT-13 for 300 bucks, so he said we had better go and have a look at it, because he thought that he and his pals might manage to raise the money. I went home that night with all heaven at my feet. *[A BT-13 Vultee Valiant was a US Army Air Corps basic trainer low-winged monoplane with a 450 hp radial engine and non-retractable undercarriage; used for navigation training and instrument flying practice. – M.T.]*

We covered a lot of ground after that night. We would drive around in the car; Lester and Freda (as I learnt to call them) and the two younger children and myself, to say nothing of Shemya, would all pile into the Doc's car while we visited airfield after airfield, scrutinizing BT-13s in various stages of dilapidation. The first one I saw, the $300 one, was just corroded through and through. Everything was rusted inside and though the engine did run, it had been run only a few hours previously, I heard.

The actual models vary quite a bit, some having laminated wood tails and others laminated wood wings. I wasn't too keen on this. I wanted a metal job all the way through and this ship that I eventually bought was much the best of the whole bunch. We started it up one dark night, Jack Ellis and the Doc and I, and as the battery was out and the starter was clogged with oil (a condition we never got around to remedying) we swung it by hand. Much to its credit, it went second swing and on run-up gave quite a reasonable performance. It did not spew out oil either on the leading edge of the starboard wing, as so many of them do. I said firmly that I liked the ship. Sure, that was fine but its price was 600 dollars.

Late that night, the Doc rang up the owner, Bob Hendricks, who agreed to drop it to 500. How nice, but where was the 500 coming from? Les was very encouraging. He said he would try around his friends who were interested in aviation and see what he could do. I racked my brains for a means of raising money. I decided at long last to buy a ticket for Vancouver, where there was a hope of putting through a business deal. I tried to persuade Jack to drive me up there in his little car but he couldn't get the time off and, in any case, I had a very dangerous effect on his vehicle.

Immediately after I had met him he had been crashed into at a crossroads and the car had had to go into dock for a few weeks. He no sooner got it out and drove me to Lester's place one night when one headlamp went and he had a flat tyre. I held a torch for him while he changed the wheel with the most awkward and unresponsive gadget for jacking the car up that I've ever seen. I had hard work to hold the torch steady because I shook so with laughter as he cursed everything all round, me included, for malignant influence on his poor little car. Thereafter the car cost him abnormal sums in repairs as bits used to fall off, as on the day when the gearbox was drained and there were loud clicks and plonks as the works fell into the tin can underneath.

Wearing the dress and the coat, I took a Greyhound bus from Seattle to Vancouver. Never having gone anywhere very much by bus I was rather nervous, but bought myself some candy and cigarettes and settled down for the run. I was a bit worried about the border line and had contacted my pal in the Immigration Office so that on my return I shouldn't get locked up. That was all OK but the question was, would they let me into Canada? Due to my dire poverty I had a sneaking suspicion that I was becoming slightly unwelcome!

When we came to the border, I lined up with the rest of them. No, no luggage, just my little despatch case and I was allowed to board the bus again after a quick inspection of my passport. I breathed a sigh of relief, settled back into my seat and lit a cigarette. Everyone else had all packed in and we were just about to go when one of the Customs men climbed on to the bus and, pointing at me, declared in a loud voice that the Customs Chief wished to speak to me. I crawled out of the bus, crimson with embarrassment as everyone stared curiously at me. I was only a few inches tall when I was led to the desk of the Immigration Chief.

"So you're Mrs Morrow-Tait, are you?"

"Yes," I answered humbly.

"I'm very pleased to meet you," said the Chief; "you've had quite a trip, haven't you?"

I nearly cried with relief.

He chatted for quite a while and then let me board the bus. I stepped, chest swollen with pride, to my seat, while everyone looked most disappointed that they hadn't had the journey enlivened by me being forcibly ejected.

When I arrived in Vancouver I found to my horror that everything had misfired. All my plans had gone wrong and I was just stuck penniless in this strange town. With the one speck of wisdom left, I went to the fuel firm with whom I had a carnet, asking them if they would lend me some money. I think they really wanted to but they couldn't do it without some authority from the higher-ups

Nearly in tears I explained how broke and stranded I was and in a fit of inspiration they called in Jack Steples of the *Vancouver Daily Province*. I told him my story and how Lester Campbell of Seattle was helping me. How he said he had already got 200 dollars and I was trying to find the other 300. Jack put it out in the papers that day and took me round to the YWCA where they let me stay free on a travellers' aid scheme. I was quite overwhelmed with the friendship that they showed towards me and when the next day I received a phone call from an elderly lady offering me 300 dollars, I could just gurgle incoherently.

I went round to Jack Steples next morning in his office, only to be greeted by the news that he, too, had received an offer from a man of 300 dollars. Dear Lord, I thought, it never rains but it flipping well pours. *"To him that hath shall be given"* this time.

Then Jack, being intelligent, got down to organising things. He rang up the two prospective donors, Miss Hughes and Bob Maclean, and asked them whether they would mind my accepting both offers. It sounded bad, I know, but I needed money for fuel too. Strangely enough they both said they didn't mind a bit and thereafter we worked, Jack and I.

I was not, of course, permitted to take Canadian dollars into the States and oh, what a wangle. We went from bank to Exchange Control Commissions. We saw people, we talked to people until I was nearly desperate. All this money and I couldn't take a cent into the States. It was eventually decided that I should be permitted to take a cheque written out for the Consul, who could cash it and then dispose of the money "as he thought fit." This was only decided after two days' hard work, rushing places, making frantic telephone calls and consuming enormous quantities of *Coke*, gum and cigarettes.

On the fourth day after my arrival I sped homewards to Seattle with 20 dollars in my pocket, the remains of a gift from a very kind woman from Victoria, and a cheque for 300 dollars and a bottle of Seagrams V.O. for Jack and I to celebrate with. I think I purred all the way into Seattle. Certainly I caught myself giggling happily once or twice. At about midnight

I arrived back and took a cab to Jack's little house. I just couldn't keep the news to myself. I just had to tell somebody and I daren't wake the Doc and his wife up, for I thought they mightn't quite see eye to eye with such insuppressible joy at this time of night. Jack and I discussed everything excitedly over the whisky. Was his navigation good enough? After all, he was only a sergeant pilot on an Anson. The very first thing next morning I sent two ecstatic wires, one to Morrow and one to Mike telling them I'd be home in a month and heaven could wait. Oh! brother, how wrong can you be?

I was at the Campbell's house so much they suggested it would be easier for me if I stayed, so I packed up my duffel bag and took up residence there. How good they were to me. Shemya was already fast friends with the younger children and it was much easier to get everything organised when I was on the spot. Lester had been an instructor on BT-13s during the war and he said he would teach me how to fly it. Brave man! He paid Bob Hendricks the 300 dollars deposit and then we set to. How he managed his dental practice I can't think, because he spent many days with me, quite a few of them unavoidably wasted because the aircraft needed so much attention.

The very first thing I did was paint *"Next Thursday's Child"* on it, both sides. Then it had to be cleaned up a bit and, as the instruments were practically all useless, they had to be checked. He had to do a compass check, and the prop was smoothed out and rebalanced. One day the back tyre went, and all sorts of little things like that needed attention and held us up. We had a lot of help from volunteers though I'm afraid they all thought the work rather useless as the current rumour was that the ship would not last 500 miles.

In all, I think we did little more than three hours' flying instruction. I found it very difficult to do neat turns as the aircraft needed so much rudder and so little stick to guide it. I found it very difficult to concentrate at this period and I know I am a maddening person to teach. My mind would keep wandering away all over the place: India, Alaska. Oh, how soon could I be back in England?

And then my mind would switch to a matter which occupied a lot of my time: why should two completely unknown people give me this money? It was more understandable perhaps in Miss Hughes' case. She was elderly and alone and maybe she just wanted to help and I know that she felt sorry for the trouble that I had encountered. But then 300 dollars is a lot of money, I think. She could have bought herself many little comforts with that, which just goes to show what a wonderful person she was, that she preferred to see me fly home. But it was Bob Maclean who worried me. He was young, about thirtyish, slightly built and pleasant-looking. He could have done so much with those dollars. He afterwards had an operation anyhow, for he wasn't strong and yet he'd wanted to help me. I am ashamed to say I don't think I would have done it if I was 30, a man and unmarried.

I'm afraid I would spend every penny, but then I get little pleasure from watching, only from doing. Bob, I believe, would be living the flight with me.

Jack, too, spent several nights at the Campbells' home, for he was with us as much of the time as he could possibly get off. He would be out all day, running round doing things to the ship, getting home very late, when we would have a hasty meal or absorb renewed vigour from Freda's wonderful pick-me-up, composed of gin, coffee & ice cream. It did wonders, that, on an empty stomach, believe you me. I'm afraid the house got a little disorganised at times. I can't think how Freda managed, anyhow. The day would begin, when Jack was there, with us congregating round the open doorway of the downstairs cloakroom, where we would watch Les wash and shave whilst talking nineteen to the dozen; then while Freda was dressing the children we would grab our own ideas of breakfast from the fridge. I only cared for fruit juice, some had bacon and toast, or maybe just a shot of Scotch. It was all delightfully informal and the kitchen was a really delightful spot. I've seen some beautiful kitchens but this was really unbelievably smooth. Lester and his father-in-law had just completed making it; everything was at the same level, the sink, the stove and the tables. There was a built-in washing-up machine, a wonderful, wonderful gadget, and all the cupboards were built especially for the things they housed. It had everything a kitchen should have. I wish it had been mine.

After I had acquired some basic knowledge from my scattered half-hours of flying, I was told to do a solo circuit. I wasn't feeling any too sure of myself, not that I thought I couldn't land the ship but I just felt sort-of shy of it. It was so much bigger than I was, so I said carelessly to Jack: "Oh! it will just be a waste of gas," but he said: "No, I think you should do it," and so with a nonchalance I certainly did not feel, I climbed into the ship, asked permission from Control, and took off. My RT technique even now is a bit vague and over-chatty, due to Michael having operated this on the Proctor entirely on his own, but after a lot of "Sorry, what did you say?" on my part, and "Affirmative, repeat, affirmative," on their part, I decided the runway was clear.

I took off, only to be told just as I was airborne, whilst fumbling furiously with flaps & throttle and fine & coarse pitch, that the wind had changed and I must now land the opposite way to the way I took off. I found this highly confusing, I remember, at the time, because I didn't have to make a circuit. I was all ready to land and facing the wrong way. Boeing Field anyhow is rather a confusing airfield, because the two runways, one for light and one for heavy aircraft, run parallel with each other and after take off you always turn *away* from the other runway. I performed a neat turn, having gained about 1,000 ft, came straight in again and taxied quietly up to the hangar, where I saw Jack and a friend of ours (Art Bell, who had helped us very considerably) standing, eyes shaded, looking the other way, waiting for my return. They were looking rather worried, too;

they thought I'd taken rather long on the circuit, yet still couldn't see me coming in!

A rather harassing incident occurred one day whilst I was under instruction, for not only did one of the seals on the prop go, covering the ship and windshield with oil, but as I was staggering rather blindly over the telegraph wires near the grass field I used to practise on, I hit a duck with the base of the radio mast, causing the aircraft to become not only tarred but feathered!

Because my efforts at getting an aircraft in Seattle were greeted even from the beginning with a reasonable amount of success, the British Consul and the Immigration Authorities gave me until the beginning of April before I had to get out. The Consul was very pessimistic and made all arrangements to have me shipped home as a distressed person, and a certain amount of correspondence was passed to my husband on this subject. However, by the beginning of April I had the aeroplane and everything was lined up – or at least I thought so – but it wasn't until I tried to leave on the 5th April that I discovered the difficulties I had run into. I was exporting a military ship and I was also applying for ownership of the aircraft, which I couldn't possibly do because I was not an American citizen. With great trouble we had already filled up, with the aid of a Notary Public, an involved and intimidating form, by which I applied for ownership. This I had signed and sent off, only to discover that I couldn't own an aircraft. Jack and I decided that the CAA would obviously ignore it and, to clinch matters, Doc Campbell asked the Seattle CAA to cancel it at HQ so it would just lapse back into Bob Hendrick's name. We asked him if this was OK and after a hurried consultation with his lawyer, he reluctantly said yes.

Meanwhile, we were facing other questions. We had to get an export permit for the ship and that would take some time. We decided that as we were bound to visit Toronto where Jack's parents lived, we would call in at Buffalo, where we would arrange for the export permit to be sent. Thus as the trip to Canada would be commenced and concluded in the United States, we solved the problem of flying a BT-13 in a country where actually they are not permitted to be flown. We started to leave Seattle on Tuesday but we didn't get out until Saturday lunchtime and then we had to do a lot of hard talking. Everyone stood around trying to say goodbye to us in the warm sunshine and we didn't go and didn't go and didn't go. I think only Doc, Freda and Art Bell were left when we finally quit Seattle for Vancouver.

The Vultee Valiant purchased by Dikki. The previous owner, Bob Hendricks, is leaning against the left wing, while Dr Lester Campbell prepares to turn over the propeller; Dikki and her navigator Jack Ellis are in the cockpit. Photo: via Bob Hendricks.

Dr Lester Campbell gives some instructions to Dikki. Photo: via Bob Hendricks.

UPPER: Dr Lester Campbell with his wife Freda and their daughter, Jack Ellis and Shemya, Dikki's Husky pup.
LOWER: Don Dorothy, the bush pilot 'saviour' from Anchorage, Alaska, but without the beard (see Ch. 30).

Dikki always enjoyed the dirty jobs; here she is seen servicing the Valiant at Buffalo.

CHAPTER 34

SEATTLE–VANCOUVER–EDMONTON

I must honestly admit I was unbelievably jittery on that flight. I felt like I was pedalling a bicycle on a tightrope. I don't know why I should, but occasionally I get spells of nervousness, usually when it is quite unwarranted. I didn't fly that ship, *it* flew *me* to Vancouver and when we found the field and tried to call up the tower, our radio wouldn't work. We flew round the airfield about four times and then decided to come in. Several people had warned me to keep plenty of speed on the last turn as she was very prone to do a flick-roll into the deck.

I was so petrified with this that the first time I came into land I missed the whole runway by about 100 yards, a mistake which I tried to pass off as trying to let the tower know our radio didn't work! The second time I came in a bit fast and was just bringing the stick back to a nice three-pointer when it became jammed. Jack had my despatch case on his knee and the stick in the back cockpit was rammed up against it. I swore out aloud at Jack, not into the microphone, but so violently that he could hear quite plainly even with his headphones on.

One special modification we carried out in Seattle was turning the little shelf behind Jack into a kennel. Jack and Shemya did not mix very well and I had to keep my navigator separate from the livestock. Unfortunately Shemya was unwell on that flight and Jack had plenty to say about that, too.

After landing we checked through Customs, Immigration and Health, and that included Shemya's papers showing that he had been inoculated against rabies and distemper. They had to have rabies injections by law, the two distemper shots were just what I considered a wise precaution. We met our patient friends, Jack Stepler of the *Province*, Miss Hughes and Bob Maclean. They had waited ages for us and I felt most apologetic. We were whisked away into town, where the second cheque, Bob's, was cashed and the money handed over to us. Jack tucked it away in his money-belt, which somewhat inadequately kept up his RAF trousers. We then bade farewell to my 'angels' and were brought back to the RCAF side of the field to see about the ship.

We had already made friends with the Duty Officer, who helped us fix up for sleeping accommodation. He parked Jack in quarters there and very kindly ran me into town to his own little flat, where I was able to sleep that night because he was on duty. His wife and I went out to see Bob Maclean, who lived not very far away, though to me it seemed miles.

I was very tired with all the strain and excitement and fast talking I had done. I had a bath and exchanged my heavy old flying boots for slippers; good enough, but for some most extraordinary reason blisters, huge painful blisters, began on the balls of both my feet. I started walking but the pain was just too much. I took my shoes off – it was dark, of course – but even that didn't ease the burning of my feet. We got a little lost on the way, having gone east instead of west or something, so went back to the house where I donned a pair of moccasins. This did help a bit but even so it was only with greatest of pain that I managed to get to Bob's house, where I shed the moccasins for my slippers and hid them surreptitiously in the rose bed. I am sure I must have burbled an awful lot of trash to Bob that night for I was overwhelmingly sleepy, though he was very good to me, making me the present of an extremely accurate aircraft clock. This now resides in my kitchen, no more timing position points, only eggs and Swiss rolls.

The next morning we trotted out to where the ship was parked in a line, only to discover, ye gods and little fishes, a fuel leak. It was the sort of thing you could smell from about a hundred yards away when you stood downwind and somehow you just didn't smoke near it. I screwed the new clock into the empty socket in the back panel and then we got out screwdrivers and cushions and lay under the ship searching for the exact leak. This was very hard to find for the fluid of course dripped off the lowest edge.

In a Vultee BT-13 there are what are known as integral tanks, being nothing more than hollow wing roots flooded to the centre section. I think they are a rotten idea. The RCAF were most sympathetic; they pushed the ship into the hangar and gave us all the help they possibly could with checking the aircraft and mending the leak. Our radio was mended, our instruments made to work and much more work was done on the ship than anyone ever said. Unfortunately I opened my mouth a bit wide to the Press, saying how grateful I was for their help, and when this in turn was relayed over the radio and came to the ears of Group, the station received a stern ticking off. We heard that that evening when, after a hard day's work on those miserable tanks, they still leaked.

I was worried stiff and binding at everybody – including long-suffering Jack – who came anywhere near me. One very charming sergeant, who had more patience than I believed possible in any human being, stood by me and he and his wife put me up that night. The next morning we taxied our ship back to the Civil side of the field where once more we drained the tanks and redoped them inside. All day we worked in the spring sunshine and still those confounded tanks leaked. I learned innumerable local oaths from Jack, who had resided longer in Canada than I.

On the Tuesday, we went round asking from other people who had flown BT-13s.

"Leaky tanks?" they said; "why, they always leak. Even if you do get them sealed, you've only got to go through bumpy weather where wings flap up and down for all the seams to spring again."

Jack and I thought: "To hell with this," so we quit. We had after all got it down to about half a gallon that morning so we decided to call it a day.

We were asked to dinner that night with a local operator of light aircraft. He and his wife had a little flat and he ran us down there in his car. It was suggested Shemya should stay in the garage as livestock were not permitted in the flats, and in any case he was not housetrained. I was quite agreeable to this as his manners were always a source of worry to me.

We had a very nice dinner, after which the two men went out with a bowl of food for the pup. The door was shut but the dog was missing. Quite definitely so. I walked round and round the block, calling "Shemya" and making the familiar whistle. This must have gone on about an hour or more and not one bit of difference did it make. The only thing we did discover, apart from innumerable cats, was that some little girl had heard him barking and, being incredibly inquisitive as well as being wicked, had opened the garage door and was then surprised when he bolted.

I realised of course that, dog or no dog, the flight must go on and late that night called in on TCA who fixed me up with a crate and promised to pack the dog off to Edmonton as soon as he was found. I was reasonably confident of this as two radio stations had already broadcast the loss and we had informed the police; I had even paid his fare.

The next morning at about midday we set off to cross the Rockies. It must honestly be admitted that Jack and I were not exactly smart on that ship to start off with and, after he had told me to circle over the field, climbing to 5,000 ft, we decided it was too high and couldn't see enough because of stratus cloud, so we came down to 1,500 ft and pressed on following the river. As we neared the mountains the conditions became clearer and we climbed on up and up to 11,000 ft without any trouble; in fact I was much impressed by the ship, I had never taken her up to that altitude before.

We found our way pretty well but got tied up in more cloud again. My gyro wasn't working as well as it should have done and, not being used to the ship, I found quite a lot of trouble in keeping her on the straight and level; in fact according to Jack I was in a screaming spiral dive at one time, though personally I don't believe it, because I was watching the needle and ball pretty closely. However, I was all in agreement with Jack when he suggested we drop in at a little airfield nearby called Princeton. We beamed into the field and I was distinctly perturbed to hear coughing and spluttering noises from the engine when I throttled back. This had me puzzled for a while but it went much better when I put it into rich mixture again. *[You 'lean' the mixture as you climb higher for optimum engine performance; Dikki had forgotten to return it to 'rich' on descending. – M.T.]*

I did two cautious circuits of the field, scanning the ground for a wind-T or windsock, and came in. Because there was nobody looking I did a beautiful landing and smiled happily at the desolate countryside. Jack slid back the canopy while we were still taxying (was he sweating too?) and had to walk back afterwards to pick up the maps which had blown out. In the tiny little radio station there, we signed ourselves in and organised a truck to take us into the village

Jack and I were ridiculously happy. We really felt we had got under way now, and it's infinitely pleasurable to fly places and drop down somewhere completely unknown and land there just because you feel you want to. Maybe too it was the relief after a certain amount of tension which had been induced by a flight over such inhospitable terrain in a comparatively unknown ship. The mountains were high, black and jagged, just rough rock with no vegetation, snow in the hollows and ice on the lakes.

Jack and I were just burbling and chortling with joy that day. All the impatience gone (and how much energy one wastes in being impatient – being impatient for a quarter of an hour can set you back all day in energy), we drove down by truck into the little town of Princeton. My first impression of this little town was: "Why it's just like the town in Western movies!" There was only one hotel on the main street and it was absolutely typical of my conception garnered from the movies of a Western town in the mid-eighties. Only the women's clothes had changed – the men still wore jeans, check overshirts and even occasionally the large flat black hat. I was utterly delighted. I almost knew where to look to find everything. We piled out of the truck, Jack with his battered suitcase and me with my duffel bag. We checked in over a large mahogany counter looking somewhat like a bank, were handed keys and found our rooms. Mine exceeded all expectations: in one corner of the room was a big brass spittoon on legs on a little rubber mat – in case you missed. I had to call Jack in to have a look at this as I did not even remember having seen one before. When I had pulled up the blind and pulled back the lace curtains, I set about trying to locate the bathroom; this entailed a long search for whoever had the key; I don't think it was used much.

When we had changed we went and ate in the little café at the back of the hotel. There a quaint and somewhat unbalanced reporter cornered us but we gave him some light-hearted gen. We strolled up and down the main 'drag' and had a quick beer before we finally went back. We were firm believers in getting plenty of sleep in, particularly as we had flight-planned to Edmonton.

The next morning, bright and early, we set off for the ship in the same truck that brought us down and, with the very little fuss and bother which is only possible when taking off from a small field, we climbed into our craft and took off, to the accompaniment of loud cheering from two small boys and a dog.

We switched on to the radio range and sat back and enjoyed ourselves. *[Most air routes in Canada and the USA were marked by "radio ranges." At convenient points and most airfields an M/F radio transmitter radiated four narrow beams approximately 90° apart. An identifying two- or three-letter call sign in Morse code would interrupt the radiated signal at intervals. The pilot would tune in to and identify the desired range station and would receive a steady continuous tone if exactly on one of the beams and an "A" (•—) if on one side of the bean and an "N" (—•) if on the other. – M.T.]* Maps were available overprinted with the beam, the callsign, the radio frequency and which side the "A" and "N" would be heard. We flew at our usual 6,000 ft which of course wasn't very high as we were in mountainous country, but we followed the river valleys and I was starting to feel *au fait* with the aircraft. It was an uneventful trip, and the sky was blue though the winds were quite strong. We decided to drop in at the little town of Cranbrook where we planned to have some lunch. I was distinctly annoyed with Jack, as when I landed he thought I touched down too far down the field and slapped open the throttle again. I flew round and came in again but was definitely huffy about it. Flying was *my* job. If Jack didn't like it, he could get out and walk. However, I soon forgot about it. We scrambled over the railway line out into the Highway, where we got a lift into the town; this was quite easy to arrange as the blisters on my feet made it difficult for me to walk without a limp.

In the café I also enjoyed the pleasure of seeing a man pick up a paper with a photograph of me in it and discuss me with his friend, without realising I was sitting just behind him.

At 2.15 we took off again, following along the valleys as before. It was more bumpy now, due to the heat of the day causing up-draughts, but the sky was absolutely clear of clouds and it was warm and bright. We nearly turned up the wrong Pass – it was just as well I noticed in time that it was a dead end for it was very narrow. Crow's Nest Pass was the one we were aiming for and as we flew in through it I remembered a movie I had seen many years before about the finding of the Pass, which led to a route through the wild Canadian Rockies. They were very majestic, high and stern but somehow a lot less cruel than those jagged Alaskan peaks. Soon they became less, the hills were lower and more rounded and the conditions were less bumpy. Then suddenly the hills ended and the level prairies stretched out endlessly beyond and to every side of us. Over Calgary we switched on to the Edmonton beam and flew a dull never-ending course over the flat monotonous country.

I was tired by now; the headphones pressed far too tightly onto my ears and they felt they were meeting in the middle. My neck felt stiff and my back ached and Jack kept binding about keeping to the right of the beam, which I thought quite an unnecessary refinement. There were no aircraft for miles around, nor cloud. After what seemed endless time, the flat field of Edmonton came into sight. We circled and landed, and taxied up to the tower. I was very pleased in many ways because I had met so many 'doubting Thomases' in Edmonton, people who said I would never get anywhere and were not all that glad when I did. I'd show 'em, I thought, as I plodded up the stairs to close my flight plan.

The first thing I did was to make enquiries as to whether Shemya had yet been found. No? Well I guess it was a bit early. We had a little money at this time so we decided to stay at the Airlines Hotel. This was a very pleasant hotel, built like a log cabin but quite pleasantly finished inside. The rooms were rather expensive, unfortunately, but they included a shower and an electric blanket – the first I'd ever met. This quite defeated me, as first of all I turned it too high and nearly fried myself, then turned it too low so that I shivered with cold, added to which, having never used any of these advanced comforts, and not being any too sure of their reaction, I got out of bed every time I wanted to have a drink, in case I was electrocuted!

That evening we paid our respects to the OC of the airfield on the RCAF side as we wished to borrow maps and ask about facilities on our way north. You see, being a very determined and conscientious person, I was firmly determined to complete the flight down to the absolutely last half-mile; thus in order to do that I had to fly into Alaska to the scene of the crash before the trip could really be considered started.

CHAPTER 35
EDMONTON–TANACROSS–EDMONTON

The next morning, a Friday, we taxied the ship across to my friends, Northwest Industries; to Gordon Best I explained the fuel situation. This aircraft carried 120 US gallons in its two wing tanks and I thought it quite possible to install one of the auxiliary tanks from the Proctor into the empty belly of the ship under my feet. We rushed around with measures for a while, wondering if such a thing was possible, but decided that the tank would be the wrong shape and would have to be altered. The firm, we were told, would help us to the extent of about 250 dollars, out of friendship and for the advertisement, such as it was. Mr Pitfield, the managing director, and the generous help his firm gave, became a very important factor in the success of the flight.

We talked it over but unfortunately we had arrived at just the wrong time. Friday was only a half-day, Sunday was Easter and Monday was also a holiday. This then would hold everything up until Tuesday. We in our impatient foolishness said we couldn't wait until Tuesday and, if they would kindly change the battery, we would press on northwards straight away and get the tank fitted on our return journey.

After two nights spent in the Airlines Hotel, we became more cautious of our dollars and spent the next night in a rooming house, struggling up at the break of day – quite unnecessarily, as we couldn't locate the battery – and we didn't get off finally until 8.50. Delays before take-off I find exceptionally maddening. There is nothing you can do and it always takes a long time to get through paperwork.

We had already made all arrangements with Northwest Air Command, by whom we were properly briefed, as to emergency measures; flying up to Alaska is taken seriously by the RCAF, as well it should be, because its very loneliness makes this a dangerous route. We were shown the emergency landing grounds, told what to do should anything happen and we were made to hire emergency kit from Hargreaves & Dick, a local firm. This firm, run by two enterprising and tough bush flyers, deals in safety equipment and, when you hire one of their kits, they guarantee to go and look for you should you crash, then they parachute down and look after you. We got to know these two men quite well later on and many wonderful tales they told us of frozen adventures.

We were allowed according to the rules to fly to Fort St. John by beam but thereafter all single-engine aircraft had to follow the Alcan Highway. North of Edmonton the prairie seemed to have dwindled into low scrub and lakes and by the time we got to Fort St. John it was stunted forest. It took us quite a while to find Fort St. John for, the beam station not being quite on the airfield, somehow we were just blind enough to miss it. However, we touched down at 11.30 and, after nobly refusing drinks from the Sergeant's Mess, had lunch and set forth again for Fort Nelson.

This was quite a short run, only 1 hour and 50 minutes. I was amused to find how well I recognised the Highway; it looks very small and winding, lonely among the wide undulating country.

We landed at Fort Nelson mid-afternoon and decided to call it a day. We had dinner with the CO that night and stayed in a Ministry of Transport hostel.

On again next morning, we were in a burning hurry. We set off for Watson Lake. There wasn't any navigating for Jack to do – though he liked to follow along the map. The journey was tedious to begin with but soon the road entered into the mountains proper again. They towered on either side of us, dwarfing us to the size of a passing crow. Maybe I did shudder a bit when I first entered their jagged maw. I have a very wholesome respect for snow-clad mountains, particularly when you fly through narrow passes.

Jack had great fun calling up Smith River in passing, for that station had been closed for two years. We made one mountain valley only just in time and as we turned round and looked back afterwards, it was filled with cloud. The weather was getting decidedly worse and we wondered what lay ahead. We got into a pretty nasty patch of low cloud near Watson Lake and in trying to dodge it we got off the beam for a short time. However, we soon picked our way up and the radio range gave us a helping hand when we were looking for the field. This was just a peninsula jutting out into a lake and we soon found it and landed, both of us pretending loudly that we hadn't been in the least bit frightened.

Here the snow lay thick on the ground, though sloshy and, having parked our ship and closed our flight plan, we looked around for fuel. We were utterly appalled – it was 98 cents a gallon. My God! we thought, dollars won't last very far if fuel is as expensive as this, but as we were told it was cheaper further north in White Horse, we decided to take only a safe minimum.

We were told we could not go on as there were low clouds and snow storms over the Pass so we tucked ourselves again into DOT headquarters and played cards. All the Air Force Base was built of logs, even the control tower, and Jack, who had never been as far north, was beginning to be quite impressed. That evening, amusing ourselves with cards and silly games on bits of paper, we got to know each other a lot better. This was away from the sophistication and the bright lights of Seattle. I think we were both beginning to respect each other's capabilities, for though neither of us was very experienced in aviation we were both determined, for different reasons, to put up a good show. We had had an evening of mutual confessions in Seattle, wherein I told him that I had only about 200 hours to my credit, and he told me that he had about the same and that his navigation was only up to pilot nav. standard, having trained on Avro

Ansons. When remembering it now I think God must have tempered the wind.

Soon Jack got into the spirit of the thing. This was the wild, wild Yukon, and Jack and I suddenly turned wild and Yukon too, as played by Hollywood. We looked the part, wearing Service pants and boots, and that night while playing cards, Jack started talking out of the corner of his mouth in blasphemous Canadian slang. I'd seen him rag around in Seattle looking American by disguising himself in a quite incredible hat but this was all new and huge fun to me and I laughed like a drain. We played pontoon, Jack holding the card up to his face but never taking his eyes off me, pretending that I would knife him if he did. The whole thing was incredibly foolish and light-hearted and tremendous fun.

We wandered down that night to the Mess known as Dan Magrew's Saloon, complete, of course with picture of Dan Magrew on the outside. All the Messes were called that, I was told, and in time it started to get a bit confusing.

From Watson Lake onwards Jack was known as "Jake, one of the 49-ers," and for quite a while we childishly assumed new personalities. Not, of course, when we were flying, for piloting, I always found, is one of the most impersonal of actions. Sometimes in times of stress I would tell myself firmly: "I am a machine. There is no 'I'. My hands and my eyes watching the instruments are just mere mechanical contrivances between the instruments and the controls. I am a machine, there is no 'I'." I used to particularly say this whilst cloud-flying when, at that time in particular, however tilted and upside down you may feel, the instruments know best.

From then onwards was a mad whirl. None of the flights were long. White Horse to Snag, 2 hours 13 minutes. From Snag we circled the spot where I believed I had crashed, 10 miles off from Tanacross, then we flew south as in a dream to White Horse, Watson Lake again. Here, foolishly, I was attacked by a wild beast.

Some airmen were chasing a mouse in Dan Magrew's saloon. I caught it, picked it up and put it into an empty barrel. The men leant over and watched the thing – much too scared to touch it, I noticed. There it stayed until I had finished my drink and was going to return to my quarters but, thinking it unkind to leave it there all night, I picked it up to put it outside, whereupon the nasty little ingrate bit me on my thumb. This swelled up and I felt no-end foolish when I reported to the sick quarters that I thought my finger was poisoned because I had been bitten by a mouse.

However, nothing serious occurred and, flying fast and furious down the eternal and inevitable and exasperating Highway, we stopped at Fort Nelson and then again at Fort St. John. The Sergeants' Mess had promised us a party there and we were determined to be in on it. We were tired with our endless little hops and I used to get very stiff sitting in the aircraft. Jake could move around a bit more than I could but, to compensate, the hot air never got back to him and several times he complained of navigator icing.

As we came in to Fort St. John Field I just hadn't the patience to do a circuit; very bad piloting, I know, but I just made my let-down on track and came in: I needed that rum & *Coke.*

We received an awful lot of kindness here. Everyone was more than good to us and the Sergeants' Mess, bless 'em, subscribed to pay for the filling of our fuel tanks, a thing that was really appreciated, as were the canned foods with which we were sent away, for we were really stony broke and had lived on emergency rations quite a bit on this part of the flight. It was very lucky we had them but RCAF emergency rations are only for the very hungry, for having been packed in a cardboard container for so long, they taste just of cardboard. The chocolate and the crackers can only be distinguished one from the other by their texture, and in the larger kind of parcel you get a small can of meat of a very pronounced and piercing taste, the sort of thing you can't forget for a couple of days; still, it was all experience. We had spent all our money on buying fuel and you can guess our absolute horror when one morning at Watson Lake, I think it was – certainly it was one of these places where fuel was very expensive – we found that the tanks had leaked 5 gallons overnight. We really did stand there, rooted to the snow with horror and tongue-tied, until Jake whispered "Jesus wept" in anguished tones. It was at a time when we really needed five dollars, even five cents was important.

At Fort St. John we stayed with Flying Officer Peter Gilham and his wife and with a very charming Sergeant and his wife, whose name unfortunately I have completely forgotten. I had tried to clean the aircraft with aviation spirit but the weather stains on the metal just wouldn't come off, so I decided that as I couldn't have a nice clean shiny ship I would exaggerate its crumminess. So that Sunday morning Peter and I got down with paint brushes and, whilst I painted patches apparently pinned onto the ship, triangular tears with large stitches, and a large inartistic cobweb on the front, he put *Morrow-Tait Airlines* in beautiful sprawling lettering, with the 'N's and the 'S's back-to-front, underneath the cockpit; in due course got added under this: *"They also serve . . ."*

Then other people started writing on the ship. Names there were in number. One guy wrote *Charlie* in big green letters when we went to Edmonton; he had to break off before he could write his surname because the foreman came. As time went by, the patches became bright-coloured, spotted and striped, and under *Morrow-Tait Airlines* was written *"Try TCA."* In the course of time, there got doped on airline luggage labels and a beautiful one of a beer bottle, *Old and Mellow,* several *Handle with Care* and two large *Fragile.* But more about that anon.

CHAPTER 36
EDMONTON

We got to Edmonton on the 24th April, absolutely exhausted, and we were directed by the tower to park our ship at the emergency equipment firm of Hargreaves & Dick. They welcomed us cheerfully as they always did, and to my timid request for floor space in their offices that night they were very generous. They gave us the keys and told us we could make quite good sleeping quarters out of piles of canvas bags they were engaged in manufacturing at that time. They also gave us the key to their little store, where they had an iced drink machine and crackers of various kinds.

The next thing I did was to find Shemya, who had arrived the day before. Oh, was I glad to see him, though I was anxious because he looked so thin and so sad. We tied him onto a long piece of string and, after a cold supper of canned food we had brought from Fort St. John, went out into the town, where we borrowed two blankets from Yvonne and then trudged homeward, wishing we had enough money to stay in the Airlines Hotel. We used to watch their neon sign, looking like a propeller, which performed several revolutions and then turned into the words "Airlines Hotel." Jake and I would walk around the airfield, watching this sign and chanting to ourselves: "Airlines Hotel bzz . . . Airlines Hotel bzz . . ."

I chose the inner office, and there I carried a row of canvas bags which I combined together to form various combinations of discomfort on the floor. Eventually Shemya and I (sure we slept together, why waste warm dog?) curled ourselves up and slept restlessly until dawn, when we were woken all too early by the morning sunlight. I never mind sleeping on floors too much, possibly because I am plump and carry my own cushioning, but Jake hated it. He chose the table in the machining room on the theory that as the table sagged considerably with his weight, it would form a curved surface upon which to lie, and thus be less uncomfortable. As the night wore on, he found this only too untrue and, according to what he told me, he tried sleeping practically everywhere in that room during that night, because he was thin on the hips. We washed in a somewhat scummy basin and breakfasted off a can of cold Irish stew. We did make some tea for ourselves, though.

We slept in the offices for four nights and we had many peculiar meals. I nearly laughed myself silly one day watching Jake eat canned spaghetti off the end of my very sharp sheath knife, though Jake could see nothing funny in it at all.

During the day we worked at Northwest Industries, where the ship was now hangared, and they were getting under way with plans for a fuel tank. After much consultation they had decided that it would be easier to make up a completely new tank and, after removing the cold air vent pipe and one strut (which didn't seem particularly important), installed the whole bang shooting match under my feet. This would amount to 60 US gallons, which we thought would be adequate. While the ship was in the hangar we looked it over and had a chat with the Chief Engineer, an Englishman, John Portlock, who said he wouldn't sign out anything on a ship as crummy as that.

"Oh! come," I said, a little hurt.

My admiration for the aircraft was very great indeed and now I was more used to her and had seen her face the kind of weather when you can "hear the wind whistling through the clouds" in Alaska, I was prepared to back her against all comers. As a matter of fact, I think that when you have full belief in your aircraft, when you really trust it, it not only seems to perform better but saves you a lot of energy expended in anxiety. I trusted that ship wholeheartedly, which I must confess I never did with the Proctor.

Jake and I knew nothing about the aircraft but, while we were in Edmonton, we decided we'd clean and overhaul and check up on everything that was possible. John Portlock came back, thumb between the pages of a book stating the mandatory requirements necessary on this type of machine. Then we set to. First we checked the inspection panels and looked inside to see what sort of condition the cables were in. John had said they were thick with rust but we found that, when wiped with an oily rag, the reddish dust wiped off, leaving shiny smooth cable.

We put in new under-wing bolts and new hose connections on the engine, and I undertook myself the heartbreaking job of getting all the plugs out. The front ones were easy enough, a piece of cake, but you had to remove practically half the engine to get at the back ones, at least that's what I thought, as oily and tired, I removed innumerable baffle plates. The plugs were pretty good, but we had them sand-blasted. I cleaned whatever I could inside the engine and checked the strainers, getting infinite pleasure, as many people do, in pottering, wrench in hand and greasy to the elbows, over an elderly engine. Jake teased me no end, for whereas he always chose the comparatively clean jobs, I plumbed straight for anything that was really greasy.

A very present help in time of trouble was more money sent to us by Bob Maclean and Miss Hughes from Vancouver whereupon, deciding the strain of sleeping on the floor was too great, we moved into a cheap hotel right next door to the railroad roundhouse and only a few hundred yards from the airfield across the lane. It wasn't much of a place, of course, but it was somewhere to lay our weary heads and it was cheap; also Shemya was allowed to sleep in my room, and that was just as well for he had got distemper. Despite the injections he'd got it, but definitely. Here we finished up our canned food and lived sparingly, very often on canned meat and crackers. A certain amount of money had to be spent in having our pants cleaned after a while for, speaking for my own, with engine oil and long wear, it was about time too.

We were in Edmonton about three weeks due entirely to the slow workings of the Department of Transport. First of all, the drawings for the tank had to be approved and the firm wanted to make sure this was done before they started building and making them up. Then there were letters and arguments about the validity of the Certificate of Airworthiness. According to what they said, any major alterations which affected the flight characteristics of the aircraft invalidated the C. of A. Therefore they said the ship could not be flown in Canada. I got most gloriously tied up in all this and, looking back on it now, I seem to have been remarkably nitwitted; all I understood at that time was that I was directed to the States.

"Go direct to the States," I was told, "by the shortest possible route." (Remember playing *Monopoly*? "Go to jail, go directly to jail. Do not pass 'Go.' Do not collect £200.")

Strange to relate, we spent about three weeks working quite hard on that ship. True, some of the time we pottered and some of the time we painted coloured patches, but at times I enjoyed myself so much just working on the engine that I started enquiring how long it took to be a fitter. I thought to myself I might take up 'fittering' when I came back. On Saturdays, after the men had gone, or on Sundays, Jake and I would dive into the scrap metal bins where dural of peculiar shapes had been discarded and there, amid the machines and the machine shop, we would be absorbed for hours using every machine that moved – and many strange machines there were, making frilly edges and things.

Jake reminded me of the mountain in Aesop's Fables, which groaned so prodigiously and produced a mouse, for after hours of concentrated labour, he proudly showed me a hook he had made in dural, on which to hang the map-board on the ship when he wasn't using it. I, spurred on to fresh endeavours, produced after a whole afternoon a little narrow shelf upon which I could rest my left elbow, keeping my hand on the throttle. This also had a hook (though I must admit it wasn't quite such a good hook as Jake's) upon which I could hang my microphone – which hitherto hung on the right side and necessitated a change of hand on the stick, a complicated arrangement when landing.

On Saturday afternoons we would bath and change and go out to dinner in the town. Some of the time this existence was incredibly tedious and humdrum and Jake and I would occasionally bawl each other out.

Shemya, poor little mite, got worse instead of better. I took him to the vet several times, spending dollars again, but though I nursed him and cossetted him and, when he could only lap, fed him on eggs and milk, he didn't get much better; then one day I noticed that his beautiful blue eyes were filming over and becoming glassy, so I had him put away. I nearly cried my heart out all day, pausing only to curse myself periodically for a sentimental fool.

CHAPTER 37
EDMONTON–MINNEAPOLIS

For many days after the completion of the work on the ship we could not take off as we were still grounded. Quite a lot of the work we had done had been signed out, but even so we were only allowed to fly straight to Great Falls, Montana. The permit came through on the 17th May and we had a sudden scrounge round trying to acquire US dollars in exchange for Canadian ones without paying more for them. We scooped a fair amount, about 60 bucks, which is all we had left, and on the 18th cleared the Customs, but were held up by the DOT who would not pass the radio. One of the valves had gone and we couldn't get the radio range from far enough distance away to please them.

I had my troubles that day. In the back of the aircraft was a canvas-walled cupboard which was opened from the outside by a metal door that you lifted up. This had a small gadget to keep it from falling down, but on a windy day it had an infuriating habit of slapping you on the head just when you were already wasting a lot of temper wrestling with a stubborn and overloaded duffel bag, which just fitted the compartment. Whilst holding the lid up for Jake, I was absolutely shaken with laughter seeing him frantically wresting our obstinate baggage from a hugging hold, till the tears ran down my face in pure joy. I tactfully refrained from making any noise for it is an incredibly infuriating process to the struggler thus employed.

A few days before our departure we acquired by devious means one large size DF loop – but without any means of fitting it, one Bendix DF gauge – with no possible means of connecting the two, a fire extinguisher, some First Aid equipment, a bag of red flares, an old straw hat with a hole in it and one empty packet of W.D. & H.O. Wills – genuine "wild woodbines."

Whilst checking the radio the day before we left Edmonton, I slid open the canopy, and when I rose briskly to my feet to get out I suddenly found it wasn't fully open. The result was painful, to say the least, and though now the bald patch the size of a shilling has grown over, I still carry the lump. I felt very sick for the rest of the day, and stretched myself out in the cot in the ladies' room, pecking disinterestedly at an Erle Stanley Gardner.

After a frightful flap, we got off at 7.10 in the morning. That meant getting up at 5 because there is always so much work to be put in before actual take-off. I can't say I wasn't glad to get away at last, and as we climbed over the little stratus clouds and flew south to the States I breathed a sigh of relief. At least the CAA are not as severe as the DOT, I thought.

Away from the world, Jake and I had a little discussion. We definitely decided that we weren't going to Great Falls but that we would check in at Cutbank, Montana, where we hoped we would meet fewer officials and less trouble. I was getting so confused now with the rules and regulations that I wasn't sure whether my Certificate of Airworthiness was valid or not in the States. The belly tank was scarcely noticeable from outside so who was to know our C. of A. was invalid, if that's to say it was? I wasn't particularly anxious to make enquiries because I didn't particularly want to know the answer. We touched down at Cutbank at 10.15. We were getting into a very nervous stage and were very official-shy. However, we put on a bold front and checked with Immigration, who quite willingly gave me a month. We taxied over to the hangar, where the American Air Force greeted us with such heartwarming gusto we could scarcely tear ourselves away.

Whilst we were there, a couple of awkward phone calls came in, to which I replied politely but firmly: "Yes, we have a Certificate of Airworthiness," but that wasn't their trouble, they were perfectly certain I hadn't got a flying licence. I had two, English and American, which I produced proudly, and at 12.35 we took off for Devil's Lake, North Dakota, intending to drop in on our friend Doc Toomai.

Another reason was that if there was going to be any trouble, and there always is wherever I go, I wanted to get as far east as possible before it started.

We didn't make Devil's Lake though. The shadows were lengthening, so we dropped in at Williston, North Dakota. The runway was only a track marked out in the grass and we did about three circuits whilst we had a heated discussion as to which was the runway most into wind. This happened all too frequently as a matter of fact, particularly when the runways were not marked.

"What, that one there, you mean?"
"Yes, that one."
"You mean the one parallel with us now?"
"No, that one, *that* one, you clot."
"You're on your downwind leg now."
"No, I'm on my base leg."
"Not that one, you fool."
"Well, *which* one?"

We were tired but rather pleased with ourselves when we landed at Williston. We had covered quite a lot of ground that day, snow-sprinkled or sandy infertile stuff, but we had moved, and tomorrow night we should be at Minneapolis (*d.v.*). We put the ship in line with the others on the grass, clambered out, stretched out creaking limbs and sniffed the sweet fresh air. Silence always seems unbearably lovely to start off with after the constant drone or "the frying sound" of the intercom and the da-dit of the beam. I hung up on the radio aerial the baby clothes we had acquired in Fort St. John and of which Jake so heartily disapproved, still it looked nice and homely, I thought; you only needed an aspidistra in the tail....

We got a lift into the town, checked in at the little wooden hotel, and then we sat and had a chat.

"Jake," I said, "we've got to get some publicity. We're practically flat broke and we need help pretty badly. We can't get help unless people know we're coming and we've just got to get a write-up somehow."

"What are you going to do?" said Jake. "Sock a cop over the jaw or throw a brick into a window?"

"No," I said, "we'd better go and tell the paper."

"We can't do that," said Jake.

"I know we can't," I agreed miserably, "but I'll have to."

I enquired of the proprietor where the local paper lived and we walked along the street to the news building. I pounded on the door but the place looked pretty deserted. Jake started protesting loudly again; he said he wanted his dinner and I said: "Well, maybe the Press will give us one."

He was very sceptical and kept asking me what I was going to say. I told him to shut up and think about a steak. He had just about reached the state when he pretended to be someone else entirely different in sheer embarrassment when the door opened and I was asked what I wanted. There ensued a very embarrassing explanation, I must confess, but eventually I was allowed in and another reporter was rung up. I gave them as good a story as I possibly could and when things got a bit warmer, Jake joined in too. How glad I am now that I did screw my courage up and insist to the disbelieving, scowling face which peeped around the door that I was flying round the world.

We had several drinks that night and the most tremendous steak I've ever seen. Jake and I ate and ate and in fact we overate, and Jake was sick next morning; I wondered why he took so long to dress. We almost kissed our Press friends goodnight and they promised to take us up to the field the next morning. We were up betimes and consumed a can of pineapple juice. Funny, neither of us felt like any breakfast. We were a trifle disconcerted by having to cart the fuel in cans to the ship from an outhouse but soon we were filled up and we took off for Bismarck. There was a beam at Bismarck and very little navigation was necessary. We were having trouble though with our transmitter, which wouldn't transmit. We landed there at 10.50 and refuelled.

The Press had already got cracking by this time for I had to speak to one lot down the telephone, doing a recording for the broadcast by telephone. I was just tickled pink by a bouncy little man who rushed up to me when I was sitting on the mainplane, hand oustretched and an eager smile of greeting on his face, announcing: "I'm Moses from the *Sun*." I really didn't know what he meant for a moment.

We put some more oil in the oleo-leg, which had a bad habit of sinking down at rather inopportune moments, thus causing two- instead of three-point landings. Then we fuelled up, taking off at 12.20 for Minneapolis.

We flew over miles and miles of chequered country, endless roads – north-south and east-west, which covered the country like a chess board. We got a little lost on this flight due, Jake said, to a town being marked on the wrong end of a lake on his maps, and we had to fly down low and look at the name of a nearby town, so conveniently displayed on its water tower; having pin-pointed ourselves, we climbed up and continued on our way – we weren't off track. I was getting more & more fidgetty and more & more sore and cramped. I handed the stick to Jake for a bit while I stretched my feet, took my headphones off and hung them up, rubbed my ears, combed my hair, ate a piece of candy and got out a new piece of gum and tried to compose myself into a better frame of mind. But for all that I was very glad when Jake said: "Well, it's somewhere over there."

We tried to contact the tower, without success, but joined in on the circuit, listening intently to a few impolite words about "an unknown BT-13 on the south-west corner without radio." We took our turn and came in and taxied up to a convenient place. Here to my great joy, hordes of reporters pressed forward.

"Jake," I squeaked with excitement, "it *was* worthwhile after all. We'll never get anywhere if we don't have publicity."

Actually, it is awfully difficult to get out of your aircraft nonchalantly under the eyes of the cameras; you either grin sheepishly at them, a thing I hate to do, or else you ignore them entirely, which always seems to me to be bad manners. As soon as we had coped with the Press, we were told to wait for a message from the State Department. This was nothing more or less than a simple statement to the effect that we were grounded and no explanation was offered us. We took it philosophically, both of us saying: "Well, at any rate we have got this far." We got driven into town and parked in quite a pleasant hotel, not too flashy but better-class than the type we had been staying in.

Our first reaction was to bath, change and go out for a drink. We knew we had time before us, for this was Friday evening and State Departments don't work Saturdays or Sundays. Jake knew Minneapolis a bit for he had spent a leave there, so we had our first drink in the Dome, which he remembered from old, and moved on from there. My, my, but it was good to buy a drink from over a bar again.

We had just spent three weeks in Alberta, which has a most peculiar drinking system. Liquor, hard liquor that's to say, may only be bought from the Government-controlled liquor store, of which there are only two in the town and they shut at 9 – or is it 8, some awful time like that? Beer may be bought from bars but you have to be seated at a table before you buy it and women may only drink with women and men with men . . . dull, isn't it? I think that is an absolutely outlandish plan for adults. I know it's to stop drunkenness, but you find there is so much illicit drinking in parked cars smooching with your girl friend, or hurried rushes to the cloakroom for your flask; or else on a Saturday night, when you've got your wages, you dive out for a crock and you and your pals sit in your hotel room in a thick atmosphere of smoke and finish the bottle (or bottles). I saw far more drunkenness in Alberta than I did in Buffalo, or Seattle, where you can drink *ad lib*.

CHAPTER 38
MINNEAPOLIS–CHICAGO

The next day, Saturday, we didn't even try to do any business or visit any of the Government Departments. We knew we would find no one there for they're firm believers in the 'long weekend.' The weather was decidedly mild and, as I had only the one woollen frock, Jake and I after much contemplation decided I should buy a thin blouse and skirt. We also agreed to skip lunch and have a couple of drinks at the Five O'Clock Club instead. Lord knows we only had a few drinks each and the clothes were cheap enough, but the money flew as money always does, so that evening we just bought cheap seats at a movie, which we saw for the sake of old times – *Casablanca*.

On Sunday we both went to Mass and spent the rest of the day loitering around. It's not quite so heartbreaking wasting time when there's two of you but we were pretty well bored at this delay. We walked round the town quite a bit, eating mainly at the cheap cafés which would entail quite a walk to fill in the time. I was much amused by a hock shop near the hotel which showed in the window a double-barrelled shotgun painted white, bearing a card inscribed "For Weddings."

After an early night we plunged into negotiations with the Customs, a senior official made a few phone calls and, to our intense surprise, word came though that we could go. Of course we complained bitterly of their "outrageous behaviour" but were secretly overjoyed that this was all and that we were free to go. As a sop to our complaints, and to smooth our ruffled feelings, we were granted a car and driver in which to do our business with the oil companies. We were flat broke again and were distinctly perturbed as to how we should obtain fuel and pay for it. We had only enough dollars to buy full tanks out of Minneapolis and we were rather worried as to the possible bouncing of the cheque which was to cover half the hotel bill. Jake wrote it on his bank in Seattle and he wasn't any too sure as to the state of his account. We were distinctly perturbed. Despite my eloquence (born of a tortured spirit) to the Shell Oil Co, they just wouldn't give us free fuel. Can't say I blame them, you know, but we would have been fools not to try. We gave it as big as we could to the Press and we had a call from one of the Chicago papers asking us in which field we would land and arranging a pick-up point, at one of the innumerable firms bordering Chicago's big Civil Airfield.

Minneapolis Tower was a bit chary of our going off when we could only receive on our radio and not transmit. We swore it was just that the battery was down so they let us out. We were getting rather to the state where we would swear that the moon was green cheese and convince ourselves. It was an easy flight, of course, we just followed the beam, but no amount of calling up on Jake's part and fiddling with the radio would enable us to emit one squeak. We didn't know quite what to do. Here was this ginormous airfield, one of the busiest in the States, and we had an appointment to land on it and we needed every bit of publicity we could get if we wanted another meal. We dithered for a while and I told Jake we had better go in. We tuned in to the tower and started circling, indicating that we wanted to land, while Jake looked all ways at the same time in case of trouble. To begin with, the tower was either dumb with horror or maybe they just didn't notice us, and then they started making rude remarks about "a dirty silver BT-13 on the south-west corner" and started warning all and sundry of our unwanted presence. The tower then tried calling me and told me to waggle my wings if I was receiving them. I dutifully waggled. In fact I waggled frantically and tried to indicate that I was coming in. I heard no more and decided they must have understood so, choosing the biggest runway of the three which lay into wind, we swooped in over the tower and landed. It was rather unfortunate that the wind lay in that direction because neither Jake nor I saw the Very pistol firing a red light beneath our wings. I don't know why they should have wanted to stop us, for the runway was perfectly clear, but they were just hopping mad when I landed.

Immediately after the ship had trailed to a halt it seemed that every vehicle on the field came screaming towards us, all the drivers gesticulating in wildly different directions where I must go. I taxied through to the pre-arranged hangar with the Press convoy where I made a call to the tower, explaining my defunct radio and giving a soft answer while they tore strips off me for my negligence and incompetence.

I always found it very difficult to appear natural in front of all the cameras and what-have-you, for if I really was natural I'd be wearing a soft and soppy grin on my face, for I always had an intense desire to giggle. This looked so unutterably horrible that I would force myself to look where the cameras weren't and retain a perfectly solemn face and, when I could no longer cower in the cockpit with a reasonable excuse, leap smartly out and dive under a wing. Besides which, if I had my way, I would always fly in a dress or shorts, but as I would have needed an inexhaustible supply as I rarely stayed long enough to get my clothes washed or cleaned, it was very much out of the question, and I had to wear the inevitable Army pants, check woollen shirt and flying boots. I grant you pigtails looked a big incongruous but they were more comfortable, even wearing headphones. My flying boots had by this time, due to the warmer weather, become pungently insanitary and when I removed them, they had instantly to be confined in a cupboard and only released at the last possible moment. To leave them lying around the room was really more than I could bear. But you can't wash sheepskin when it's inside a boot.

We bummed a ride in the last Press car going back into town and they dropped us at a building which they said housed the British Consulate. We shouldered our bags and piled out, only to discover that it had since moved. However, we tracked it down in due course, only to be told – inevitably –

that however broke we were we could expect no help from HM Government. In vain we pleaded that if we had no money we would have to sleep on a park bench. I was worried, but somehow or other a woman reporter had discovered where we were and I took a call in the outside office. After a little natter she said she would like to see us and we waited around until she arrived. We explained our plight to her – we just didn't have a bean – and she said she would see what she could do. She called the Hotel Sherman, where they run a breakfast radio programme called *Welcome Travelers*. They agreed they would like us on their programmes and said we could stay for a couple of nights. We were wildly excited and on thinking back I can still feel that thrill of pleasure when I was shown to my room at the Sherman Hotel. With pleasant furnishings, soft lights, a wide inviting bed, and a real bathroom all of my own, to say nothing of the built-in radio, it seemed to me the acme of worldly wants. Unfortunately we didn't have enough money to tip the porter, so with assumed nonchalance we waited until he had hovered out of sight, after which I remember rushing to Jake's room, screaming with excitement and doing a little impromptu dance in front of the window out of pure joy. This was Chicago.

When my excitement had worn a little quieter, I went back to my own room, shut my boots in the cupboard and proceeded to undress and bath, emitting ecstatic sighs of sheer content. I called up on the telephone to have the radio switched on in my room and while I bathed listened to dance music. I distinctly remember hearing for the first time *Riders of the Sky*. Having bathed and showered, turned on all the lights, tried all the chairs and finally dressed myself, I pounded on Jake's door. He, too, had run the gamut of all available pleasures; he was even one up on me, having written a free postcard, and together we went forth to investigate dinner, which was also 'on the house.'

Later that evening, despite one of my shoes being worn to paper thinness (it had been reinforced by a postcard already), we sauntered down a few blocks gazing in the lighted windows of the shops, and being absurdly happy over nothing in particular. It's not usual when you're so utterly down and out to land so very well on your feet. Let tomorrow take care of itself, tonight we had fed, and back at the hotel there were rooms waiting and everything we could want. The only drawback was that we invariably lost our way in the meandering deep carpeted passages between the elevator and our rooms. It was while we were standing by the elevator that one of those regrettably embarrassing incidents occurred. A man came up behind Jake, his footsteps unheard on the deep pile, and at that same moment a woman came round the corner and, facing Jake, smiled broadly and said "Hi"; to this Jake responded enthusiastically before he had realised that it was not him that was being addressed. In the embarrassed pause which followed, during which Jake wished he had died some time ago or his mother had strangled him at birth, the elevator made an opportune arrival.

The next morning, Wednesday, we made our way at the appointed hour for our breakfast assignment in the College Inn. The room was crowded with people from all over the States, all travelling places, or having come to see the other travellers. We consumed large quantities of coffee and doughnuts, while to my intense amusement I was given a form to fill in. Not all the travellers who filled in forms were picked to speak but just before zero hour, I was parked on the platform with a ticket round my neck, awaiting my appointed interview. Being an exhibitionist, I'm lucky in that I can not only rise to the occasion unafraid but enjoy it too when I have an audience to play to. It's perfectly true; if I'm talking to a gathering of disinterested businessmen I can make absolutely no impression but if the audience is interested, I can do things I never believed I could – and plain cold sober. You try broadcasting at 10 o'clock in the morning on coffee and doughnuts.

As a reward for my effort, I was given a fill-up of fuel for my ship, free dinner that night in the College Inn including cabaret, two pairs of slacks (which I wouldn't be seen dead in), two wizard nylon sweaters and – being a Proctor & Gamble show– a packet of *Tide* and a can of *Crisco*. This stands now on the top shelf in the kitchen of my little Cambridge flat, a silent symbol of those faraway days. By the way the clothes were not given me there and then but arrived in Montreal two months later.

Later on that morning Jake and I changed into our flying kit for a television film which was made up at the field. I never saw the actual showing of it although they promised to send the reel to me, but it never arrived. The rest of the day we filled in seeing innumerable people and papers, trying to scare financial backing out of somebody or some organisation. We were remarkably unsuccessful and all our excitement and happiness slowly ebbed away. Maybe it was our intense disappointment that instigated the stormy scenes that evening.

Jake and I quarrelled violently, all strangely enough over a girl friend of his and a lot of hypothetical women that I would meet in the course of my life. He knew a most attractive girl in Chicago and quite naturally wanted me to meet her. I was tired and I didn't want to be stared at, summed up, tried in the balance and found wanting. I know very few women at all well. I had two elder sisters, no brothers, and it has kinda put me off the feminine sex. There's very few women I would ever trust. Too many smile sweetly at your face in order to hear more so that they can discuss you with vixenish pleasure to their friends. Maybe I am being unjust. Anyhow I was quite determined not to be judged. For hours we argued until Jake told me to go to hell, stormed out of the room and left me weeping with anger.

I was so infuriated, I picked up my automatic and sat looking at it on the bed, wondering whether I would shoot myself or Jake and then decided that I wouldn't shoot myself just to spite him. *"Lord, what fools we mortals be."* Strange to relate though, after I'd bathed and showered and changed, I rapped docilely on Jake's door, apologised and said that of course I would meet his girl friend. Jake also apologised, quite sincerely, and said that no, he quite understood if I didn't feel like it. This started everything all over again as each party wished to be self-sacrificing, until tactfully Jake quit and we went down to our dinner in the College Inn, a little exhausted but quite amicable.

We were allowed to choose what we wanted for dinner, even though it was 'on the house,' and we decided that as asparagus was on the menu we would have it, not as a vegetable in the American style but before the sweet in the English way. This needed an enormous amount of detailed explanation to the waiter, who couldn't seem to understand that we liked melted butter with it in a separate container. When at last it appeared, everyone gazed entranced as we dipped the asparagus in the butter and ate the stalks between our fingers. I was getting quite embarrassed and had almost decided to use a fork when the lights dimmed and everybody's eyes turned to the cabaret.

Over a drink after dinner, I politely became acquainted with Jake's friend, then excused myself and retired to bed, only to find that there were still more reporters to be coped with. When I finally went to sleep that night I was very, very tired.

On the Thursday morning we again rushed hither and thither talking furiously to everybody. We were taken to see the Attorney General, who very nicely asked us to lunch. It was a good lunch, too. And then, bless him, he even slid us a 20-buck note as he said goodbye.

We quarrelled again that afternoon, according to my diary. It was probably something appallingly trivial but I suppose we were in the mood for it and, after all, it's difficult when you're thrown together as closely as we were not to get on each other's nerves. Besides which, I was terribly tired and worried. The excitement had worn thin and I didn't know where I was going from there. We had that 20-dollar bill and a full tank but what next?

I had dinner that night with one of Chicago's important state officials. He gave me an excellent dinner and I ate soft-shelled crab for the first time, but things are not always what they seem. What I took for pure friendliness had ulterior motives. I ought to have realised, it was silly of me. The suggestion with which the evening wound up was so indelicately framed that I didn't know whether to laugh or be sick. I was quite shocked and I thought I was wise to most things by then. It has often amused me, when thinking it over at other times, how the respectable citizens of these different towns would react if they heard of the offers I received and the suggestions made by other equally respectable citizens, often quite outstanding in their town's businesses.

On the Friday morning, we got up early and took a lift in a Press car to the ship. They were going to do a write-up about our take-off but as we went towards it, tied to the counterweights on the prop and the throttle in the front cockpit were two little red labels left by the CAA. In addition there was a little lead seal affixed to the label in the front cockpit. Yes, my heart sank, and I was even wearing boots for it to sink into in the traditional way. We could take the one off the prop but not the one on the throttle without breaking the seal, and the throttle couldn't be moved as it now stood. My first instinctive reaction was: "How unfair, they never even told us," and the second: "Well, we'd better get round it somehow."

We immediately got in a huddle with the CAA to find out where we had erred. Firstly, I was told, I had made a false declaration. I had made application for the ownership of the Vultee. This form had been made out by a notary and quite unwittingly I'd signed that I was an American citizen. Then a couple of days later I'd been told that foreigners can't own aircraft and, in the flap and panic of leaving Seattle, I'd presumed that my application would be treated as null and void and left it at that, assuming that the ownership would fall back on to the previous owner.

I was told that this was very far from the case.

"Well, who does it belong to?" I asked.

I was told: "No one."

This seemed strange to me.

Then I was secondly accused of not having a valid C. of A. I argued that if it didn't belong to anybody it didn't need a C. of A. but they weren't playing that one. We talked all the morning and half the afternoon, until I was utterly and completely balled-up and I didn't know whether I was standing on my head or my heels. I was as confused as only I can be and in a state where I was ready to swear that the ship did not even exist. By 3 o'clock I'd reached the climax of desperation on hearing that the paperwork would take at least three days to organise and that the CAA officials would shortly be knocking off work for a long weekend. They don't work Saturdays or Sundays and Monday was Decoration Day. That meant that when they started work, if they cleared it up by next Friday we'd be damned lucky. Seven days and 20 dollars for two people! It just wasn't possible.

Then the devil came and whispered in my ear. Attractive things, devils, aren't they? And they have such wizard suggestions!

"Why don't you just beat it?"

Conscience said: "Naughty, naughty! How?"

"Oh! just fly out, just take off."

"What, get past the tower on the busiest airfield in the States?"

"Well, you can but try. Faint heart never won anything."

It took about half an hour to convince Jake it was the one thing left to do, but finally he agreed. We would wait until the CAA had gone home and then we would take off. No, that wouldn't do. We would get into trouble with the night coming down on us. No, we would fly out at crack o'dawn. Exhausted and silent, we extracted a toothbrush each from our bags and plodded along to a cheap hotel near to the corner of the airfield. It was a crummy old dump and the never-ceasing stream of traffic under my bedroom window was no help in inducing sleep to an over-tired body and an over-strained mind, to say nothing of the over-greasy food on an over-hungry stomach.

CHAPTER 39
BREAKING THE SEALS

We were up at 5 am and after flapping round in a panic we did a quick run-up, taking off at 6.50. The run-up was over-hasty and it wasn't until I had slapped the throttle wide open and was speeding down the runway that it suddenly dawned on me that with the propeller in take-off (fine) pitch we were only getting 1,800 rpm instead of the usual 2,100. However I thought she could do it and that it wasn't too great a risk to run. Maybe I should have said something to Jake but he soon realised that there was something amiss when he realised our slow rate of climb. It seemed an appallingly long time before we climbed out over the smoke at 1,500 ft where we flattened out and set course. In coarse pitch she was only running at 1,500 revs, still 300 too few. We crept along discussing over the intercom where we should go and what we should do. We unanimously decided that we should find a small airfield to fuel up at when our tanks were low for we weren't using the belly tank, in fact it was sealed.

We decided on a place called St. Clare County, which proved to be small enough and took a good 20 minutes' circling to find. I did a circuit and touched down on the rough turf. Jake said: "Look out, there's another aircraft coming in," so I darted off the runway like a scalded cat, cursing Jake furiously when I saw it was a good 500 ft up still. However, we were in a much more cheerful frame of mind. At least we had got out of Chicago and as we drank *Cokes* in the hangar while the ship was being refuelled, we were laughing happily, whispering excitedly as we tried to make plans.

Now, should it be Toronto or Buffalo? We weren't particularly popular with the Department of Transport in Canada and it certainly didn't look as if we were going to be loved by the CAA in the States. Which was the lesser of the two evils? We had some Canadian dollars, at least we hoped we had, which in reply to our SOS were mailed by Bob Maclean to Jake's mother's address in Toronto. If we had to have any work done on the ship, it would be cheaper in Canada but would they be able to sign us out, as we had an American ship? Then again, we'd have to live in the meanwhile, and Jake living with his wife and his mother would cut our expenses down quite a bit. It was quite a problem and the main point in Toronto's favour was that Jake's wife was waiting there for him. This was worrying Jake a lot because she was getting decidedly impatient with the delays and I'm sure she suspected Jake of all sorts of things – until she met me. So we flew in to Toronto.

"Don't you worry, Jake," I sang out blithely; "I'll be right behind you."

"What?" he said in mock astonishment; "are you going to fly from the back cockpit?"

As we taxied bumpingly to the end of the runway, it suddenly dawned on Jake and me that here we were on a short rough runway with full tanks and only half power. It was silly of us not to have thought it out before. We did our straps up, even my shoulder harness, and with the tail on the boundary fence I kept my feet on the brake and opened the throttle. I crossed myself and smartly released the brakes. We had already agreed that if we hadn't left the ground by the intersection, we'd slam on the brakes again. I think it was will power only that got that ship in the air and I certainly shouldn't like to do that again, for as we whipped between the branches of the trees at the far end, they were a darn sight too near.

We landed unannounced at Toronto about midday. We weren't exactly welcomed but we insisted we had made a forced landing and that was very nearly true for, if it hadn't been for absolute necessity, I certainly would not have flown the ship that day. In fear and trepidation Jake put his call through to his home only to find everybody out but his kid brother. We had a milk shake in the bar where we were met by the Press. I tried hard to sell my story ("back me and I'll give you the exclusive gen") but no go.

We got a lift into town, though, by a couple of reporters who were in a hurry to knock off. I told them to drop me at some hotel which wasn't too expensive, not at either of the two big ones but one of the smaller ones. They pointed out that this might be difficult as there was a Convention on in town (I've never yet been to a town where there wasn't a Convention of some sort going on). However, they were in a hurry and they couldn't be bothered so, trundling through the cheaper districts, they dropped me in Jarvis Street, a road which bore signs at nearly every house saying 'Bed & Breakfast.' They left me on the pavement with my duffel bag, hurriedly said goodbye and left me whilst I made enquiries for accommodation for the night.

I was tired, so the third rooming house I called at was good enough for me. All rooming houses are much the same, but you can't tell from the hall really, which is always dark and smells of stale cabbages. I wasn't to know that this was the red light district. In my home town, Cambridge, England, the rooms are eminently respectable and run by University landladies, and it never crossed my mind that this should be otherwise until I had to pay a price out of all proportion for a night's accommodation. The room I had was a section partitioned off another one with wallboard inartistically decorated by hand with sundry rhymes and obscene drawings. The battered double bed was covered by a greasy quilt, which harboured a nauseating smell. The pink and blue flannelette sheets smelt of other mens' feet and there was another woman's lipstick on the pillow. It was a crummy joint, I tell you, and to add insult to injury there was a crack in the lav seat which pinched one's posterior painfully.

I washed and dressed in case Jake should want me and played endless games of Patience until nightfall, when I undressed and slept fitfully until awakened by a pounding on the door. Jake brought me a whole batch of letters and in hurried whispers gave me a brief outline of how things stood with the family. He looked utterly exhausted, poor kid. So I didn't like to worry him with my own troubles and even forgot to mention that I had no money. This was rather careless on my part for it entailed my being stuck there unable to move out until he made his reappearance. Accompanied by the daughter of the house I went to Mass on the Sunday morning. The rest of the day I did absolutely nothing at all. I read each letter many times and played the inevitable games of Patience. I had no money to go out and buy food, so I had no meal from Friday night in Chicago – barring the milk shake on arrival – until Monday night, when Jake got me out to a small private hotel and left me with some money. That is the longest time I've ever been without some sort of nourishment but it's amazing really how long you can subsist on cigarettes and water.

On Monday afternoon Jake called with a bunch of papers and, pointing to one article, finger quivering with indignant rage, insisted something must be done about it. It was rather a hasty paragraph insinuating that Jake daren't face his family and that we were living in Jarvis Street together.

We called on the paper in question that afternoon and while we were there, a call came through from Buffalo. The telephone operator, who had spent a long time trying to catch up with me, had lost the first party by this time, but arranged to contact me in my hotel. This turned out to be an offer to appear in Buffalo the next day to do sundry broadcasts and generally 'show off,' for a fee of 50 bucks. I leapt at the offer and put out frantic calls for Jake. First of all, we were to have flown by airlines there but, the appropriate aircraft being fully booked, we went by train. After frantically washing out my blouse and skirt that evening, and even more frantically ironing it the next morning, Jake and I caught our train.

I was somewhat worried by not having the necessary papers for entry into the States. These had been taken off me on my entry into Canada and, what with that and my fear of some steps being taken by the Authorities subsequent to my unusual departure, I nearly had kittens when together standing beside a big car waiting to greet me were two cops on motor bikes. My heart sank. "Now we're for it," I thought. What would I get? Six months? To my surprise, however, we were royally greeted, and to my intense embarrassment to begin with, and intense pleasure afterwards, we were driven through the town in this open car, my name splashed on both sides, between the two cops bang in the middle of the road.

It's childish, I know, but the pleasure I got from going through red traffic lights legally was quite out of all proportion. I can grin with pleasure just to remember it. I often wondered what it must be like to be Royalty or a film star, and just for those few brief hours I knew.

I did four broadcasts that day, I had a lunch date, attended the trotting races (consuming dinner meanwhile), and later went to a very big night club, where I appeared on the stage.

Our accommodation that night was at a good class hotel, where we had a whole apartment each, even including a kitchen. The startling change from my previous quarters in Toronto to the magnificent wastefulness of these just left me gasping. But then, of course, I found over the whole flight I'd either get three meals, all excellent, in one day, or none at all.

We flew back next morning, June 1st, from Buffalo to Toronto via Niagara Falls. These looked rather magnificent from the air but I can't say I was madly impressed. Maybe it's because flying over them you get no sense of height.

As always on June 1st, I did a little mental stocktaking, for eight years previously that day my mother had died and I had left childhood behind. I had come a long way in those eight years, though whether really I was any further forward it was difficult to say, but I was very conscious of having grown up a lot since then. I thought at that time that I really could cope with anything, which included public speaking. Somebody once said that the human brain was a very wonderful thing: it started working when you were born and only stopped when you got up to speak in public – a remark which I heartily endorsed.

On our arrival at the airport we clambered into the ship to do a run-up. Instantly one of the fuel trucks and two officials from the Admin. building rushed out to stop me. The silly things thought we were taking off, whereas all we were doing was sadly counting the lack of revs. The same thing happened the next morning when we started clambering over the ship: they weren't taking any risks this time. We had a few words with Customs and the airport manager and the Department of Transport. I was told to go back to the States. This was getting tedious.

I spent the afternoon in my quiet little room in my hotel, writing letters and then reading. I would rather economise on food, buying only a slab of chocolate and some peanuts, in order to spend the two bits on an Erle Stanley Gardner thriller. For at least that kept me sane and not so desperately lonely.

I arranged to meet Jake the next day, Friday, at 12 o'clock at the airfield. Incidentally, this field was 18 miles out of town and entailed considerable manoeuvring to get up there. I always carried a pocket compass, which was a help, for the best thing I found was to get to the edge of the town and bum a ride on an outgoing truck. I arrived there at about 12.15 but couldn't find Jake anywhere. I had a prolonged milk shake at the bar but still he never arrived so I went out to the ship to contemplate. The sun was sweltering down that day and I got very hot and angry; firstly because I couldn't get anyone to swing my ship (the battery of course was u/s) and, secondly, the only repair firm on the field would have absolutely nothing to do with the ship. Apparently they had only the week before repaired one and as it was being tested it killed their test pilot. On the run-up I had noticed the drop was still there though how it had come, God knows, for it was all right when we landed in Chicago. At first I thought it was due to some low grade of fuel, but though I added 100 octane it made no difference. I talked or rather tried to talk to some of the Airline engineers to hear their theories on the subject, but they were all so madly busy and, anyway, they were not supposed to help anybody else. I was getting hotter & hotter and crosser & crosser but I eventually found one man who said: "I'll give you a hand in a moment. Take the cowling off and then I'll come along." At least this was a start so taking my boots off – my feet were very hard and I cared not a damn for my dignity under that blazing sun – I set to work.

It's completely impossible as I've said before for me to remain at all clean anywhere near an engine and anyway that cowling was grubby. I was just well in the throes of it when Jake's wife arrived with half the family, looking cool and feminine in a summer frock and gossamer nylons. This was my first meeting and though she is only about my age I wanted to make a reasonable impression as I knew Jake so well. I was too oily to shake hands but I tried to pretend that I had done, and immediately after introductions, my pal the engineer arrived. I turned on him eagerly; I thought he had forgotten all about me and together we dived under the engine, discussing the ship earnestly. When next I looked up, everyone had disappeared bar Jake, who was speechless with anger,, swearing I had insulted his wife etc. etc. I tried to explain that I had waited for that engineer half the afternoon and soon anger flamed up and we were calling each other all the names under the sun. I know I lost my temper for I hit Jake in the face with my fist. With considerable restraint Jake did not retaliate and of course I immediately felt madly apologetic. I do not know what the control tower must have thought.

It's always interesting, hitting somebody, for they invariably change colour. Some people flush, while others whiten and their expression, fluid before, sets like a jelly. Then they either hit you back, swear at you or turn and walk away. Jake chose the middle course. He always could swear well and, after calling me a few unrepeatable names, he went on with what he had been doing. Almost instantly repentant, I apologised to him for the display of temper and tried to explain that the afternoon hadn't been easy for me either. I told him about the engineer, for whose aid I had waited for so long, it seemed. Jake accepted my apology and pointed out that it wasn't very easy for him when his wife thought I had been rude. I agreed but for the rest of that afternoon we weren't exactly chatty and when Jake went to check up on the bus times and didn't return, I realised he must have gone home.

I decided I might as well pack up myself so I screwed on the engine cowling, struggled into my boots and stood at the entrance to the airfield where the cars slowed down to join the main road, waiting to cadge a lift. I soon got one, overtaking Jake's bus, and got off at the city limits; there I joined Jake on a streetcar and told him that I would call his wife up as soon as he got back and suggest a convivial evening at some hotel or other. This I did, and after a slight misunderstanding as to the location we finally met and spent a very cheerful evening, during which everything was explained and everybody was happy.

I had already decided that, even though the engine was not doing what it should, I should fly her out alone the next day, so this was really our last evening together and my only evening out in the city of Toronto. The next morning, Jake gave me a hand with my bag up to the airfield and handed over the money which Bob Hendricks had sent in the form of a money order from Vancouver. It was all there was and I hoarded it like diamonds. God bless Bob for sending it; I should have been absolutely stuck without it.

We sorted out our possessions, Jake giving me back the Benzedrine tablets and sundry maps and I returning his passport and such papers as there were. Then we organised my departure: Customs, Immigration, showing the Ferry Permit and finally a flight plan. I decided that as the engine hadn't been doing so good I wouldn't fly *over* Lake Ontario but *round*, and actually it is, I believe, forbidden for single-engine ships to fly over the Lakes.

Jake swung the prop for the last time and gave me a kiss, then I taxied to the runway. Poor Jake. He looked so sad. He had loved the adventuring, though many people, Press included, had tried to insinuate he was in love with me. That only showed how little they knew about human beings. Jake wasn't in love with me, and the way we argued anybody could have seen that. He was in love with adventure. I think he thoroughly enjoyed all his RAF career because it wasn't quite 'everyday' when there was the pleasure of flying. I didn't realise, as I waved to him, standing wistfully on the tarmac, that I should never see him again. I thought he would probably follow me to Buffalo and we would go on again from there, or maybe I just didn't think.

CHAPTER 40

BUFFALO INTERNATIONAL

As I did a run-up at the end of the runway, I noticed happily that the revs, for some reason best known to God, were back up to normal. I was overjoyed as I opened the throttle and, busying myself with the controls, I was suddenly very happy. I levelled off at about 1,500 ft and though there was a slight haze beneath me I was flying contact. Having throttled back and trimmed the ship, I checked the map and this unaccustomed piece of drill suddenly awoke a panic in my heart. Oh my God, I thought, I'm up here alone. I don't know the way and I'm going to get lost.

For about a quarter of an hour as I flew round the corner of the lake, I sweated blood. I cannot think why; I had flown the aircraft unassisted for hundreds of miles and I've flown it alone since then with no more thought than in driving a car alone but for some incredible reason I was scared stiff. I was even more afraid when I noticed the aircraft (how light in the tail she seemed without Jake) was rocking, until I realised it was my own trembling hand on the stick. That promptly sobered me up, if you can put it like that, and by the time I was looking for the third river on the right, I was quite organised again. No longer had I the fear or the feeling that I was riding a bicycle on a tightrope, but I was sitting in an armchair over a large-scale map.

I found the right river and flew down, circling the Falls once more. The inevitable rainbow was there and it looked very beautiful. Yet once again, I felt vaguely disappointed that they didn't impress me more. I followed on into Buffalo, circled the field and came in. I couldn't call up the tower because my radio was out but they knew I was coming and gave me landing instructions. These I misheard and came in on a runway which was out of commission. There were wooden barricades across it, which faded into the surrounding terrain so well that I never saw them until I had all but touched down, in fact, I think I *had* touched down. I really don't know how I missed them. I must have squeezed past by sheer inches and when I slid back the canopy to wave joyously to the fire truck and for the air to cool my streaming brow, my knees were doing a samba. Coo, I wouldn't go through that again.

I parked the ship, feeling oh! so glad to be alive, and cursing Toronto for not having told me one runway was out and myself for not having heard the landing instructions correctly, and singing, too, between my teeth, a little rhyme which I always catch myself singing when I've just got over something difficult: *"I don't care if it rains or freezes, I am safe in the arms of Jeezes."*

Immediately on arrival I rang up the tower from the Customs office to apologise. I gave them the benefit of the doubt though quite honestly I was perfectly sure I had obeyed what they had said and no one had told me the runway was out. Then I turned back to Customs. There was a lot to be done and a lot of people to see. I had to organise a firm who would park my ship and give it the necessary overhaul for the Certificate of Airworthiness.

It was a really hot day and in my woollen shirt, Army pants and thick flying boots I really noticed it. I just caught the CAA representative before he went off for the day. I'm not sure he didn't stay that morning especially for me for normally they don't work on a Saturday. We had a discussion about the ship but the only thing we decided was that we would leave it until Monday.

I had a lift down to town late that afternoon by one of the Press, who kindly took me to buy a set of sun-tans (US Army tropical shirt and slacks) from an Army surplus stores and a pair of sandals. He then dropped me at a big cheap hotel where, after a little chat with the manager, I was given a little room on the twelfth floor for $11.50 a week, which was a reduced rate for me. I was very grateful for this and rather enjoyed that little room, so high up, where I could watch out of my window several streets and the little crawling cars.

I like Buffalo. I made many good friends there and my room was clean and the sun shone. It's much easier to be happier when the sun shines.

When I had changed into cooler clothes that night, I wandered out into the busy streets in the evening sun to look around, to choose a café in which to eat and just to walk and look at the citizens. Some places are hostile and some are not, and quite by chance I wandered into a novelty shop, which sold an incredible assortment of things from china pigs and cruets to curiosities and cheap jewellery. I spent the rest of the evening chatting happily to the proprietor and fingering everything in the shop. It was after 11 before I went back to the hotel, happy at the friendliness of complete strangers. I expected to be there at least two weeks and I decided I liked Buffalo. The next morning I went to Mass but spent a quiet day washing my hair and sleeping.

Monday morning I got up to the airfield keen and ready to have long talks with the CAA, and I had to decide which would be the best way to license the ship and also submit to their decision to immobilise it. I realised that my past actions rather justified that so I made no demur. Incidentally, that aircraft was parked on the grass for a month and people would walk over to it and sometimes look inside it but nobody stole anything.

On Monday night I was asked to address the monthly gathering of Quiet Birdmen, an organisation composed of flyers and which, I believe, is very difficult to enter. It is not at all well-known as it is not advertised in the least but an enormous proportion of the people at Buffalo airfield belong to it. It is an entirely male show so I was very interested to see what the evening would be like. I'd often wondered what a whole lot of men did when they got together and now I know. Brother, how they drink! Everybody got most incredibly high and I suppose I must have been quite moderately happy myself for I thoroughly enjoyed the evening, and though

I don't remember what I spoke about, I do remember the CAA representative laughingly announcing me in the most derogatory terms and my starting my speech with "Gentlemen – and CAA." The next morning, feeling slightly under the weather and deciding that it would be a show of weakness on my part not to put in an appearance up at the field, I was tickled pink to notice that a large proportion of people wore dark glasses that day.

Day after day I went up to the airfield but I just could make no headway. Certain papers had to be organised with the CAA Head Office and there was really nothing to do but sit and wait. I put calls through to Washington and submitted a report to be forwarded by the CAA about my mix-up with papers which caused the grounding by the CAA. I tried to be as patient as possible but the longer I sat and waited the poorer I became. Meals became scarcer and scarcer. I didn't want to break into the notes Jake had handed over that Bob had sent from Vancouver. I knew I should need every cent of those for fuel and what-have-you for the flight home. The result was that I subsisted on one evening meal which would cost me about 75 cents in the little café round the corner, where I alternated between egg salad and cream cheese salad, with soup and dessert. I would drink a bottle of *Coke* for lunch and the rest of the time consume gum and cigarettes.

I went out when I could and I soon got to know many people. I made two very good friends. One was the telephonist Clairebelle Spencer, who had contacted me regarding the publicity stunt when I was in Toronto. She had spent all the afternoon putting calls through trying to find me and somehow became interested. She called me up one day at my hotel and asked me to come and have lunch with her. I thought her adorable as soon as I met her and we immediately became firm friends. She was awfully good to me and I only hope that I can see her again one day.

Another very real friend I made came about in a rather roundabout way. I was lying on my bed one evening reading – I spent a lot of evenings that way – when a voice on the telephone told me that it was coming up. I had no indication as to who he was and I wasn't given the chance to enquire. It turned out to be two detectives from Police headquarters. They had received information that I had a gun, for which I was not licensed. Was this true? Sure it was, I said, and if you went the places I went, you'd carry a gun, too. We discussed it in a friendly way and they told me that I was not really entitled to have one so they confiscated it and asked me to come up to headquarters the next day.

Everyone was frightfully friendly at headquarters too, and I told them that I had had quite a lot of bother with anonymous telephone calls. One man in particular used to bother me. He would ring up, offering me money, quite large sums, for intimate articles of apparel or for looking at me undressed, and other equally impossible offers. I tried and I tried to get some indication as to who this importunate caller was until I finally scared him off by telling him there was a 'tec downstairs watching him.

Being a fervent admirer of Erle Stanley Gardner, the American Police headquarters interested me immensely, so I was shown over that morning and was photographed with the fingerprint expert holding in a pot a pair of hands which had come off a dead sailor. I saw over the cells, some of which were occupied, and the room with a lie detector in. Does it really work, I wondered at the time, and I still feel convinced that I could lie so my pulse remained perfectly still. I met a great many cops there, of course, and that night, when I had my supper and was sitting down writing letters, I had a call from one of them, Neil O'Donnell, an enormous specimen of 6 ft 4 in. Would I come and have a drink? I was delighted. What I thought was going to be another dull evening turned out to be enormous fun and from then onwards we were firm friends. Surely I wouldn't be safer than with a police escort?

These were two of very many friends I made in Buffalo and though I was eager to press on and anxious to get home, I was very happy. I many times went over the Peace Bridge to bathe in the lakes in Canada, and after a few times of taking my passport and going through all the involved formalities that being English entailed, I used to become quite adept at sitting tight and saying, when I was asked where I was born, saying Buffalo in the best American accent I could muster. It saved much time, that, on a busy Sunday. With all the sunshine and all the swimming and despite the somewhat erratic feeding, my skin tanned and my muscles hardened until I was fitter than I had ever been in my life before. To me Buffalo will always bring memories of sun. I just can't imagine it, despite the photos I've been sent of it knee-deep in snow.

All this while I was making very little headway with the aircraft. I fixed up with a friend of mine, Bill Deramo, to become, at the cost of a dollar, the official owner of the ship. I was advised to do this to simplify procedure somewhat so that I could register it in his name. He was awful chary of doing it, feeling certain I would let him down and it would involve him in some financial difficulty but I convinced him in the end, for the last thing I wanted was to repay that kindness by settling any trouble on him.

Then suddenly the blow fell. I was called out to the field urgently one Monday morning by the CAA and there I met an official specially sent down from New York to tell me that either the ship was interned or I was to pay a fine of 300 dollars. My first reaction was: "You can't, you can't do this to me," but it was pointed out carefully that oh yes, they could, and that I was getting off lightly according to them. If I cared I could take the case to court, which would in itself be a very lengthy procedure, particularly as they would seize the ship in the meanwhile and I would have to pay hangar costs. They gave me 24 hours in which to find the money and if I didn't pay it by 11 o'clock on Tuesday morning the aircraft would be seized.

And that's quite something. It would be quite hard for someone on a much sounder financial footing to rake up 300 bucks by the next day, let alone myself living, as I was, on a shoestring.

I didn't know what to do. With my hoarded dollars and what I had earned speaking at luncheon clubs, over the radio and on television shows, what I had added up to 250 bucks. I'd got to find 50 bucks by next morning. I went to the Chief of Police and I met with much kindness though no dollars. Then again, the dollars I had were Canadian and by being changed into US dollars I would lose at least 5%. I flapped around so much seeing people that I almost left it too late the next day and if Neil had not leaped into his car and grabbed some money from his bank, I should never have made it. As it was, the CAA official had already started making arrangements for the ship to be seized and I had to change the money into a money order at the last moment, which also took up time. What a hopeless feeling it is, just handing money over for which there was no return, and not only that, but handing over more money than I had. I was in debt to Neil to the extent of about 70 dollars and that only left me with three in my pocket.

The next week or so I lived incredibly thinly. I had to quit smoking and drinking *Cokes*. I almost had to quit eating and you kinda miss that, you know. But nearly all my friends stood me a meal, at least one meal, so I scraped along somehow.

I had had several letters from Jake, who told me that the rest of the journey was definitely off. It wasn't a great surprise to me that he and his wife were on their way to Seattle. I had told Mike Townsend this and I think he knew before I asked him that he would navigate me back. As soon as I was sure about Jake, I wired Mike, though at that time I wasn't awfully sure about whether I would even have an aircraft to fly. Luckily he had just completed his exams at Cambridge and, immediately after the Degree ceremony, he set about getting himself across the Atlantic. As a civilian and only a reserve RAF officer he did not have enough pull to wangle a free flight with the RAF or USAF and had to buy a ticket to Montreal with Trans-Canada Airlines.

[Richarda's manuscript was discontinued at this point when in 1950 it became clear that it would be unwise to publish it. The final chapters were written after her death by Michael Townsend and were based on the original flight records. – Ed.]

UPPER: Clairebelle Spencer, a telephonist who worked tirelessly to get Dikki publicity in Buffalo and who became a firm friend.
LOWER: Neil O'Donnell, a Buffalo cop who came to Dikki's rescue.

A friendly Police escort for Dikki in Buffalo.

Disreputable adornments on *"Next Thursday's Child"*; these were removed shortly afterwards as they didn't enhance Canadian officials' feelings about the reliability of the aircraft.

The Valiant all cleaned up and ready to go.

CHAPTER 41

BUFFALO–MONTREAL

I arrived back in the USA via Montreal on June 29th and was first off the train at Buffalo, but I did not see Dikki, so phoned her and took a cab to the Richford Hotel, whither she had returned after missing me at the station. She had just paid up the $300 fine that morning with the aid of a loan from Neil O'Donnell, a Buffalo city policeman. Even with this help Dikki had used all the money saved to pay for expenses on the flight across the Atlantic. It was just as well that I had turned up as I had still a small reserve of money in an account with the Royal Bank of Canada, left over from my wartime service with the RAF Atlantic Ferry Group in Montreal.

In the evening, we went for a big dinner of roast duck at the club of a luckless admirer of Dikki's who had been rash enough to issue one of those typically generous American open invitations. Next day, dressed up in old khaki shirts and slacks, we caught the bus to the Municipal Airport, where I had a first look at the Vultee Valiant *"Next Thursday's Child."* It appeared reasonably complete and in fair condition but for paintings of cobwebs, mottos and messages all over it. The engine particularly looked in good shape, although the inertia starter was inoperative and needed overhauling. As it was, the propeller had to be swung by hand – rather a tough proposition, seemingly, with a 450 hp engine. However, Dikki claimed that the previous navigator, Jake, had managed it, so I had a try. Surprisingly, the engine started perfectly on the first swing, but our hopes fell when we were unable to increase its speed above idling. Eventually one of the CAA officials came out and told us that he had disconnected the throttle linkage as a precaution against another of Dikki's illegal exits. On reconnecting it the engine went like a bird; this was not bad, considering that the plane had been standing idle on the apron for two weeks.

Now that the fine had been paid, the aircraft was released to fly anywhere within the States. As we wished to fly to Montreal next, however, an export licence was necessary and this meant applying to Washington. The State Department were in no hurry and no doubt wished to make sure that they were not sticking their necks out over us. So we spent 10 days in Buffalo, during which time I became acclimatised to Dikki's economical subsistence diet of one meal per day, with a few *Coca-Colas* thrown in when everybody else went to lunch. After the first day I insisted on some form of breakfast and we usually called in at a snack bar near the airport bus stop for fruit juice and cereal.

There was plenty of work to be done on her aircraft under the direction of the Civil Aeronautics Inspectors, who proved to be surprisingly helpful. The interior of the plane had to be cleaned of oil and dirt to reduce fire hazards, leaks in the integral wing fuel tanks had to be stopped and the "NC" markings on the wings and tail had to be changed to "NX," the "X" indicating that we had an experimental category, due to the extra fuel tank. The weather was very hot and sunny and I, for one, found the manual work in the open a pleasant change after being cooped up writing exams in England during the preceding weeks.

Hanging over our heads all the time, however, were two fears: first, that the State Department would not issue the export licence; second, that our money would not last the trip. Every extra day that we were forced to spend in the States cost several of our precious dollars, in spite of restricting ourselves to a 30 cent breakfast and a 75 cent soup and cottage cheese salad supper. There were our bus tickets to and from the airfield and the cost of our two rooms. We could hardly expect officials at Washington to take all this into account, however, and as far as we could see, the *status quo* might remain indefinitely.

Meanwhile, we had done all the jobs on *"Next Thursday's Child"* to the satisfaction of the CAA, including the messy work of sealing the leaks in the fuel tanks. This involved removing about a dozen inspection plates, working leak-proofing paste into likely angles inside the tanks and sealing them up again. When it is realised that all this had to be done lying flat on our backs under the wings and that the sealing paste was very like tar, it will be appreciated that we presented a somewhat dishevelled sight on returning to the hotel each night. It was with evident reluctance that a hairdresser in Buffalo allowed me to sit in his chair for a haircut on the way back to town one day. He even seemed to think that his (by British standards) exorbitant charge of a dollar for a mere trim would scarcely recompense him for the damage done to his chair and apron.

After a week in Buffalo we decided that something must be done to hurry up our export licence and even the expense of a phone call to Washington was justified. I made this from a call box in the airport terminal building with Dikki sitting on the floor outside and hugging a mysteriously bandaged wrist. Eventually I contacted the correct department and after the insertion of several more 25 cent pieces I even managed to speak to the official who had the misfortune to be dealing with our case. He turned out to be an ex-Air Force pilot who had flown Vultee Valiants during the war and was sceptical enough about crossing the Atlantic in one to promise me a box of cigars if we made it successfully. Anyway, he promised to expedite matters and to phone the Customs Office in Buffalo when the export permit was on its way.

He was evidently as good as his word, but the Customs officers at the airport must have been fed up with the sight of our inquiring faces by the time they eventually heard from Washington. This was in the afternoon two days after the phone call and we had already returned to the Richford, despondent of getting away that day. In fact we had wired friends in Montreal to cancel arrangements for a party at the Royal St. Lawrence Yacht Club that night. However, we hurriedly packed, said goodbye to our kind friend, Clairebelle Spencer, and Neil drove us out to the airport, all set to dash off before the official world changed its mind about the export permit. We could hardly believe that we were free to go at last and I think that the friendly mechanics of the Buffalo Aeronautical Corporation (outside whose hangar our aircraft had been parked) were as surprised as we were when they saw us finally pack in our luggage and taxy out to the runway.

I was a little apprehensive about my first trip in the back of the Vultee, particularly as much of it took place over Lake Ontario and the weather was poor. There were also little disturbing memories of reports in the English Press about the condition of the aircraft. Yet another factor was that I had never flown the machine myself, whereas I had flown solo on the Proctor a few times before the flight had started nearly a year before. The sliding canopy over the cockpit rattled rather alarmingly during take-off but thereafter the 2½-hour flight became one of increasing confidence. There was heaps of room to move about in the back cockpit and I noted with satisfaction that there would be room for two vital pieces of navigation equipment, the drift meter and the astro-compass.

The last part of the flight, from Kingston along the St. Lawrence to Lake St. Louis and Montreal Airport, passed uneventfully and we landed in the pleasant coolness of a summer evening. There followed the usual customs and immigration formalities and the taxying of the aircraft to its allotted parking space on the enormous expense of tarmac which, now deserted, had only four years ago been crowded wingtip to wingtip with every conceivable American and Canadian warplane waiting to be ferried to Britain, Italy or the Far East.

We were asked how long we wished to stay and whether we were carrying on to Goose Bay that night. Little did we know our mistake when we made arrangements for a five-day stay. The purpose of this self-imposed delay was to fit *"Next Thursday's Child"* out with full navigational and safety equipment before making the ocean crossing and to visit old friends and places in Montreal in the evenings. On the night of our arrival we finally did get to the Royal St. Lawrence Yacht Club dance, but of course the rest of our party were not expecting us and had not turned up. Next day was Sunday and we took the airport bus into Montreal and went to St. James' Cathedral where, not being familiar with local Roman Catholic procedure, I was astonished to be given 15 cents change when I contributed a quarter to the collection. Apparently a dime was the regulation charge for occupying a pew!

In the evening we heard that there was a big International Light Plane Rally at Grey Rocks Inn, St. Jovite, and we were given an introduction to the organiser by the Dorval representative of Wheeler Airlines, a company that operated between St. Jovite and Montreal. It was already late when we decided that it would be a good thing to fly up there and meet as many enthusiastic and influential people in the flying world as possible; so we hastily packed our overnight bags and, after some argument with the

Department of Transport Authorities, we climbed into *"Next Thursday's Child"* already dressed for an evening out at Grey Rocks. The DOT apparently looked askance on the 'experimental category' of our aircraft and wished to ground it until the arrival of their local chief on Monday. It was only after making firm promises to return to Montreal next day that we were allowed to take off. St. Jovite was a small summer resort in the mountains about 60 miles north and the journey should not have taken more than half an hour, but nothing like an airfield appeared on ETA. This may or may not have been because we had been rather hastily briefed on its exact location, or it may have been that we only had a small-scale map with insufficient detail. Anyway, repeated flying back and forth over the road which should have passed quite close to the airfield failed to reveal it and we had to return shamefacedly to Montreal before nightfall.

CHAPTER 42
MONTREAL–BURLINGTON–MONTREAL

The next day, Monday 11th July, was the first of our 'black' days. We had breakfast in the caféteria and then visited the local DOT boss, Monsieur Fournier, who had just returned from his weekend. He coolly informed us that, subject to confirmation by Ottawa, we would not be allowed to fly the Vultee in Canada at all due to its 'experimental' registration, nor, if that had been waived, could we fly across the sea to Greenland in a single-engined aircraft. This was quite a shock as the United States authorities in Buffalo had said that, so far as they knew, there was nothing to prevent us completing the flight to England.

The question of Canadian objections had not arisen at all when complete clearance for the round-the-world flight had been obtained in England prior to setting out. In fact, the flight had been cleared by the DOT for "entry into Canada at Whitehorse and departure from Goose Bay, Labrador, subject to carrying the correct radio frequencies." Unfortunately, since the clearance, Canada had taken over control of Newfoundland and Labrador, thus supervising flights to Greenland.

M. Fournier freely admitted that, had we pushed on to Goose Bay on the evening of our arrival, no one would have asked any questions. As it was, our plane was positively grounded pending a decision from his boss in Ottawa. He was not going to take the responsibility. This was not so bad really, as we were confident that Ottawa, having once cleared the flight (albeit 10 months ago), would not stand in our way when we were so close to achieving our objective at last; in any case, we had planned on five days in Montreal for checking up on our aircraft, buying dinghies and *Mae Wests* and fitting a drift meter and astro-compass (the astro-compass was for checking the accuracy of the magnetic compass against the sun's azimuth as datum).

Days passed and no official word came from Ottawa. Eventually we bearded Fournier in his office and he blithely informed us that neither his boss, a Mr Travers, nor the Minister of Transport (Mr C.D. Howe) were prepared to waive any of the regulations. Each had apparently tried to pass the buck to the other, Howe maintaining that Travers was boss of the air division of the DOT and that it was his responsibility. There were rumours, even, that the question had gone to higher authority than the Minister and that the buck had been smartly passed back again. Seldom can there have been such lack of confidence in an aircraft and its crew and seldom can anyone have been less keen to accept responsibility and more keen to rest on the letter of the law. Independent unofficial approaches had also been made to the DOT by mutual friends in an effort to convince them of the technical ability and experience of the crew and of the unlikelihood of their using an unairworthy aeroplane.

All was to no avail, however, and the argument that we had already completed successfully a sea crossing twice as far as that from Labrador to Greenland in far worse weather and in a smaller aircraft was worth nothing compared to the almost hysterical fear of having anything to do with the flight, engendered in official circles no doubt by reading the more sensational reports in local newspapers. Eventually, out of the goodness of their hearts or, more probably, out of their anxiety to get rid of the responsibility as soon as possible, the DOT promised a Ferry Permit to the nearest customs airport across the American border.

It became obvious that we must review our position and make new plans if we were to reach Greenland and the way home. Unlike Dikki, for whom *"Next Thursday's Child"* and the flight had become something of an obsession, I was able to take an objective view of the position and could more easily understand outside opinion. The first thing that struck me was the shocking appearance of our aircraft. The fact that Dikki had flown to the Yukon and back without any mechanical trouble was liable to be forgotten when one saw its bizarre and unprofessional daubs of paint. Humorists in various parts of Canada and the States had painted cobwebs, patches, slogans and even messages to pals in Goose Bay on wings, fuselage and tail surfaces until there was hardly a square foot of the original silver showing. No doubt these had served a purpose during the trip across Canada by attracting the attention and publicity necessary for raising money, but they had obviously been a strong contributory factor to the very low opinion of the aircraft's efficiency held in official circles. Moreover it became increasingly obvious that, from now on, the less conspicuous we were the healthier it would be. We no longer needed money so badly from publicity and any plan that we adopted to reach Greenland would, of necessity, have to be executed swiftly and inconspicuously.

Stormy interviews with Fournier, characterised by considerable heat and abandon on both sides, had convinced us that there was not only lack of co-operation but hostility – a hostility which made one all the more determined and sharpened the wits to combat a situation that was obviously becoming difficult. The first thing to do was to clean every daub of paint and writing off *"Next Thursday's Child,"* including even the name. The next was to speed the work of getting her ready for the ocean crossing. With the active co-operation of Canadian Pacific Airlines, who had the misfortune to occupy the hangar nearest to our parking place, we soon made the slight modifications necessary to fit the extra navigation equipment. I think that the interest shown by the CPA types and their readiness to give us a helping hand during their lunch hour was one of the few highlights of our three weeks' stay in Montreal. A similar helping hand was offered with charts and expert navigational advice by the chief navigator of Trans-Canada Airlines.

There was no problem in obtaining items of navigation and survival equipment, but it meant a trip to Ottawa, where I purchased a drift meter and astro-compass at a government surplus store and maps of Labrador, Northern Quebec and Baffin Island. There was no detailed topographical mapping of these areas in 1949, only white for land and blue for water, but that would have to do.

During our stay in Montreal there were several approaches from the media. The reporter from *Newsweek* met us in downtown Montreal and gave us $10 for a steak dinner; his subsequent article, however, was not in very good taste. We were also taken out to dinner at the La Salle Hotel by a smooth-looking lady radio commentator (who shamed us by eating very little) and then made a broadcast. This all went off pretty well, but I was rather embarrassed by Dikki asking her (so strong was the habit by now) to keep an eye open for possible sponsors or opportunities to lecture. We should have been keeping a low profile at this point, rather than courting publicity.

The Royal Canadian Air Force, who had invited us to one of their Mess parties, supplied us with large quantities of paint stripper to clean up our aircraft. We were warned not to put it on any fabric parts or any clothes as it would eat its way through anything but metal. One pair of my tropical worsteds never recovered. The paint remover was very effective and the job was nicely under way when, in my eagerness to run and turn off the water tap that was drenching us as well as washing off the loosened paint, I tripped over the hosepipe and sprained an ankle. I was carried off to Dorval Inn on a tractor and I was not to see *"Next Thursday's Child"* again until several days later, when it had finally emerged from Dikki's efforts, all clean and shining silver.

My sprain had recovered sufficiently for us to make a move by Wednesday 26th July and we availed ourselves of the promised Ferry Permit, having decided on a tentative and flexible plan of action to be followed when once clear of Canada. Our first stop would be Burlington, Vermont, because DOT would only allow us enough petrol to complete the necessary 60 miles with a small margin. M. Fournier even went to the trouble of ensuring that we were refused flight clearance until one of his men had personally inspected our fuel tanks and dipped in a measuring rod to make certain that we had not popped in an extra 5 or 10 gallons. We were finally warned not to land again in Canada except in an emergency. Eventually we were allowed to clear customs and immigration and took off on our 30-minute hop over the border.

Everything went well at Burlington at first. There was no crowd, no reporters and no fuss. We told Customs of our next intended port of call, Presqu'Isle, Maine, and were completing immigration formalities when, to our dismay, we were told that Dikki's visa had expired a few days previously. This was a blow as it meant returning to Montreal to get it renewed by the American Consul there. However it should only be a matter of 48 hours and that was a small price to pay for staying on the right side of the law. So, with cheerful promises to "see you tomorrow or Friday" to the immigration officer, we flew back to Montreal – where our aircraft was promptly impounded!

What fools we were! If only we had played safe and left *"Next Thursday's Child"* at Burlington whilst we returned to Canada by bus for the new visa! But somehow it had seemed such a trifling little trouble and easily settled by a 30-minute trip to Montreal, a visit to the consul and a 30-minute trip back again. The thought of being impounded never crossed our innocent minds.

Worse things were still to come, however. Fournier telephoned the customs officer at Burlington and asked where we had intended calling next. Of course, when he was told "Presqu'Isle" the fat really was in the fire. Having a nasty suspicious mind and realising that Presqu'Isle was the most north-easterly airport in the United States, he put two and two together and guessed that either Goose Bay in Labrador or Gander in Newfoundland would be our next stop. This thought evidently disturbed him greatly, for he started pulling strings in all directions regardless of whether he was going beyond his province. First, the Customs and Immigrations authorities at Burlington were warned not to accept our aircraft without special written authority, in addition to a visa, from the United States Consul in Montreal. Next, he called up one of the senior officials in the consulate and persuaded him that we were undesirables and should not have visas. Finally, he telephoned Travers, in Ottawa, to fix us in higher quarters!

The first thing we did on our return was to call on friend Fournier to find out just why he was being so small-minded about the whole procedure. At least he was honest in admitting that he was determined not to let us fly back to England. He also admitted warning the US consulate and Burlington about us. Outraged at this treatment, Dikki immediately phoned the consulate. They appeared to be as surprised by Fournier's demand for special written authority to enter the States as we were and said that all Dikki needed was a renewal of her visa. Accordingly, we toiled into the city next morning and obtained a rather douce and innocent-looking passport photo at a 'five and ten cent' store which boasted a 4 ft-square studio and an ill-mannered photographer. We then repaired to the US Consulate and queued up with sundry other characters waiting to see the great man.

The consul was typically American in appearance, busy, abrupt and reasonable. After his opening words of: "Well, what's on your mind?" (one felt he should have added "sister" or "lady" after it to fit in with correct movie style), I was dismissed from the proceeding and he and Dikki argued the case for her visa. Evidently she was successful and the consul was cooperative, as she emerged not only with a visa but with one stamped "good for transit through the US *en route* to the United Kingdom." It looked as if we should be off to Burlington next day.

We had not reckoned with the intransigence of Fournier, however: when we triumphantly presented him with the visa, he looked at it unbelievingly and calmly refused to give us a Ferry Permit! It began to look as if we would have to settle down and live in Canada. This admittedly had its attractions but they were dwarfed by our overwhelming impatience to finish the round-the-world flight that we had started, and anyway Dikki had her family waiting for her at home.

Friends in Montreal kept asking us when we were going and what the hold-up was, and one friend in Trans-Canada Airlines actually made two round trips to England whilst we were hanging around. Furthermore, newspaper reporters were on our heels again and impatient of being stalled off by promises to let them know when we were going. We still had to give the impression that it was just a matter of red tape and would be cleared up any day soon.

Further attempts to persuade Fournier that it was unreasonable and financially embarrassing for us to remain at the airport indefinitely at his pleasure were to no avail. Unfortunately he had heard about a light-hearted suggestion of Dikki's when in the Control tower that the controller should look the other way or be attending to the calls of nature whilst we took off illegally! Even the walls had ears for Fournier. We could not discuss our route or plans with a soul. Meanwhile he was issuing horrible threats that Mounties with drawn guns would be waiting for us at Goose Bay and all other airfields near the east coast.

The position was getting desperate and we even listened to a plan by some of our well-wishers that we should take off clandestinely from the long hangar apron which was out of sight from the control tower, whilst the test crew revved up the engines of a Lancaster to drown the noise of our own engine! Such a plan was very much of a last resort, however, and Dikki was determined to do things legally if possible. A last straw to clutch at was the suggestion that the DOT might allow our flight if we were escorted the whole way to Goose Bay (about 800 miles) and the whole way from there to Greenland, another 800 miles. The RCAF transport squadron tentatively offered to escort us to Goose, but the plan came to nothing, partly due to the fact that they only had fast four-engined *North Stars* available.

CHAPTER 43
ESCAPE FROM MONTREAL

Feeling that we had exhausted the legal possibilities at our Montreal base and not yet being desperate enough to risk the penalties of a failed clandestine departure, the only option was to go right to the top. Accordingly, Dikki boarded the train for Ottawa and visited the Deputy Minister of Transport. He proved to be most reasonable and directed Fournier to issue the required Ferry Permit. This time we would not return to Montreal at any price.

Once again we went through the rigmarole of the measuring sticks in our fuel tanks and this time we were made to drain off 10 precious gallons to satisfy the DOT inspector before we could take off. Burlington was the nearest United States customs airport, so we had to call there first of all. After that, Presqu'Isle was obviously out as Fournier was expecting us to land there; Goose Bay was also out for the same reason and Fort Chimo, on Ungava Bay in Northern Quebec, was another obvious leaping-off point for Greenland. The trip from anywhere in the north-eastern States was several hundred miles further than we could fly in *"Next Thursday's Child."*

There was, however, a landing strip hundreds of miles from anywhere on the border between Quebec and Labrador. This was called Knob Lake and was operated not by the DOT but by a private mining company (the Hollinger-Ungava Mining Co.). It had no radio aids to help us find it and was in poorly-mapped country on the edge of one of the many thousands of similar lakes in the area; but it was about halfway between Bangor, Maine, and Frobisher Bay in Baffin Island, both of which bases were operated by the United States Air Force.

As the USAF had been thoroughly helpful wherever we had met them and had already given us official permission to land at their base in Greenland, the projected route seemed fairly secure. Both Goose Bay and Fort Chimo would be cut out and Knob Lake would only be a refuelling stop. Moreover, Knob Lake and Frobisher would be unlikely to have heard of our wrangling with the DOT in Montreal and were probably not connected to Ottawa by regular communications, one being in the wilderness of Labrador and the other being situated on one of the Arctic Islands.

Our route would now have to be from Montreal to Burlington (78 miles), Burlington to Bangor (188 miles), Bangor to Knob Lake (595 miles) and Knob Lake to Frobisher Bay (534 miles). The hop to Greenland would then be over the shortest possible sea crossing to the USAF base at Stromfjord, a distance of only 500 miles. A further useful factor was that daylight would last virtually all night long so far north, and if necessary the trip could be flown in the evening after stopping off at Frobisher merely for refuelling. With any luck we could be in Greenland the day after leaving Montreal.

After our take-off for Burlington, a RCAF *North Star* transport plane circled round us and we were so anxious in case we had done something wrong again in the eyes of the DOT that we phoned Montreal tower after landing just to check up. Fortunately it turned out to be a farewell gesture from the squadron; so we cleared Customs and Immigration at Burlington, extricated a couple of bottles from a complicated *Coke* machine, refuelled and set off for Bangor. No one had asked our destination and we were told that no flight plan was necessary, which was all to the good in avoiding publicity.

One of the main reasons that we had for choosing Dow Air Force Base, Bangor, as a stopping point was our hope of getting a USAF escort aircraft to Greenland. This should satisfy the Canadian DOT. Dow turned out to be a jet fighter base where civil aircraft were only allowed to land in emergency. We were therefore received with some surprise by the 'officer of the day,' but he rallied well and obtained rooms for us in the visiting officers' quarters pending enquiries about an escort. For this we were advised to ring Westover Field, which was the headquarters of the Air Sea Rescue Service for the Atlantic Seaboard. This could not very well be done until Monday, so we had a day to while away. In typically American fashion, we were offered hospitality within an hour or two of our arrival, in the form of an invitation to dinner by one of the weather officers whose wife was English. Incidentally, she had hardly a trace of her English accent left.

On Monday the Base Commander offered us any help we needed to get our aircraft absolutely shipshape to fly the Atlantic and we gladly availed ourselves of the services of a Master-Sergeant rigger to check the angles of our propeller blades at the 'coarse' and 'fine' pitch settings. We had had some difficulty in getting the maximum permissible revs on take-off and wondered whether this was due to incorrect adjustment of the propeller pitch control. I had already moved it once at Montreal and thought that perhaps I had not made a good job of it. However, after very careful measurements with special equipment the adjustment was pronounced to be exactly right. This was quite a feather in my cap, to have my amateur work approved by such an experienced man. (He must have had more chevrons on his arm than any other man in the USAF; his upper arm was covered by his insignia of rank and the lower sleeve was almost hidden by the rows of service chevrons.)

Whilst the Master-Sergeant was tackling our propeller problem we telephoned Westover Field. They had a Catalina flying boat to escort us, but permission would have to be approved by Washington. Our contact gave us the name of the appropriate department to call up and we gave them a ring. Dikki made the call but, not unreasonably, the staff officer on the other end of the line had to refer our request to higher authority. He would call us back on the following day. Meanwhile, newspapers had found us again and even the *Daily Mail* in England knew our whereabouts and phoned all the way from London for a story. They were told, as were all the other papers, that we were trying to organise an escort aircraft from the USAF and were still waiting for an answer from Washington. The very word Washington sent little niggling pangs of doubt through our minds, but we had to pretend optimism to anyone who questioned us. Besides newspaper reporters, there were many officers on the base who wanted to take photographs of us and the plane. All were as helpful and enthusiastic as they could be and more than one volunteered quite unsolicited subscriptions to the cost of our flight. How nice it would have been to refuse! But we needed literally every cent we could get, particularly as we did not know how long we would be delayed *en route*.

On the next day, which was Tuesday 2nd August, we had a mysterious visit from the Customs officer. We had to convince him that we had an export licence for the Vultee (was this more of Fournier's work?); this involved persuading him to telephone the official in Washington State Department who had granted it. Until he had done this he refused to allow us to leave Dow AFB. Meanwhile, the Base Commander suggested that as our aircraft was fully serviceable and was not really allowed at Dow, we should move to Old Town, the civil airfield 10 miles to the north, pending a decision from Washington on the escort question. We were still expecting a call from them and after waiting until the afternoon, Dikki eventually borrowed a handful of quarters from me and called them. We used the phone box in the "PX" and I had to keep dashing off to waylay airmen for change to put in the box, whilst Dikki was obviously pleading desperately for a cause that at the Washington end was already lost. Their attitude appeared to be that they were not worried whether we had an escort or not and, if the Canadian DOT were, well, let them provide one!

Dikki was obviously upset about the position, but it merely confirmed the suspicions long latent in my mind and at least we now knew exactly where we stood. We must not admit to anyone that we had been refused an escort; instead we would say that there was a delay and that we hoped to hear tomorrow.

In the late afternoon we climbed into *"Next Thursday's Child"* and flew over to Old Town, which turned out to be a quiet little airfield, some miles from Bangor. It had, however, very long tarmac runways and no air traffic control. We might need the long runways for take-off with our overload tank full and if there was no air traffic control there would be nobody whom we were obliged to notify of our destination. The evening was warm and sunny and the few airport employees about were cheery and helpful. We filled up all three tanks on our aircraft, parked it in line with various Piper Cubs etc. and accepted a lift into the township of Old Town, where we secured rooms in a modest hotel.

Fuel had been dripping out of the overload fuel tank vent when we had left the airport and we thought it best to check up on whether it had stopped; so we phoned the servicing company and asked them to have a look. They reported that it was still coming out quite fast and the only thing to do was to spend money on a taxi back to the field. The remedy turned out to be quite simple: apparently the end of the air vent pipe was at a lower level than the tank and fuel was syphoning out. It was merely necessary to bend the end of the pipe up to the requisite level and the syphoning stopped. We had resolved to take off at dawn and organised a taxi to collect us at 4 am. For once our plans were clear and the time for action had come. We had a pleasant dinner in a local restaurant and went early to bed after indulging in the luxury of a couple of bottles of beer.

By 4.30 am we were loading up *"Next Thursday's Child"* at a deserted and barely light airfield. The engine started first swing and idled normally but when opened up would only give 1,700 rpm instead of the usual 2,000. No amount of running up would improve it; our only hope was that power would develop fully on the take-off run, so we taxied out to the end of the runway and opened up. It was useless, in fact we could now barely get 1,600 rpm and had to throttle back and taxy back to the apron. What a thing to happen on the very morning when it was vital to slip away early and when we were more heavily loaded than ever before! We checked the mixture control, the propeller pitch control and everything else that we could think of. Finally, the only thing left was to remove the engine cowlings and check the plugs. We were engaged in this laborious procedure when the airfield mechanics came on duty at 7 o'clock and we summoned the expert assistance of one of them. He checked everything that we had and carried out some extra investigations of his own but everything, including the plugs, was in good order. Finally, to our astonishment, he suggested carburettor icing as the cause of the trouble.

On the face of it this seemed ridiculous as the weather was as warm as an English spring morning. However, the air was heavily laden with moisture as well as being fairly cool at 5.30 am; so we followed his suggestion and waited until the sun had warmed things up a bit before starting the engine again. Meanwhile we had the fuel tanks all topped up and paid the bill.

At midday we started up again and the engine went like a bird. So much for our idea that carburettor icing could only occur in cloud! At last we were airborne again and the old feeling of relief came flooding back. No one could worry us or tie us up in red tape again for at least six hours and by then we should be another 700 miles nearer to England with any luck.

We decided to follow the radio ranges as far as the St. Lawrence and then map-read our way to Knob Lake. For obvious reasons we had been unable to get a Met forecast and, even if we had done so, it is not certain that it would have been able to foresee the blanket of fog and low cloud that rolled in over the whole of New England and Eastern Canada shortly after our take-off. The area around Old Town itself was clear and sunny when we left, but gradually more and more of the ground was covered up. Further north we ran into solid cloud. We battled on, sometimes flying by instruments and sometimes between cloud layers, always listening to the steady signal of the radio ranges, the 'MT' of Millinocket, the 'PQI' of Presqu'Isle, the 'YY' of Mont Joli and the 'ZV' of Seven Islands. At 30-minute intervals the weather report for each place in the area was transmitted. They were not encouraging: to the east all stations gave cloud ceilings lower than 700 ft; Seven Islands and Mingan, our two best emergency landing places, both on the north bank of the St. Lawrence, were almost closed in by low cloud.

Two and a half hours after take-off gaps appeared in the cloud and presently the south shore of the St. Lawrence passed beneath us. The whole river was clear and we crossed it at 7,000 ft in high hopes of picking up a pinpoint on the north shore prior to setting course for Knob Lake. We did in fact identify our crossing point as Baie Comeau, a mining town with a landing strip, but the low cloud soon started thickening up again, at first only in patches, which encouraged us to press on in the hope of it clearing to the north. This was not to be, however, and we were very soon on instruments again, occasionally glimpsing the barren, rocky wilderness beneath us. Dikki suggested a descent through one of the holes in an attempt to map-read our way to Knob Lake at low level, as it was becoming more and more certain that we should never find it by ploughing along in cloud. As I still had a good idea of our dead reckoning position, I agreed.

We soon found ourselves following a deep, narrow valley with a river flowing along the bottom. At intervals it widened out into lakes which in any other type of terrain would have been good landmarks, but which here could have been any of two or three similar north-south features in an area packed with long thin lakes connected by rivers. The fact that the low cloud forced us to fly along below the level of the valley sides eventually rendered any hope that we still had of finding our way to Knob Lake quite vain. The only thing to do was to climb up into the cloud and reconsider our position.

There were three alternatives: return to Baie Comeau, which was only 300 miles from Montreal, but probably lacked regular communications, attempt to reach Fort Chimo on the north coast of Quebec or fly to Goose Bay on the east coast of Labrador. Fort Chimo was tempting, but it was barely within our range and also might have been closed in by fog or low cloud (both common in the Arctic in summer); Baie Comeau was the nearest but was too far inland for a leaping-off point for Greenland. At the psychological moment a weather report came through over Seven Islands radio range announcing that they had a cloud base of less than 400 ft, but giving conditions at Goose Bay as "4,000 ft, broken cloud." It was literally the only airport with safe landing conditions and it remained only for us to call Fournier's bluff of armed Mounties waiting for us there.

Accordingly we headed eastwards and after a couple of hours broke cloud. It was not long before we picked up the big Hamilton river which, according to the map, flowed right past the high, sandy plateau occupied by

Goose Bay airport. After 7½ hours with barely a glimpse of the ground until the last 30 minutes, we saw the three great runways surrounding the centre triangle of forest. We were safe, anyway, and within a single hop of Greenland and freedom, but what reception awaited us down below?

CHAPTER 44
GOOSE BAY

It was with some trepidation that we taxied to the hangar as directed by the Control Tower and our fears were not allayed by being told to report to the Tower immediately! At least there were no redcoats to be seen on the tarmac though.

We need not have worried ourselves. Our reception was most cordial. The Royal Canadian Air Force Commanding Officer was away but his deputy and the station adjutant welcomed us most hospitably, asking when we wished to take-off for Bluie West 1 and whether we would like to refuel now or in the morning. Foolishly and trustingly we suggested the morning as we had a slight leak from the starboard fuel tank. We should have learned by now that it was fatal not to press on whilst we had the chance. Customs and immigration wanted to know why we had landed at Goose Bay without prior clearance. The quite truthful answer was that bad weather had made it impossible to land anywhere else and this was readily accepted.

We parked the aircraft outside No. 2 hangar, covered the engine up and went along to the Mess, where Dikki was allotted a room in the nurses' quarters and myself in the bachelor officers' wing. It was 'bingo' evening in the officers' club on the American side of the camp. The RCAF acting CO took us over for the party. We were amazed at the quality of the numerous prizes, which included cameras and radios. The club itself was most impressive, the central feature being a dance floor with a stage and soft, coloured lighting like a night club. Round the floor were tables and chairs in groups. After the bingo there was a dance but we were so tired after being on the go since dawn that we excused ourselves for an early bed in order to wake up ready for the trip to Greenland next morning. We needn't have bothered.

The met. forecast for the 800-mile flight to Bluie West 1 was good and our hopes were at first high. It was not until we had taken our luggage out to the aircraft that the news was broken gently to us: there was a conference of DOT officials from Ottawa who had just arrived at Goose Bay on the very same day as us! Apparently they had not known of our presence until that morning. It must have come as rather a surprise, not to say embarrassment, to them as they could not very well send us back to Montreal or Bangor since it was their ruling which prohibited single-engined landplanes from flying over the uninhabited stretch between Goose Bay and the St. Lawrence. They finally conceded that we could fly on to Greenland provided that we had an escort all the way. They could not arrange an escort and to make sure that we did not pull a fast one, they ordered the RCAF and the petrol company to refuse us fuel. If only we had refuelled yesterday! Once again we had made the fatal delay.

Our despondency was soon cleared away, however, when the USAF Colonel immediately volunteered a Catalina flying boat as escort. It would not be serviceable until Saturday; meanwhile he would check up with his immediate superiors for permission to lay on a training flight to Bluie West 1. This did not sound at all bad: two days' rest and good food at Goose Bay and the prospect of leaving Canada legally at last seemed a very pleasant outlook.

Saturday 5th August dawned and we went to visit the American Colonel. The Catalina was now fully serviceable, but it could not escort us. The question had been referred to Washington and permission refused on the same grounds as before: the USAF did not insist on us having an escort: Ottawa did and it was their responsibility to provide one. The problem was referred back to the DOT at Ottawa and we waited, 800 miles nearer home but otherwise not much better off than we had been in Montreal. At least the natives were friendly at Goose Bay, though.

We waited in a state of stalemate for five days, with no reply from Ottawa. There was nothing wrong with our aircraft, so we could not occupy ourselves working on it as we had done at Buffalo and Montreal. We did occasionally run the engine and made small adjustments such as retrimming the aileron tabs as we had noticed a tendency to fly one wing low recently. For the rest of the time we tried to think up new answers to the daily recurring question: "Haven't you gone yet, Mrs Tait?"

We also delved into the problem of filling *"Next Thursday's Child"* with petrol and kept an eagle eye on weather conditions over the Atlantic. The refuelling problem became more and more acute as our hopes of a favourable answer from Ottawa faded. The Service tankers had been ordered not to refuel us and the civilian fuel company at the airport dare not as Goose Bay was a military airfield and they were answerable to the RCAF Commanding Officer. Of course, there were ways of abstracting petrol from one aircraft and transferring it to another but, apart from being somewhat nefarious, the job was very laborious. To drain 30 six-gallon cans from a Dakota locked in a hangar and transfer them across 100 yards of partially floodlit apron would be a job requiring no mean skill and stealth. Such was the position, however, after a week at Goose Bay that serious consideration was given to the plan and a detailed reconnaissance was made during a heavy storm one night. Fortunately, information was gleaned next day from the RCAF adjutant that rendered our clandestine refuelling plan unnecessary.

The days at Goose were spent in walking across to the American Base, badgering the met. men, walking in the forest and sunbathing. On one afternoon we went hunting in the woods and shot five spruce grouse with the Walther PPK automatic (Dikki's protective weapon during her adventures in the Yukon). The birds seemed quite unafraid of human beings and none of the shots was taken at over 20 yards. One bird was sporting enough to sit still whilst three bullets hummed past it. It then evidently decided that it was needlessly exposing itself to danger and flew off into a nearby fir tree. When we returned with the four grouse that we had been able to find, Dikki insisted on presenting them (I suppose as a sort of peace offering-cum-bribe!) to the RCAF Station Commander. They were rather small and scrawny, but perhaps the CO accepted them in the spirit in which they were given rather than in the light of their rather doubtful culinary properties.

Evenings at Goose Bay were mostly spent at the station cinema or in the Mess, where there was a pleasant group of university research students up for their long vacation as well as the RCAF officers. It was in the cinema on August 11th that we received our "marching orders," framed in the terms of a barely uttered hint that we should be on our way tomorrow; which way was left for us to conjecture. It was to be hoped that the civilian fuel company had been briefed or we would look extremely foolish with our bags packed at the aircraft at 6 am and no fuel.

At that time next morning we phoned up the fuel company to come round to refuel *"Next Thursday's Child."* Surprisingly enough they obliged. Thinking it unwise to appear anywhere near the air traffic department, we made a hasty call to the duty met. forecaster instead of visiting him and found out that a strong headwind was forecast for the route to Bluie West 1, but there were likely to be clear conditions in the fjord leading to the airfield. My flight plan gave an 8¼ hour trip, leaving us a margin of only 1¾ hours – much less than I had hoped for. However, there was nothing for it but to go; it was now or not at all and we should be very unlucky if the winds were any worse than forecast. Also, the entrance to Tunugdliarfik Fjord would be easy to find with clear weather off the Greenland coast.

There was a slight delay due to the refuelling, so that we were champing at the bit in case the whole airfield should be up and about by the time we were off. Eventually we just made it and at 07.18 local time were heading out for the coast of Labrador and climbing slowly to 7,000 ft, our operational height, in sunny clear conditions, so very different from those in which we had first seen Goose Bay. Map-reading was easy here, where we were within sight of the Hamilton river estuary almost the whole way to the coast. We soon began to lose faith in our somewhat hasty weather forecast, for repeated alterations of course were necessary to keep on track and a wind velocity found by observing the drift on three separate courses was widely different from the one expected in the area. Had I had more faith in my navigation and less in the met. forecast I should have been greatly cheered. as the 20-knot forecast headwind was definitely non-existent according to my calculations. However, I knew that weather forecasts were usually excellent over the area and little doubts began to arise in my mind about the serviceability of our compass and drift meter. Besides, the wind that I had found might only exist in the local area over which we were flying when the drift observations were made. We decided to review our progress when we reached the coast; if we were late on our flight plan we would have to turn north and go either to Fort Chimo (420 miles) or Frobisher Bay (650 miles); if we were ahead we would press on to Greenland (550 miles).

As we obtained a pinpoint on the coast slightly ahead of schedule we elected to carry on. Shortly after leaving the coast a layer of low cloud appeared to cover the sea, but all was clear above us and navigation was simple. We followed the north-east leg of Goose Bay radio range to keep us on track and crossed it with sun position lines at intervals to work out our MPP (most probable position). The only slight worry was that the forecast headwind was absent and there was thus a risk of the fjord leading up to our destination being "socked in" by low cloud. There was no blind landing system and no instrument approach at Bluie West 1. It was necessary to follow a winding 45-mile fjord with steep sides and then land uphill on a runway laid on the moraine at the foot of a glacier. No overshoot was possible as the glacier rose up to the Greenland icecap at a steeper angle than that at which our plane could climb.

Five hours after take-off we had reached our point of no return, i.e. the last point from which we could turn back to Goose Bay. We had just picked up the BW3 radio range (located on an island at the entrance to the fjord). At about the same time the west coast of Greenland appeared on the horizon like a jagged battlement.

It was whilst we were congratulating ourselves that we became aware that we had company. Zigzagging behind us at about a mile's distance was an RCAF Lancaster. Whether this had been intended originally to escort us back from Goose Bay to Montreal or whether it had been hastily scrambled from one of the Eastern Seaboard RCAF Stations to search for us after our departure from Goose Bay had been discovered we never found out. At all events it did very well to find us. At this stage of the flight we were not going to let a tagging Lancaster alter our plans and we homed to the radio station BW3 (callsign SI) but never saw the island (Simiutak) where it was located as the entrance to Tunugdliarfik Fjord was covered by low cloud.

However, the tops of the mountains on either side of the fjord were in the clear, as was the distant icecap, so we pressed on hopefully towards our designation. To our relief, about halfway along the fjord the low cloud cleared and it was possible to see the last kink in the route, with the glacier and landing strip beckoning us. We landed in brilliant sunshine after a flight of under 7 hours, instead of the flight-planned 8½. What a glorious relief, to be welcomed by the United States Air Force and to have escaped at last from our month-long imprisonment in a mesh of governmental bureaucracy and buck-passing!

On landing we still had a slight leak in our starboard wing-tank and the American Base Commander, insisting that he was responsible for our safety, made us take four days' rest whilst his men gave the aircraft a thorough inspection. The delay was disappointing to me as it would make me miss a planned Cambridge University expedition to Norway. However, his plan was obviously sensible and three days of brilliant sunshine with temperatures well into the sixties gave me an opportunity to make two very useful local expeditions to study glaciers and their accompanying landforms. This would provide material for the "regional" essay which, as a second year Geographer, I had to write during my long vac. On the most adventurous of these trips Dikki and I managed to recruit one of the USAF Met. Officers, Bud Browdy.

"Next Thursday's Child" at Dow Air Force Base, Maine, with USAF Thunderjets in the background.

The approaches to Bluie West 1, Greenland (see Ch. 45); this view was from a wartime survey.

A poor surface for a forced landing: Narssassuaq glacier, Greenland (see Ch. 45).

LEFT: Bud Browdy (Met. Officer) negotiates a difficult ledge (see Ch. 45).
RIGHT: Dikki and Bud share out the dry clothes after Bud's dip in a glacial stream (see Ch. 45).

Dikki and Michael finally arrive at Croydon in *"Next Thursday's Child"* on the 19th August 1949.
Photo: courtesy of PA Photos.

Dikki exits the Valiant's cockpit on her return to Croydon, exultant that she's "done it at last."

CHAPTER 45
BLUIE WEST 1

We set out bright and early, intending to climb up the mountain on the south-east side of the glacier, drop down onto the ice, make our way across and return on the north-west side. To get back to the airfield we should have to wade the shallow stream which separated the foot of the glacier from the terminal moraine. All went well on the way up, although lack of a climbing rope made one traverse tricky. I have a photograph of Bud Browdy facing outwards on a narrow ledge looking anything but happy! We descended onto the glacier but none of us had really expected to meet the type of surface that it presented. It was not a nice smooth snow-covered slope as it had appeared from the air. Instead, it was a broken mass of ice pinnacles, separated by chasms of varying width and depth. It was a long job finding a way across it to the safety of the land on the other side, but we all made it eventually and set off towards the airfield, looking forward to a bath and a hot meal in the officers' club.

The water, when we reached it, looked just like your average Scottish or Welsh mountain stream, fast-flowing but shallow – definitely fordable. Bud, as behoved the host, took off his shoes and socks, rolled up his trousers and tried it first. Alas! As soon as the depth reached about 18 inches the force of the current knocked him off his feet and he crawled out wet through. I could not believe that was possible, so in I waded. I have never, ever known such cold water and the tug of the stream would have bowled me over if I had tried to continue. The situation now began to look worrying: only one of the party, Dikki, had completely dry clothes; Bud was wet from top to toe and I was wet from the waist down. We had to climb up on to the glacier, cross it and climb a 3,000 ft mountain in order to reach home and it was already late in the afternoon. The first thing to do was to re-allocate the dry clothes so that no one froze or caught pneumonia: Bud stripped off to his underpants and put on Dikki's thick shirt. Both he and I made the rest of the trip with our wet trousers over our arm and Dikki had her own trousers on but was stripped to her bra up top. We must have made a weird picture clambering over the ice but there was no one to see us as it was dark by the time we reached Camp. Our solicitous American friends put Dikki straight into hospital for a warm-up night; Bud and I collapsed thankfully into our own beds.

None of the mountaineering party suffered any long-term effects and all were invited on the following Sunday to a "fish-fry" on the hillside above the Camp. Unlike my previous visit to Bluie West, which had been during the war, Service personnel were now accompanied by wives and families, so it was a jolly and colourful picnic, with great square trays of sizzling fish and French fries washed down with *Coca-Cola* and followed by similar trays laden with squares of pink iced cake.

CHAPTER 46

GREENLAND–ICELAND–UK

On our fifth day in Greenland *"Next Thursday's Child"* was declared fully serviceable by the engineers and the weather forecast for Keflavik, Iceland, was favourable. The normal military route to Iceland was direct at 13,000 ft (the official safety height) under instrument flight rules. The visual flight rules (i.e. map-reading) route avoided overflying the icecap and followed the west coast of Greenland down to Cape Farewell – it was 150 miles longer. Our morning of departure, August 17th, was so brilliantly clear, however, that we tacked up and down the fjord climbing for 45 minutes and set course direct across the icecap at 9,000 ft. That flight across Greenland in clear weather is perhaps the most beautiful in the world. The two lines of jagged peaks along either coast, converging to a chaotic mass of frost-shattered 'horns' and corries in the south and diverging on either side of the dazzling dome of the icecap to the north, present a picture almost impossible to do justice to in words; but it is a very cruel beauty.

A pinpoint was obtained on the east coast, and drifts and sun shots kept us fairly well on track until Keflavik radio range was picked up 4½ hours out. The last 2½ hours of the flight to Iceland were made at 7,000 ft between solid layers of cloud and a radio range let-down was made to bring us to Keflavik below a 1,000 ft ceiling. Flight time, including the 45-minute climb out of Bluie West 1, was 7¼ hours. Keflavik, the wartime USAF Meeks Field, was now operated by Lockheed Overseas Corporation and the Lockheed manager was the first person to welcome us and offer us free landing (normally a fixed $40 fee) and hospitality at the excellent modern Airport Hotel.

The weather forecast for the last leg of this flight, to Prestwick, was bad for the following day, and during our enforced stopover the President of Iceland did us the honour of asking us to meet him. At 6.20 am on the day after, we took off for Prestwick in drizzling rain below a 600 ft ceiling, climbed to 7,000 ft and were in brilliant sunshine. The 740-nautical mile flight from Keflavik to Prestwick was the only leg of the North Atlantic crossing on which serious navigation, as opposed to radio range flying, turned out to be necessary, and the weather was so perfect that it was a pleasure. Friends in Trans-Canada Airlines' Montreal office had persuaded me, rather against my will, to try using the *Consol* radio direction-finding system and had given me a set of coordinate tables and a Lambert Conformal Conic chart upon which long-range radio bearings could be plotted as straight lines. *Consol* was a wartime invention by the Germans intended for U-Boat navigation in the war against Allied shipping in the Atlantic. The rather rudimentary security code had been broken and the Allies had not only been able to use German *Consol* stations in Spain, Brittany and Norway, but had introduced their own station, Bush Mills, in

Northern Ireland. To my surprise Bush Mills beacon came in loud and clear directly we reached cruising altitude and the coordinate tables turned out to be quite simple to use. No special equipment was required in the aircraft other than a radio range receiver. Any pilot or navigator who knows how to count and can tell the difference between a dot and a dash can obtain an almost instantaneous accurate position line. The Bush Mills position lines gave a track check the whole way from Iceland to the Scottish landfall and fixes were obtained at hourly intervals by crossing these with sun position lines which cut the track approximately at right-angles.

Five and three quarter hours after take-off the higher peaks of the Outer Hebrides appeared, projecting above the solid layer of low cloud. An immediate about-turn was made, followed by an attempt to descend below cloud without hitting anything solid. However, this plan did not work as the aircraft was still in it at an indicated 300 ft. A climb back to 4,000 ft was necessary for safety, but fortunately breaks began to appear below and a second descent, this time through a clear hole, brought us down off the coast of Arran, only 17 miles west of Prestwick. The Tower had been calling us frantically, probably having watched our attempts to descend on their surveillance radar, but our transmitter was unserviceable and they were quite relieved when we eventually appeared in the circuit.

At Prestwick we were still not 'home' as our round-the-world flight had started at Croydon, but it was there that we had our first taste of fame – or was it notoriety? – in England when we were applauded by a welcoming crowd. Our attempts to respond verbally to their greeting were sternly curtailed by our escorting immigration officer. It was all rather embarrassing.

Fortunately it transpired that we were not to be interned or otherwise delayed for long, and two hours later we were on our way to Croydon, which we reached after an uneventful trip of 2½ hours. This time there was no mistaking the crowd assembled to meet us. *Gaumont British News* was filming and the *Daily Mail* had transported Morrow and Anna in one car and my parents in another to meet us. The media had a bit of a field day. We decided to leave *"Next Thursday's Child"* at Croydon for the time being and were driven home to Cambridge in the *Daily Mail* cars, both of us, I think, with a big sigh of relief that it was all over and that we were still alive, and not detained in some faraway land.

EPILOGUE
(by Norman H. Ellison)

Having completed her journey around the world, Richarda could now rightly claim to be the first woman to pilot an aircraft all the way around the world. So, today, why is her name not listed along with the other great names of feminine aviators? Amy Johnson, Jean Batten, Beryl Markham, Mrs Victor Bruce, Amelia Earhart: none of these actually flew all the way around the world but their names are so well-known that most people now assume that they did.

Richarda was the first of several post-WWII lady pilots to make the circumnavigation journey, and so her name should be at the head of that list that includes Sheila Scott, Jerrie Mock, Joan Merriam, Ann Pellegrino, Judy Chisholm, Linda Finch & Polly Vacher. This author believes that the reason Richarda's name is not recognised nowadays is because of envy and, at the time, this materialised as a form of ridicule.

When Richarda completed her circumnavigation flight it was only four years after the end of WWII. Conditions in England at that time were very different from those nowadays at the beginning of a new century. Wartime rationing was still in force for many of the basic commodities. Currency restrictions were very tight, especially when American Dollars were involved. In 1949 the Exchange Rate was the long-established 4 US Dollars to 1 British Pound Sterling.

However, post-war conditions in the UK, especially the Socialist policies of the Labour Government, caused the Pound to come under severe pressure in the Exchange markets around the world. The ensuing currency crisis caused severe hardships in the UK. Most imports from the USA were banned, especially aircraft and aeronautical products. Britain was a land of austerity and travel restrictions. For many years we existed upon products that were almost 'sub-standard,' and clothing, furniture and household products featured the infamous *Utility* label that looked similar to the later famous *Packman* electronic creature. Holiday travel abroad was restricted to non-dollar areas of the world and, for a time, fuel for private pleasure-flying was rationed.

Growing up in this environment after the war we generally did not appreciate how poor was the general quality of life when compared to the rest of the world. After all, there were now no blackouts, no doodlebugs or rockets falling out of the sky, and life was peaceful. We did not miss having a car, as we had grown up using other forms of locomotion, and travel abroad was for the 'rich and famous.' The only thing we had to endure was National Service in the armed forces.

It was against this background of doom and gloom that Richarda managed to fly herself around the world. A lot of people were envious of the opportunity she had taken, and those who were in a position to moan about it did so, particularly the magazines and newspapers that were then the self-appointed moulders of public opinion. So instead of lauding the achievement, that Richarda had become the first lady to pilot herself around the world, they ridiculed her flight. One newspaper even went to the extent of publishing an "Open Letter" to her. This said in effect that, instead of carrying out an adventurous, personal achievement flight, she should have stayed at home to mind the baby, and that she was failing in her duties as a mother.

Richarda said after the flight that she did it because "she was so depressed with the failure of our people to retain the lead in sport and other activities that she was determined to show what an ordinary housewife could do to show the world that the spirit of adventure and endurance was still very much alive in the British."

Instead, all she managed to achieve was to alienate the aviation establishment, and the technical aviation press dismissed her accomplishments as a high-spirited romp. Consequently the same aviation establishment which was also responsible for making awards for personal achievements took no action to recognise the flying and navigating skills that had been so amply demonstrated. In retrospect, to sum up the situation, as everything in those days was ordered hardship and austerity, Richarda's flight could be excused as a case of bad timing.

However, Richarda probably did not help her own situation. There were several times when her off-the-cuff remarks were picked up with glee by reporters looking for material to fill column inches in their write-ups. These comments were enthusiastically reported by all the newspapers, usually ahead of her arrival at any one point. Constant remarks about her glamorous appearance, her former occupation as a model, and baby Anna left at home, took the seriousness out of the occasion. In retrospect it would have been wiser if Richarda had employed or hired a Press Agent to handle all the Press interviews.

In an interview after the flight, she said: "I had more trouble on the ground than I ever had in the air." To raise money whilst in Alaska she sang, modelled, gave talks to lunch clubs, and was interviewed on the radio. The top fee for a talk was $25.

Her constant remarks about the lack of finances to complete the required servicing of the aircraft and their engines did not help her image as a competent pilot. At the many British and American Air Force Bases at which she landed, much aid and work was provided by the air force personnel. Perhaps the glamour appeal worked in her favour on these occasions. Nevertheless, her flying abilities, and Michael's navigation skills, were never in doubt. They did not get lost at any time.

However, in her last Press interview she said that she was fed up with all the poor publicity she had received, and was "going to retire to the kitchen and shut the door." Apparently this is roughly what she did, as she dropped out of circulation and was not heard of again in the national Press.

POSTSCRIPT

(by Michael Townsend)

Although Richarda deliberately avoided further contact with the national Press, she continued her flying, as a Sergeant Pilot in the Women's Royal Air Force Volunteer Reserve. We both flew, under the guidance of CFI Squadron Leader Leslie Worsdell, at No. 22 RFS, Marshalls Airport, Cambridge. There Richarda flew Chipmunks and I navigated Ansons at first and then remustered as a pilot, also flying Chipmunks.

We eventually married, after her first marriage broke up, and she joined me on my regular RAF Station in Germany. Here she very nearly managed another 'first' – at least for a British woman – when the Air Ministry gave her permission to fly Meteor jet fighter aircraft "subject to being thoroughly checked out by a Meteor QFI"! The QFI and the dual-control Meteor 7 were both available on the Station but, alas, she failed her annual medical and had to retire from the WRAFVR. Her eyesight was still good enough for Private Pilot Licence standards and she maintained a PPL until 1960. Thereafter, she flew light aircraft with me until a few months before her death in 1982.

During our retirement in Maldon, Essex, Richarda developed a successful insurance business, took a prominent part in local politics and lived life to the full on the Blackwater Estuary, sailing, wildfowling, sail-boarding and finally (at the age of 55) qualifying for her BSAC Diver's Certificate. She died of a rare, incurable blood disease on 17th December 1982 at the early age of 59.

APPENDIX 1
FINAL PRESS COMMENTS

(by Norman H. Ellison)

After Richarda and Michael arrived back at Croydon, the Press were there in force to meet them, as shown in the photographs here. Short (and sometimes terse reports) appeared in the aeronautical magazines to note their return, but the national newspapers were in a critical mood and trivialised the occasion. Typical of the reports were these included here:

1. From the *Seattle Post-Intelligencer*, dated 19th August 1949, quoting reports received from London:
"... *Britain's flying housewife landed at Prestwick today* .... *The attractive 25-year-old former model and mother of a 30-month-old daughter thus became the first woman to pilot a plane around the world. She and her navigator, Michael Townsend, 25, handsome Cambridge University undergraduate and childhood friend, landed at this wartime bomber base after a flight from Iceland.*
The two flyers had taken off from Britain August 18, 1948. Mrs Morrow-Tait kissed her husband goodbye and told him she would be back in six weeks. 'Please look after baby until then,' the aviatrix said ....
From Prestwick, Mrs Morrow-Tait and Townsend will fly to London. Her husband, Britain's most publicized babysitter ... is waiting for her there. He told newsmen he is tired of changing diapers."

2. From the *Sunday Pictorial* of Sunday 21st August 1949:
"The *Sunday Pictorial* frankly expressed its view on this adventure two months ago. We said: 'All the flight has proved is that an obstinate redhead has spent ten months flying round the world ....
With her round-the-world ambition realised – forty-six weeks behind schedule – Mrs Morrow-Tait had time yesterday to think about her home responsibilities. 'Anna has grown wonderfully,' she said. 'I am not sure that my daughter knows me, but she is a very friendly and happy girl.'
On her husband: 'His anxieties are over now. I know that the year has been one of strain for him. There were times when I thought I would never see home again, and that the end would come for me by death in the sea.'
We hope that Mrs Morrow-Tait's appetite for adventure has now been sated but, quite frankly, we can't join in the chorus of praise for the 'flying housewife'."

APPENDIX 2

TECHNICAL DETAILS OF EACH AIRCRAFT

(by Norman H. Ellison)

CHRISLEA CH.3 SERIES 2 SUPER ACE

A 4-seat light aircraft, designed by R.C. Christophorides and manufactured by the Chrislea Aircraft Co. Ltd. at Exeter Airport, Clyst Honiton, Devon, England, in 1947.

The fuselage was of welded steel tubular construction, fabric covered. The high-mounted wing was of light alloy construction, also fabric covered. The tail unit consisted of twin fins and rudders, mounted at each end of the light-alloy constructed tailplane.

Power was supplied by a 145 hp de Havilland Gipsy Major 10 engine, and a tricycle undercarriage was fitted.

Dimensions were: wingspan 36 feet 0 inches; overall length 21 feet 6 inches; height overall 7 ft 7½ inches. Wing area: 177 square feet.

Empty weight was 1,344 lb; all-up weight 2,342 lb. Max ceiling: 16,000 feet.

Maximum speed was 126 mph; economical cruising speed 112 mph. Normal maximum range: 420 miles.

The fourth production aircraft, serial number 104, was built in 1948 and sold to Richarda Morrow-Tait with a new Certificate of Airworthiness on 30th June 1948; it was registered G-AKUV. After being damaged at Cambridge on 16th August 1948, it was sold in 1951 to Mr J. Chapman. It was damaged beyond repair at Thruxton Airfield on 23rd June 1953.

PERCIVAL P.31 PROCTOR IV

As originally designed by Percival Aircraft Ltd. at Luton Airport, Bedfordshire, in 1943, the Proctor IV existed in two convertible versions, one as a 4-seat communications aircraft for the Royal Air Force, the other as a radio-navigation trainer for either the RAF or the Royal Navy. It was a larger version of the original Proctor III that had been developed from the pre-war Percival Vega Gull. Production was either by Percival's at Luton or by sub-contractor F. Hills and Sons Ltd., Trafford Park, Manchester.

The aircraft was of all-wood construction, spruce and plywood, three-piece folding wings, with faired main wheels on the centre section and a normal tailwheel. Power was a 208 hp de Havilland Gipsy Queen 2 engine.

Dimensions were: wingspan 39 feet 6 inches; overall length 28 feet 2 inches; height overall 7 feet 3 inches. Wing area: 202 square feet. Aspect ratio 7.72.

Empty weight 2,370 lb; all-up weight 3,500 lb. Wing loading 17.3 lb/sq ft. Power loading 16.8 lb/hp. Max. ceiling: 14,000 feet.

Maximum speed was 160 mph; economical cruising speed 140 mph.

Fuel: 20 imp. gallon tank in each outer wing-root. Normal max. range 500 miles.

Richarda's Proctor IV was originally built in 1944 by F. Hills and Sons Ltd., and issued to the Royal Air Force with the RAF serial NP353. Declared surplus by the RAF in 1947, it was one of a batch of 16 aircraft purchased by Field Aircraft Services, Croydon Airport, and was registered by them as G-AJMU. It was then modified by them to have the long-range tanks, of 10 gallons each, in the ends of the centre section in a similar manner to the special long-range versions of the Luton-built civilian Proctor 5 aircraft, which then had a maximum range of 780 miles. In addition to these extra tanks, two large 38-gallon tanks were fitted into the rear of the Proctor IV cockpit to give a total of 136 imperial gallons, for an estimated maximum range of 1,850 miles.

G-AJMU received its Certificate of Airworthiness on the 16th August 1948, but crashed in Alaska in November of the same year. The airframe was broken up at Edmonton, Alberta, but the engine is still on display in a Calgary, Alberta museum.

VULTEE MODEL 74D VALIANT

This was a 2-seat basic training aircraft, of all-metal light alloy construction, designed and built by the Vultee Corporation at Downey, California from 1940. It was awarded a US Army Air Force contract and 11,537 were built in several versions, as the BT-13, 13A, 13B and 15 for the Air Force and SNV-1 and 2 for the US Navy. Production continued up to 1944, during which time Vultee Corporation was combined with the Consolidated Aircraft Corporation of San Diego, California (in March 1943).

Power was supplied by one 450 hp Pratt & Whitney Wasp Junior R-985-AN-3 engine, and a normal tailwheel fixed undercarriage was fitted, with unfaired mainwheels.

Dimensions were: wingspan 42 feet 2 inches; overall length 28 feet 8 inches; height overall 12 feet 4 inches. Wing area: 239 square feet.

Empty weight 3,345 lb; all-up weight 4,360 lb. Max. ceiling: 21,650 feet. Maximum speed: 182 mph.

Normal fuel capacity: 120 US gallons; normal maximum range 725 miles.

The BT-13A aircraft Richarda purchased was built by Vultee and completed on 19th May 1942 with a manufacturer's serial number of 5837; it received a US Air Force serial of 41-21998.

It was declared surplus by the Reconstruction Finance Corporation, pursuant to the Surplus Property Act of 1944, on the 27th December 1945, and sold to Wichita Falls Air Transport Co., Texas, for $776.50. It was then registered to them as NC54084. The initial Annual Inspection was completed on 1st February 1946, and the Valiant was sold to C.T. McLaughlin, of Midland, Texas for "One Dollar and other valuable considerations."

In July the same year it was again sold, to a W.D. Kellogg, also of Midland, Texas, for "Ten Dollars and other considerations." However, in January 1947 it was sold for a declared value of $1,100 to W.S. McNeal in Everett, Washington State. In March 1948 it was sold again, for $700 to R.B. Hendricks of Seattle, who in turn sold it to Richarda for $500 on the 6th April 1949.

As mentioned in Chapter 40, Richarda had to sell the Valiant to a US citizen and for $1 the next owner was William Deramo of Niagara Falls, New York State. However, Richarda flew it on to England.

The eventual fate of the BT-13 aircraft was very unglamorous, and no respect was given to an aircraft that had earned an honourable place in aviation history. After their arrival at Croydon, Richarda flew the Vultee back to Cambridge on the 2nd September; it then sat there, neglected, apart from one rumoured flight for possible certification in the UK.

In the archival records received from the Federal Aviation Administration, Flight Standards Service, Civil Aviation Registry Records Office, Oklahoma City, there were many entries after the "sale" of the aircraft for one dollar. These stipulated that the BT-13 was only certified for Richarda to complete her flight to the UK. The Airworthiness Certificates specifically stated that she could only fly it up to the 5th September 1949. After arrival in the UK she applied for, and received, an extension up to the 24th of September, to allow her to display it at the RAF Battle of Britain Display at RAF Beaulieu, Hants on the 17th September.

There were no further entries in the archives until the BT-13, registration of N54084, was cancelled on the 14th December 1955 as "no reply to audit questionnaire" from the last registered owner, William Deramo of Niagara Falls.

In the meantime, it was reported in UK aviation magazines that the BT-13 was "sold" to a Mr M. Dumont of Stockton-on-Tees in August 1950. The aircraft was then flown north, and it was photographed at Greatham, near Hartlepool on 27th August 1950, where it remained until at least the 11th November. It was last seen in 1952, on a scrapyard dump of aircraft parts, at RAF Balado Bridge aerodrome in Scotland, where it was broken up for scrap metal. Whether the parts were ever used for spares will never be known. The nearest BT-13 Valiant aircraft at the time were some in use by the Israeli Air Force.

The Valiant aircraft was never certified for flying in the UK, as it never received a British Type Certificate. It also had an American engine, so it may have been rejected for certification under the general ban on importing anything from America due to the currency restrictions. Only the photographs remain to give us some reminders of a forgotten achievement.

APPENDIX 3
AIRCRAFT PERFORMANCE DATA COMPARED
(by Michael Townsend)

A/C Type	Max A/U Wt.	Max Fuel Cap.	Economical Cruising Speed	Fuel Consumption at Economical Cruise	Predicted Max. Range to Dry Tanks	Service Ceiling	Landing Speed
Chrislea Super Ace G-AKUV	2,342 lb	45½ imp. gal.	112 mph	6½ gal/hr.	780 st. ml.	16,000 ft.	50 mph
Percival Proctor IV G-AJMU	3,500 lb	136 imp. gal.	140 mph	10 gal/hr.	1,889 st. ml.	14,000 ft.	55 mph
Vultee BT-13 Valiant NX54084	4,496 lb	144 imp. gal.	120 mph	12½ gal/hr.	1,380 st. ml.	21,650 ft	60 mph

APPENDIX 4
A BRIEF HISTORY OF ROUND-THE-WORLD FLIGHT ATTEMPTS

(by Norman H. Ellison)

1) Phileas Fogg (fictional), in *Around the World in Eighty Days*, the novel by Jules Verne. The book was first published in 1873; the film version was made in 1956.

2) The first real attempt to fly round the world started from Croydon on 24th May 1922, with Maj. Wilfred T. Blaske, Capt. Norman Macmillan and Lt. Col. L.E. Broome, in a DH.9 registered G-EBDE. In Calcutta they changed aircraft to G-EBDI, a Fairey IIIC seaplane, but they crashed into the Bay of Bengal with engine failure.

3) In 1924, a Vickers Vulture amphibian, G-EBHO, left Calshot on 25th March. The pilot was Flg. Off. W.N. Plenderleith, with Sqn. Ldr. A.S.C. MacLaren as navigator; they crashed at Akyab Island, Burma on May 24th. The flight was continued in Vulture G-EBGO, which reached Nikolski, Kurile Islands, but was damaged when landing in the Bering Sea on 2nd August 1924. 13,000 miles had been covered in the two aircraft.

4) The first successful flight around the world was made by two US Army Douglas World Cruisers, fitted alternatively with wheels or floats. This lasted from 6th April to 28th September 1924, and covered 27,500 miles in 371 hours flying time. The route was: Sand Point, Seattle, then Japan, China, Hong Kong, Indo-China, Siam, Malaya, Burma, India, Persia, Mesopotamia, Turkey, Romania, Hungary, Austria, France, England, Iceland, Greenland and return to Seattle. Four aircraft had begun the flight; one crashed, one ditched near the Faroe Islands.

5) Vicomte Jacques, the French WWI air ace, and his wife Vicomtesse Violette de Sibour, departed Stag Lane on 14th September 1928 in DH.60G Gipsy Moth G-EBZR named *Safari*. The route was: France, Spain, Gibraltar, North Africa, Cairo, Baghdad, – the aircraft then developed engine trouble and was taken by sea to Karachi – India, Bangkok, Indo-China – then by sea to the USA – Chicago, by sea to Havre, then to England in mid-1929. 33,000 miles in 10 months.

6) The German airship *Graf Zeppelin* flew around the world, covering 21,873 miles in 21 days. It started out on August 8th 1929 at Lakehurst, New Jersey, USA, then flew via Germany, Japan & Los Angeles, arriving back at Lakehurst on the 29th August.

7) In 1930 the Hon. Mrs Victor Bruce flew Blackburn Bluebird IV G-ABDS on the route: England, Europe, Turkey, Middle East, India, Burma, Hong Kong, Shanghai, Tokyo; the aircraft was then taken by sea to America and by sea to France, from where she flew back to England. She left Heston on 25th September 1930 and returned 20th February, 1931.

8) Wiley Post flew around the world in June/July 1931; he left from Long Island (Roosevelt Field) in a Lockheed Vega Model 5 NR105W, named *Winnie Mae*, with Harold Gatty navigating. The total time taken was 8 days, 15 hours and 51 minutes. The route was: Berlin, Königsberg, Moscow, Novo Sibirsk (Siberia), Irkutsk (Siberia), Rukhlovo (Siberia), Khabarovsk (Siberia), (Flat) Alaska, Fairbanks, Edmonton, New York. The aircraft is now on display in the Smithsonian Museum, Washington.

He repeated the flight in July 1933 (15th-22nd), the first true solo flight around the world, in 21 hours less time than previously He covered 15,596 miles from Floyd Bennett Field, New York via Berlin, Moscow, Irkutsk and Alaska.

He was killed in 1935, along with the comedian Will Rogers, in a Lockheed Orion 9E/Explorer hybrid NR12283, in Alaska. Further details are in *Who's Who in Aviation*, page 152.

9) Amelia Mary Earhart, born 24th July 1897, left Miami on the 1st June 1937 in a Lockheed Electra, for a flight around the world as near to the equator as possible. She took off from Lae, New Guinea on 2nd July 1937 for Howland Island, never to be seen again.

10) In August 1936 Howard Hughes had to file a request with the US Bureau of Air Commerce for permission to make a foreign flight. He left New York on Sunday 10th July 1938, and flew around the world in a Lockheed 14 in the record time of 91 hours, 41 minutes. The Lockheed had a crew of four on board and a Sperry Gyropilot. Its range was 5,000 miles at 15-16,000 feet, so oxygen was carried.

The route was: Floyd Bennett Field, New York, via Newfoundland & Ireland to Le Bourget, Paris by the Great Circle route: 3,641 miles in 16 hours 37 minutes. He then continued to Moscow via Belgium, Germany, Poland, Lithuania and Latvia; then on to Omsk, Yakutsk, Fairbanks, Minneapolis and New York, arriving on the 14th July.

11) On the 31st August 1939, a Japanese Air Force crew flying a Mitsubishi Navy Type 96 Freighter named *Nippon* arrived at Boeing Field, Seattle from Whitehorse YT, on its third leg of a round-the-world flight. The Chief Pilot was Sumitoski Nakao, and it was planned to go on through South America to Africa, then through Europe, covering 34,000 miles over a month. The flight was stopped by the outbreak of WWII, and the crew toured the USA instead, including Chicago and New York.

12) In April 1947 Capt. Bill Odom flew a Douglas A-26B Invader (*Reynold's Bombshell*, owned and navigated by Milton Reynolds, and accompanied by engineer T. Carrol Ballee) 19,000 miles round the world, starting and finishing in New York, in a record time of 78 hours 56 minutes, beating Howard Hughes' 1939 flight time. Bill Odom later flew round the world solo in a record time of 73 hours 5 minutes, at an average speed of 269 mph, beating Wiley Post's previous solo record. He left Chicago on the 7th August, thence to Paris, Cairo, Karachi, Calcutta, Tokyo, Anchorage and Fargo, arriving back at Chicago on 10th August.

13) In September 1947 there was a proposed non-stop flight round the world flight in a Piper Super Cruiser, NX4478M, from New York. It was planned to pick up fuel, food & spares in flight over Gander, London, Paris, Marseilles, Rome, Athens, Basra, Karachi, Allahabad, Calcutta, Rangoon, Saigon, Hong Kong, Tokyo, Chitosi, Shemya, Anchorage, Vancouver and San Francisco. The pilots were Ted Thompson and Nelson Brown, who flew with RAF Transport Command during WWII. The flight was postponed in December due to the "unsatisfactory weather conditions currently prevailing."

14) Piper Super Cruiser NX8761M *City of the Angels* and NX2365M *City of Washington* left Teterboro Airport, New Jersey together on 9th August 1947, and returned on 20th December 1947 after 133 days, 276 flying hours and 25,162 miles. The pilots were George W. Truman and Clifford V. Evans. *City of the Angels* is now airworthy at the Piper Aviation Museum, Lock Haven, Pennsylvania, and *City of Washington* is in the Paul Garber Facility of the National Air & Space Museum, Maryland.

15) The subject of this book: 1948–49 – Mrs Richarda Morrow-Tait and Michael Townsend, travelling eastward. This was the first successful circumnavigation of the world by a woman pilot completed entirely by air.